BRITAIN'S SECRET PROPAGANDA WAR

BRITAIN'S
SECRET
PROPAGANDA
WAR

Paul Lashmar & James Oliver

SUTTON PUBLISHING

First published in the United Kingdom in 1998 by
Sutton Publishing Limited · Phoenix Mill
Thrupp · Stroud · Gloucestershire · GL5 2BU

British Library Cataloguing in Publication Data
A catalogue record for this book is available from the British Library

ISBN 0 7509 1668 0

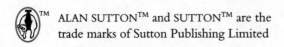

TM ALAN SUTTON™ and SUTTON™ are the
trade marks of Sutton Publishing Limited

Typeset in 10/12pt Bembo
Typesetting and origination by
Sutton Publishing Limited
Printed in Great Britain by
MPG, Bodmin, Cornwall.

Contents

List of Plates

Abbreviations

ACUE	American Committee on United Europe	ISC	Institute for the Study of Conflict
AEU	Amalgamated Engineering Union	KOSTRAD	Indonesian Army's Strategic Reserve
AKEL	Cypriot Communist Party	LSE	London School of Economics
ANA	Arab News Agency	MCP	Malayan Communist Party
BIS	British Information Services	MENA	Middle East News Agency
BPI	Indonesian Intelligence Agency	MEW	Ministry of Economic Warfare
CCF	Congress for Cultural Freedom	MI5	Military Intelligence (State Security)
CFR	Council for Foreign Relations	MI6	Military Intelligence (Espionage)
CIA	Central Intelligence Agency	MIR	a research branch of the War Office
CND	Campaing for Nuclear Disarmament	MOI	Ministry of Information
COI	Central Office of Information	MPAJA	Malayan People's Anti-Japanese Army
CPGB	Communist Party of Great Britain	NAFEN	Near and Far East News Ltd
CSCE	Conference on Security and Cooperation in Europe	NASAKOM	United ideologies of Indonesia: nationalism, religion and Communism
ECOSOC	Economic and Social Council (UN)	NBC	National Broadcasting Company
EEC	European Economic Community	NCL	Non-Communist Left
EH	Electra House	NGO	Non-governmental organization
ELEC	European League for Economic Cooperations	NICRA	Northern Ireland Civil Rights Association
EOKA	National organization of Cypriot fighters	NUM	National Union of Mineworkers
ETU	Electrical Trades Union	OID	Overseas Information Department
FBU	Fire Brigades Union	OSS	Office of Special Services (USA)
FCO	Foreign and Commonwealth Office	PKI	Indonesian Communist Party
FM	Field Marshal	POLAD	Political adviser to the Commander-in-Chief, Far East
FO	Foreign Office	POW	Prisoner of War
FWF	Forum World Features	PPS	Policy Planning Staff
GCHQ	Government Communications Headquarters	PWE	Political Warfare Executive
		RFE	Radio Free Europe
GSI	'Gustav Siegfried Eins'	RIAS	Radio in the American Sector
HMG	Her Majesty's Government	RIO	Regional Information Officer
IFTU	International Federation of Trades Unions	RL	Radio Liberty
		RNS	Regional News Service
INRAR	International News Rights and Royalties	ROK	Republic of Korea
		RSIA	Royal Society of International Affairs
IPD	Information Policy Department	SEA	South-East Asia
IRA	Irish Republican Army	SEATO	South-East Asian Treaty Organizations
IRD	Information Research Department		

SHAEF	Supreme Headquarters Allied Expeditionary Force	UN	United Nations
		UNCURK	United Nations Commission for the Unification and Rehabilitation of Korea
SIS	Secret Intelligence Service (MI6)		
SO1	Special Operation (1)		
SOE	Special Operations Executive	UNESCO	United Nations Educational, Scientific and Cultural Organization
SS	*Schutzstaffel*		
SSCM	Society of Socialist Clergy and Ministers	USIS	United States Information Services
		VOA	Voice of America
TASS	Soviet news service	WFS	World Feature Services
TUC	Trades Union Congress	WFTU	World Federation of Trade Unions

Acknowledgements

This book could never have happened without the help of Richard Fletcher. His work on IRD was the inspiration, and without his voluminous files there would have been no book.

In addition we should like to thank Richard Aldrich, Nick Anning, Brian Brivati, Duncan Campbell, Susan L. Carruthers, Mary Carson, David Chipp, Mark Curtis, Phillip Deery, Steve Dorrill, Gen Sir Anthony Farrar-Hockley, Phil Kelly, Dianne Kirby, David Leigh, Scott Lucas, Tom McCarthy, Katherine Murray, Greg Neale, Michael Nelson, Richard Norton Taylor, Richard Oliver, Hugh O'Shaughnessy, Robin Ramsay, Gary D. Rawnsley, Andrew Roth, John Savile, Ramesh Sharma, Tony Shaw, Sue Steward, Andy Weir, Hugh Wilford, and the many others who assisted us in one way or another.

In the United States, thanks go to Scott Armstrong, John Jenks, Kathy Kadane, Ralph McGhee and Lou Wolf.

We also appreciated those who gave us time for interviews on the record, including Sir Richard Body, Roland Challis, John Cloake, Brian Crozier, Col Dodds-Parker, Fred Emery, Michael Ivens, Hugh Lunghi, Lord Mayhew, Lord Owen, Norman Reddaway, Geoffrey Tucker, Hunter Wade, Colin Wallace, J.H.A. Watson, Fay Weldon, Ernest Wistrich, Sir Oliver Wright, and those former members of the IRD who gave us off-the-record interviews.

We should also like to thank Phillip Whitehead of Brook-Lapping.

Introduction

In early 1972, Richard Fletcher noticed an odd advertisement in the *Guardian* that raised his suspicions. Fletcher, a long-standing Labour Party activist and occasional investigative journalist, was engaged at the time in a major inquiry for the *Sunday Times* into the CIA's (Central Intelligence Agency) subversion of the British Labour Movement. This inquiry revealed that the CIA had extensively funded British politicians and trade unionists of a 'moderate' and anti-Communist stance and had helped overthrow leftist leaders in British dependencies. Fletcher's research had also revealed that the CIA had covertly funded anti-Communist publishing. The *Guardian* advert, Fletcher had noticed, was for a bibliography, *Books on Communism*, written by one R.N. Carew Hunt of St Antony's College, Oxford. Fletcher was well aware of St Antony's close links with US and British intelligence. 'I also knew that it was not financially viable to publish books on such a boring subject as Communism. I suspected the book was subsidized in some way,' he said.

As part of their CIA investigation, one of Fletcher's team went to Companies House and checked out the accounts of the book's obscure publisher, Ampersand Ltd. These showed that the company had been set up in 1946 by one Leslie Sheridan, 'a public relations consultant'. On the surface, everything indicated an ordinary small publishing house, but the accounts had some odd features. There appeared to be little business activity – the company had few expenses in the way of postage or telephone calls. More significantly, it seemed to make negligible profit from sales. Costs, however, were met exactly by an unidentified donor. 'It looked to me as though it was another CIA publishing front,' said Fletcher. He put any further investigation on the backburner while he concentrated on other stories. It was not until 1976 that events led him to look at Ampersand again.

In London in the mid-1970s British intelligence was shaken to the core by the intensity of the light being shone on its Atlantic cousins. In November 1976 the Labour Home Secretary, Merlyn Rees, announced that on the advice of his security advisers he intended to deport two Britain-based Americans who had been active in bringing the CIA to account. One was Phillip Agee, a former CIA officer whose revelatory book, *Inside the Company*, had become a bestseller. The other, Mark Hosenball, was an American journalist who was working for the *Evening Standard*.

Rees claimed that these men posed 'a danger to national security', without giving details. Support for the two men was mobilized from the radical left, still vibrant from the heady days of 1968. A campaign was launched to stop the deportations. The campaigners set out to publicize evidence of the CIA's malevolent involvement in the domestic politics of many countries friendly to the US. Richard Fletcher was a founder of the Agree Hosenball campaign. An ad hoc group of journalists and students assembled round him to help him to reveal more of the hidden activities of the CIA.

Fletcher asked Richard Oliver, at the time a research assistant at North London Polytechnic, to follow up the lead on the mysterious anti-Communist publisher Ampersand. The assumption was that the company's founder, Leslie Sheridan, was working as a front for the Americans – either the CIA or some other linked organization. Oliver set out to St Martin's Lane Reference Library, near Leicester Square, to find out more about the company and its directors. A few hours later, Fletcher received an excited phone call from Oliver: 'It must be British!' He had unearthed Leslie Sheridan's obituary in *The Times*.[1] Although cautiously written, the obituary revealed that Sheridan had worked for the British wartime propaganda organization the Political Warfare Executive (PWE). 'It was fascinating to watch the sureness of his professional approach on a subject like propaganda', the obituary said. After the war, it continued, Sheridan had 'carved himself a new career in the difficult field of public relations and later in an advisory capacity to the Foreign Office'. In addition, Fletcher and Oliver discovered that another of the directors of Ampersand was a wartime MI5 officer; this had to mean that the company was a British, not an American, front.

Next Fletcher located and contacted Sheridan's widow, Caroline. Although guarded, she told him that a Foreign Office section called the Information Research Department (IRD) was central to her husband's work. She suggested that Fletcher should talk to a former colleague of Leslie Sheridan's called Adelaide Maturin. She did not mention that Maturin was Sheridan's previous wife or that Maturin had become an MI6 career officer after the war. Unsurprisingly, Maturin, now retired to the country, declined to talk with Fletcher.

Fletcher's team, though, had been back to Companies House and noticed that Ampersand was linked to a range of other odd companies through its solicitor, Victor Cannon-Brookes. Over the next months the team unravelled a vast array of interlocking companies and establishment directors for a range of publishing and news agency companies. Interviews with well-placed intelligence sources had by now revealed that the Foreign Office's IRD was a secret anti-Communist propaganda organization, closely linked to MI6 and with a wide web of journalist contacts. The individual companies pieced together at Companies House were part of a global network of media organizations jointly run by IRD and MI6 over a thirty-year period. Bolstered by a growing pile of hard evidence, the team took its discoveries to the *Observer*, where they were published early in 1978 as 'How the Foreign Office Waged Secret Propaganda War', bylined Richard Fletcher, Phil Kelly, Paul Lashmar, Tony Smart and Richard Oliver.[2] The in-house reporter was George Brock.[3]

A day earlier a *Guardian* article by investigative reporter David Leigh revealed that Foreign Secretary David Owen had closed down IRD a few months before for unspecified reasons.[4] Leigh had been tipped off about IRD by a Foreign Office insider.

Since those first revelations were published, further details of IRD's activities have gradually trickled out in the media over the last twenty years. Every year or two another article has popped up in the press revealing some new facet of IRD. Many featured George Orwell's curious relationship with the department. Strangely, interest in IRD has grown rather than declined. This is, in part, a reflection of widening appreciation of the enormous impact that its covert operations had over the years.

The genesis of this book lies in one of those strange moments of synchronicity. One of Fletcher's researchers, Paul Lashmar, joined the *Observer* after the story appeared. Sporadically, he kept up his interest in IRD, with occasional articles in the paper as new material became available. In 1995 he was called by another of Fletcher's old researchers, Richard Oliver, who told him that his nephew, James, was writing a postgraduate thesis on IRD. Lashmar had taken on the IRD archive from Richard Fletcher and James Oliver was able to examine twenty years of collected evidence. In 1996 Paul Lashmar and James Oliver decided to join forces to write this history of IRD.

Both authors feel that the history of IRD provides important historical insights into postwar Britain and the nature of the Cold War – a conflict in which almost every move was made with one eye to its propaganda value. IRD also raises serious questions regarding information, secrecy, the intelligence services and the democratic state – not least because of the ability to manipulate public and political opinion which skilful propaganda work can provide.

In 1978 a Fleet Street editor remarked dismissively to Lashmar, 'Oh, everyone knew about IRD.' What he meant was that the Fleet Street establishment knew about IRD and were happy to keep the matter quiet. As the editor of another liberal broadsheet remarked, 'They are our friends.' Similarly, many ex-IRD staff say that it was not secret; it was referred to in the Foreign Office List. However, its function was *never* disclosed in the that list or in any other open material. Also, neither the British public, who paid for it, nor Parliament, to whom it was in theory accountable, knew about it. That, to us, is secret.

Even the former IRD staffers admit that it was considered to be a 'hush-hush' department from its inception. Ironically, despite that designation, the Soviets knew of the existence of IRD within weeks of its creation in 1948 through Guy Burgess, the traitor, from that same British establishment. The cosy relationship between the Foreign Office, Fleet Street and Broadcasting House (marred only by the Suez Crisis) was only broken by a new generation of journalists, unconstrained by the assumptions set during the Second World War, who did not believe that the agenda of the British State and journalists should be synonymous.

Secrecy has continued to prevent the full disclosure of IRD activities. For many years the public's right to know was restricted as IRD's records which should have been made public were withheld past the thirty-year period. While some former Foreign Office officials have maintained that the IRD had nothing to do with the secret services, IRD files have been treated as though they were those of an intelligence organization. Some early anodyne briefing documents were released in the late 1970s, but the rest only began to be released from 1995.

At the time of going to press, the documents for 1950–2 had just been released. However, at least 10 per cent of those documents remain withheld. Several people have suggested that this book is premature and that it would be better to wait until all of the IRD papers have been released. Extended retention of documents aside, at the current rate of release, the documents covering IRD's 1977 closure will not appear until 2020. By then the shenanigans of the Cold Warriors will look very strange indeed. We feel that there are some very important lessons to be learned now. In the absence of full documentation, we have fallen back on the journalist's tool and interviewed as many of those who took part in the events as we could. Oral history is still underrated in the UK, yet it is a central tool, especially when it leads to, and can be confirmed by, documentary material.

As students of propaganda will know, the subject is categorized by shades from white through myriad greys to black. We have not entered into the finer elements of debate about calibration. For our purposes, white propaganda is attributed and accurate material, while black propaganda is untrue and deliberately misleading in its source. Anything else fits into varying shades of grey. IRD propaganda was never white and rarely black, but spanned a range of greys.

There are some things that this book does not try to do. It is not a history of Soviet foreign policy machinations or propaganda. This has been dealt with extensively elsewhere, not least of all in IRD's own publications. The reader can be assured that we fully understand that the Soviets were no amateurs at propaganda and agitation, and, throughout the period we cover, exploited every opening provided by British policy to their advantage. Equally, this book is not a history of CIA cultural intervention, but we have attempted to provide enough background context to show how the British and American operations paralleled and mirrored each other. It is also not a history of psychological warfare. The military application of propaganda did, during various crises, dovetail with IRD operations. Nevertheless, it is a separate discipline that has been the subject of a number of good books.

We believe that IRD is relevant to several areas of historical research and enquiry. Not only should IRD interest those investigating the origins of, and Britain's role in the Cold War, but also historians studying the development of the postwar Anglo-American relationship. Perhaps more importantly, IRD is revealing to historians of postwar British propaganda and its influence on postwar British history. Given IRD's covert intervention into British politics, its activities and influence provide a new dimension to those investigating the development of politics during the Cold War – specifically, to what degree IRD influenced the development of the British Left during this period.

Finally, we believe that the history of IRD provides an important historical insight into the development of techniques used by governments to persuade the people they represent. Here are the early spin doctors, lobbyists, tight controls on information, and the use of rebuttal units that have become familiar to a new generation with the election of the New Labour government. The context may have changed, but the methods remain essentially the same.

CHAPTER ONE

Indonesia: Prelude to Slaughter

The Far East in the mid-1960s may seem a strange place to begin a book on British Cold War propaganda. However, events in Indonesia show how far the hand of the British government's secret anti-Communist propagandists – the Foreign Office's Information Research Department – had extended within twenty years of its discreet formation. Indonesia also reveals how highly effective IRD's covert operations were and how closely it worked with Britain's secret service, MI6.

While researching this book we uncovered evidence that the British government secretly helped overthrow President Sukarno of Indonesia, assisting the rise of General Soeharto, the pro-Western leader who ruled from 1965 until 1998, into power. As a result of Sukarno's overthrow some 500,000 Indonesians – suspected Communists – were killed. Ten years later in 1975 Soeharto's regime invaded East Timor and proceeded to kill a third of the population.[1] Soeharto's reign was one of the most brutal and corrupt in recent South-East Asian history. Nevertheless, the operation to bring him to power was considered a success by the Foreign Office as Soeharto remained firmly anti-Communist and favoured British companies and arms suppliers.

British intelligence agencies and propaganda specialists carried out covert operations to subvert the Indonesian President from at least 1963 to 1966. The extent of British involvement in the fall of the nationalist leader in 1966, one of the most important non-aligned Third World leaders of the time, has never been revealed before. The British Foreign Office's mandarins were furious at Indonesian efforts to destabilize the British-backed Malaysian Federation through Sukarno's policy of Konfrontasi. Plans were made by MI6 and British Special Forces to take the war to Sukarno and undermine his regime.

In early 1965 a special unit of the IRD was sent out to Singapore to join MI6 and Army Psychological Warfare officers who were already conducting anti-Sukarno black propaganda operations. The IRD had been set up in 1948 as a 'hush-hush', anti-Communist propaganda department. By the 1960s it employed some 400 people at its Thamesside headquarters and around the world.

As Sukarno's future hung in the balance in late 1965, following a failed dissident army officers' coup and a vicious army counter-coup backed by the CIA, Britain sent a Foreign Office propaganda specialist with £100,000 'to do anything I could do to get rid of Sukarno'. Meanwhile, MI6 was running its own covert operations, assisting anti-Sukarno elements in the Indonesian military. By 1963 Sukarno had become a thorn in the side of both the British and the Americans. They believed there was a real danger that Indonesia – considered a vital strategic country – would fall into the hands of Communists.

However, the consequences of the rise of Soeharto for the people of Indonesia were grave. In one of the worst wholesale slaughters in recent history, the Indonesian Communist Party, PKI, was physically eliminated in the massacres which accompanied Soeharto's seizure of power. An Amnesty International report compared the massacres in Indonesia with those carried out by Pol Pot and the Khmer Rouge in Cambodia a decade later. 'The government-instigated killings in Indonesia in 1965 . . . rank among the most massive violations of human rights since the Second World War. A conservative estimate of the number of people killed in Indonesia is 500,000.'[2]

The tremors of this intervention continue. Over the last decade, Britain's relationship with President Soeharto's regime has been one of the most vexed issues of foreign policy. On the one hand, Indonesia has been one of the most important markets in the world for British arms manufacturers. But, on the other, the use of those arms for internal repression, both in Indonesia itself and in East Timor, has provoked much criticism. The story of Indonesia, one of many, begins to explain why IRD was so important to postwar British history.

*****

Indonesia had not even been a colony of Britain or the United States. The Dutch had run the country until the Second World War when the islands were occupied by the Japanese. The colony produced vast profits for the Netherlands, which were estimated in 1940 to give the Dutch a return of $100 million per year. The country was important economically and strategically, and in 1952 the USA noted that if Indonesia fell out of Western influence, neighbours such as Malaya might follow, resulting in the loss of the 'principal world source of natural rubber and tin and a producer of petroleum and other strategically important commodities'.[3]

The Japanese occupation, which to the Indonesians amounted to another period of colonial rule, succeeded in revitalizing the nationalist movement which, after the war, declared independence and assumed power. The most prominent of these nationalist leaders was Ahmed Sukarno who had founded the Partai Nasional Indonesia in 1927 and had been banished to internal exile by the Dutch in 1931 in a then successful attempt to emasculate the divided nationalist movement.

Indonesia gained its independence from the Netherlands in 1949, less because of the strength of Indonesian nationalism than because of the weakness of the Dutch and the view taken in Washington that Indonesia was not on the anti-Communist front line and Dutch troops could be better employed in defending Western Europe.

Nevertheless, Indonesia was important both economically and strategically to both Britain and the US. Britain had substantial interests in Indonesia including a 40 per cent stake in Royal Dutch Shell, which controlled three-quarters of oil production before the war, and investments totalling some £100 million.[4] By 1959, Britain's investments in Indonesia were in the region of £300 million.[5] Strategically, the Straits of Malacca were considered vital to British and American interests, especially as a route for warships. A Foreign Office report of December 1945 stated, in reference to Indonesia, that: 'it is of great importance to the British Commonwealth that these islands should be under the control of a friendly power.'[6]

The US also had substantial commercial interests in Indonesia and serious concerns about the impact of the leftist nature of the Indonesian government on regional stability. In 1952 the United States noted the danger that if Indonesia fell out of the Western sphere of influence, other neighbours, such as Malaya, might follow and that this could lead to the loss of the principal world source of natural rubber and tin as well as a major producer of petroleum and other strategically important commodities.[7]

Ahmed Sukarno was declared Indonesia's first president in 1945 during the struggle for independence. Western concern regarding Sukarno's regime grew with the strength of the Indonesian Communist Party, the PKI, which by 1965 had a membership of over 10 million – the largest Communist Party in the non-Communist world. Concerns were intensified by Sukarno's internal and external policies, which included the nationalization of Western assets and a governmental role for the PKI. And in 1955, Sukarno held the Bandung Conference of the Non-Aligned Movement, increasing suspicion in both Britain and the USA.

Against this background covert US intervention in Indonesia started as early as 1958 when the CIA supported a rebellion against Sukarno in Sumatra. According to CIA veteran, Victor Marchetti, and John Marks, an ex-intelligence analyst in the State Department: 'Contrary to denials by President Eisenhower and Secretary of State Dulles, the CIA gave direct assistance to rebel groups located on the island of Sumatra. Agency B-26s even carried out bombing missions in support of the insurgents. On May 18, 1958, the Indonesians shot down one of these B-26s and captured the pilot, an American named Allen Pope. Although US government officials claimed that Pope was a "soldier of fortune", he was in fact an employee of the CIA-owned proprietary company, Civil Air Transport.'[8]

Importantly, British antipathy to Sukarno was already such that, according to Secretary of State Dulles's private memorandum, the British Foreign Secretary Selwyn Lloyd had encouraged the Americans to support the anti-Sukarno rebels. The Prime Minister then ordered MI6 to assist the CIA operations. However, the CIA-backed anti-Sukarno rebellion was crushed by loyal Indonesian army units and only succeeded in exacerbating the political and economic situation. As a BBC memorandum observed, 'President Sukarno and his semi-military regime look to an economic solution to quell regionalism and to check Communism, but the rebellion in itself hampers reconstruction. . . . Thus the Government regards with admiration China's rapid economic progress. From President downwards, ministers and civil servants speak of the need to imitate Communist techniques while rejecting the political ideology.'[9]

As a consequence the PKI continued to gain influence. One of the symptoms of the increasing strength of the PKI was Sukarno's creation of NASAKOM (an acronym for the united ideologies of Indonesia; nationalism, religion and Communism) in 1961, by which Sukarno hoped to preserve 'national unity' and give the PKI formal representation in the government. Sukarno's strategy was divide and rule. By playing off the PKI against the armed forces, he hoped to dilute and curb the power of each of the two main political forces.[10] By 1965, to balance the army's growing power, Sukarno aligned himself more closely with the PKI.

Writer and human rights activist Carmel Budiardjo[11] (who was living in Indonesia at the time) said 'For the US, Britain and other Western powers, Indonesia appeared to be on a headlong slide to the left . . . the PKI, with a membership of three million, enjoyed the political support of organizations whose joint membership probably exceeded fifteen million.'[12]

Following the rebellion's defeat, the US adopted a longer term strategy. The emphasis became training and aid for the Indonesian army. The theory was that the nationalist army élite could provide an effective barrier to Communist subversion, a successful policy used some years later in Chile.

The first indication of deliberate British involvement in Western attempts to remove Sukarno appears in a CIA memorandum of June 1962. According to this memorandum, Prime Minister Macmillan and President Kennedy, at a meeting in April, agreed to 'liquidate President Sukarno, depending on the situation and available opportunities.' The CIA officer noted: 'it is not clear to me whether murder or *overthrow* is intended by the word liquidate.'[13] A senior MI6 officer at the time later denied knowledge of the discussion and also denied that the word 'liquidate' meant assassination. He was also reported as saying, 'However, they might well have discussed the best way of getting rid of the awkward fellow.'[14]

Hostility to Sukarno was intensified by Indonesian objections to the Malaysian Federation. Malaya had been granted independence in 1955 under a pro-British government. Britain retained its neighbouring dependencies of Singapore, Sarawak and Sabah, the latter two neighbouring Indonesian Kalimantan on the island of Borneo. In May 1961 the Malaysian leader, the Tunku, declared his aim to create a Malaysian Federation including Singapore, Sarawak and Sabah. The British supported the project, as did the US. Sukarno complained the project was 'a neo-colonial plot', pointing out that the Federation was a project for Malayan expansionism and continuing British influence in the region, and in 1963 his objections crystallized in his policy of Konfrontasi, a breaking off of all relations with Malaysia, soon coupled with low-level military intervention. As Hunter Wade, the New Zealand Commissioner for Singapore and British Borneo, recalled: 'He was trying to stop Malaysia from being formed. He said that no rearrangement should be made in that area without his agreement, not just without his being informed. He insisted he should be party to it. And, of course, the Malaysians and the Brits said, like hell! We and the Australians didn't make any noises, but it was obvious that we were following the same policy. We'd all decided that Malaysia was the only solution . . . and so it had to go ahead.'[15] A protracted border war along the 700-mile front in Borneo started in which specialist forces played a major role, including the SAS and the young Major Peter de la Billière who was later to lead Britain's Gulf War army. Secret cross-border raids were initiated to force the Indonesians back from their forward jungle bases as British troops and the Gurkhas were joined by special forces from Australia and New Zealand. According to Tony Geraghty, special forces historian: 'Slowly but surely, toward the end of 1965 the Indonesians were forced to abandon their front-line bases. Nothing had been said publicly by either the British or the Indonesians about the "Claret" operations, but within Indonesia Sukarno was rapidly becoming discredited among his military commanders.'[16]

Documents recently released at the Public Record Office show that in 1964 Britain and Australia planned extensive bombing raids over Indonesia if Jakarta had stepped up its confrontation. At this point even more ambitious plans were being developed by the British: 'The British . . . were making plans to undermine the regime by spreading the guerrilla war to other parts of Indonesia including, if it were expedient, Sumatra and Java. Plans for these operations embraced such external Intelligence agencies as MI6 as well as the SAS.'[17]

Getting rid of Sukarno was not only a Western concern. Konfrontasi and Sukarno's friendly policy towards the PKI caused increasing worry in the Indonesian army. Hunter Wade, sometime New Zealand High Commissioner for the Malaysian Federation, says: 'Soeharto and most of his senior officers were looking for ways in which they could topple Sukarno, or ease him out. He was very much in their way at that stage. They did have to proceed very cautiously, that was why it was a long time before the army felt able to move.' According to BBC correspondent Roland Challis: 'Sukarno must have been a supremely annoying person for them in many ways. You know, flying, flitting here and there, in and out, making these wonderful speeches of his, which probably had nothing whatsoever to do with the realities that they were trying to deal with. So it's not particularly surprising . . . you would get army people saying, look, this old fool is past his time. You know, he's going gaga, he's in bed with 700 wives. And of course, one would get rid of him.'[18]

Challis continued: 'It is not difficult in that sort of situation for the manipulators to come in, whether they be Chinese, American, British, or whatever, and to try to – and perhaps succeed in sometimes exploiting that sort of situation.'

According to Foreign Office sources the decision to get rid of Sukarno had been taken by Macmillan's Conservative government and carried through during Wilson's 1964 Labour government. The Foreign Office had worked in conjunction with its American counterparts on a plan to oust the turbulent Sukarno. According to sources we have spoken with, a covert operation and psychological warfare strategy was put in place. MI6 plans were approved by the secret service chief Sir Dick White – the only man to head both MI5 and MI6 and a veteran of the wartime Double Cross system. The operation was controlled from Phoenix Park in Singapore, the British headquarters in the region. Initially in charge was Desmond Parkinson, a former wartime POW and life MI6 officer. One of MI6's Far East specialists he was based in Singapore between 1963 and 1965 before returning to Century House to become a head of section. Around him gathered an impressive bevy of MI6 officers including former SOE hero Hubert 'Terry' O'Bryan Tear. In addition, MI6 kept close links with key elements in the Indonesian army through the British Embassy in Jakarta. Officers constantly travelled back and forth between Singapore and Jakarta to handle the increasingly tense situation.

A senior IRD expert was discreetly sent out to Singapore from the Foreign Office to head a small team from IRD working out of Phoenix Park, and was sent there to reinforce the work already being done by MI6 and the military psychological warfare experts.

The opportunity to isolate Sukarno and the PKI came in late 1965 when an alleged PKI coup attempt was the pretext for the army to sideline Sukarno and eradicate the

PKI. On the night of September 30/1 October 1965 a dissident group of left-wing army officers launched a coup against the army high command whom they accused of plotting with the CIA against Sukarno. Six key army generals were killed and a number of strategic points in the capital were seized.

But the Untung coup, as it became known, was to be short-lived and unsuccessful. General Soeharto, commander of KOSTRAD, the army's strategic reserve, who had surprisingly not been targeted, swiftly organized suppression. Hours before the kidnap squad had set out, one Colonel Latief, a member of the Untung group who had been working with Soeharto's forces over the previous days, visited his chief at the military hospital where Soeharto was visiting his son. In his trial in 1976, Latief said that he had warned Soeharto of the imminent action. If he did, Soeharto took no action to forestall it and save his comrades.[19] Who exactly instigated the coup and for what purposes will probably remain a matter of speculation. However, within days it was crushed and the army was firmly in control. Soeharto accused the PKI of being behind the uprising and set about suppressing them in its the aftermath.

A hint of British involvement, or at least knowledge of army plans to overthrow Sukarno, emerged in 1965. Indonesian intelligence obtained a cable from Sir Andrew Gilchrist, the British Ambassador in Jakarta, to the Foreign Office, hinting that the British were aware of Indonesian army intentions. The crucial sentence reads: 'It would be as well to emphasise once more to our local friends in the army that the strictest caution, discipline and co-ordination are essential to the success of the enterprise.'[20] At the time this was dismissed by the army as a forgery produced by the Indonesian intelligence agency, the BPI. But years later, according to Budiardjo, Sir Andrew Gilchrist wrote to an Indian academic confirming its authenticity.[21]

Immediately following the attempted coup Britain set about exploiting the situation to bring an end to Sukarno and Konfrontasi because it was possible that Sukarno might just have been able to reassert his control. Gilchrist was not happy with the British propaganda operation. Back in London, he visited Foreign Office mandarin Joe Garner (Later Baron Garner and head of HM Diplomatic Service) and discussed the IRD and MI6 operations against Sukarno. Garner was convinced that action was needed and at Gilchrist's suggestion, agreed to send Norman Reddaway out to Singapore to bolster the propaganda operation. Reddaway arrived in Singapore immediately following the attempted coup in October 1965. He was put in charge of the IRD operation working side by side with his MI6 counterparts. They had adjacent offices at Phoenix Park.

Reddaway had, in fact, been given £100,000 by Joe Garner at the Foreign Office and the brief, 'to do anything I could do to get rid of Sukarno'. This included manipulating local and international media to follow an anti-Sukarno line.[22] According to Reddaway: 'Gilchrist had been supplying me in Singapore with about four top secret telegrams a week about the shortcomings of Sukarno and the immorality of confrontation – what they were doing in Borneo and so on. And it was up to me to decide what to do with these things.'[23]

As a means of getting this information out to the world from non-government sources, Reddaway used the press, including *The Times* and the *Daily Mail*, but concentrated on Roland Challis: 'What I decided to do was to form a good relationship with the most suitable customer who was a very bright BBC Overseas Service man called Roland Challis. And so Roland Challis was offered, in effect, what had come out of Jakarta in the morning. By lunch time it was off to London and in the evening it came pouring back into the region.'[24] According to Challis: 'I got out there just before Norman Reddaway, and he approached me at a reception in point of fact. Coming up and saying, "Well you and I are going to be seeing quite a lot of each other." And it was very clear that he had already spoken to other BBC people before he came out. I mean, he came out and he made a beeline for me.' But Challis was unaware of Reddaway's real mission or IRD. 'As far as I was concerned he was simply a Foreign Office bloke, you know, concerned with Malaysia and its relationship with Indonesia.'[25]

Although not the most listened to radio station in the area, the BBC was undoubtedly effective. According to Challis: 'It was the English language broadcasting . . . that really counted most. We had a Malay service at that time . . . I would say that the first influence was undoubtedly Radio Australia. Possibly followed by Peking Radio and co-equal with the BBC. The Voice of America was always there, but in all honesty I don't think people listened to it very much.'[26]

In Indonesia, Soeharto and the army began moving against Sukarno. As Carmel Budiardjo, who was imprisoned for several years following the coup attempt, recalled: 'Following the events of 1 October 1965, the army began to discredit him, claiming that he had been "involved" in the coup attempt which, they had initially said, was aimed at deposing Sukarno.'

Behind the scenes the propagandists at Phoenix Park were also getting down to work. On 5 October, Alec Adams, Political Adviser to the Commander-in-Chief, Far East, who had worked in the wartime Ministry of Information, advised the Foreign Office: 'We should have no hesitation in doing what we can surreptitiously to blacken the PKI in the eyes of the army and the people of Indonesia.' The Foreign Office agreed and suggested some 'suitable propaganda themes' such as PKI atrocities and Chinese intervention. On 9 October, Adams reported that, 'arrangements for distribution of certain unattributable material' had been made.[27]

Two days previously, on 7 October, IRD had produced a background briefing on the Indonesian situation, which argued that, 'The extent to which the Communist Party of Indonesia (PKI) was implicated in the attempted coup in Jakarta on September 30, is gradually emerging'.[28] IRD suggested that the composition of Colonel Untung's Indonesian Revolutionary Council provided evidence of PKI involvement. The evidence itself was somewhat contorted: 'The council of forty-five members was chosen so as to give it an appearance of being based on "NASAKOM" . . . Only five known PKI members were included, and these were low-ranking – an even more convincing façade. The Council is not one which anyone except a Communist would have chosen.'[29] IRD also pointed to a statement made by Soeharto suggesting PKI responsibility for the murder of the generals and the fact that the main Catholic and Muslim parties both assumed PKI involvement. Essentially, IRD backed the army's version of events.

Coincidence or not, on 10 October the *Sunday Telegraph* reported: 'Western intelligence experts have uncovered startling information which appears firmly to implicate President Sukarno in a gigantic double-cross'. The article claimed that the chronology of events revealed Sukarno's advance knowledge of the coup attempt and the full complicity of the PKI. This theme continued to dog Sukarno as he attempted to preserve his power and to prevent an all-out bloodbath, and was a major factor in his eventual downfall. It was also a story which IRD papers show the British were anxious to promote.

Over the winter and early spring, as the massacres in Indonesia continued, Sukarno and the army presided over the country in an uneasy coalition. But the political balance between the army, the PKI and Sukarno had been upset and although Sukarno was struggling to maintain and reassert his authority the army was clearly gaining the upper hand. A symptom of Sukarno's loss of power was that his efforts to bring a halt to the killings and preserve the PKI as a balance to the army were unsuccessful.[30]

The British continued to exploit the situation with Norman Reddaway receiving intelligence for exploitation from Gilchrist in Jakarta via Stanley Budd, the IRD man in the Malaysian capital, Kuala Lumpur. But Lord Healey, then Defence Minister, became aware of some IRD black operations and he was not happy: 'They began to put out false information and I came to my horror across an incident where IRD had forged documents to be put on the bodies of Indonesian soldiers. These were designed to give the impression that the Indonesians were adopting a position that was very much more hostile to Britain than in fact it was. I tackled Norman Reddaway and said that this was absolutely disgraceful and must stop.'[31] Healey's intervention did not stop the operations.

Reddaway blames MI6 and military psychological warriors for the less effective black propaganda operations: 'We made a complete nonsense of what you might call the influencing of opinion because we let all the professionals in – the black propagandists and the secret service. They devised dreadful things out of Phoenix Park in Singapore – floating bottles down the river in Sarawak with messages saying how awful Sukarno was.' Some of the projects verged on the ludicrous. Reddaway continues, 'Then there was another idea of having a shipload of anti-Sukarno intellectuals broadcasting from a steamer. Oh yes, and landing a rubber boat on the south side of Java when the moon was dark so people would conclude the Chinese were influencing Sukarno.'[32]

Although others were involved in the propaganda offensive, Norman Reddaway was at its heart and according to Challis, the most effective and ubiquitous. 'One went around talking to anyone one could and you listened to see how they differed from one another, but Norman was the most urbane and the most persuasive and the most frequently present.'

One of the main themes pursued by IRD was the threat posed by the PKI and 'Chinese Communists'. Newspaper reports continually emphasized the danger of the PKI. Drawing upon their experience in Malaya in the 1950s, the British appear to have played the ethnic card by emphasizing the Chinese nature of the Communist threat. Roland Challis says:

One of the more successful things which the West wished on to the non-Communist politicians in Indonesia was managing to transfer the whole idea of Communism on to the Chinese minority in Indonesia. It turned it into an ethnic thing. It is a terrible thing to have done actually, I mean in the way of inciting the Indonesians to rise and slaughter Chinese people . . . it was forced into that framework. The Indonesians were given the idea that it was these wicked Chinese who were actually the Communists. I'd be very surprised if it wasn't IRD – it was certainly someone in the British camp that was putting that idea out.[33]

Rumours about the state of Sukarno's health were spreading like wildfire, as Terence Prittie of the *Guardian* noted in a report on 2 October 1965:

> All reports from Indonesia seem to be coloured by speculation and there has been little reliable news from there for a long time past. Thus, 'authentic' reports about President Sukarno's health have been legion. He has been stated at various times to have had one or both kidneys removed, to have serious heart trouble, to be suffering from abdominal complaints and venereal disease, to have dropsy and be losing the use of one foot, and to have cataract and to be losing the sight of one eye.
>
> At Christmas his feet were reported to be in such a condition that he could no longer wear shoes. Shortly after this report the President performed with some agility on the dance floor at a Government ball.[34]

According to Carmel Budiardjo, the question of Sukarno's health was extremely sensitive: 'Early in August, Sukarno suffered a relapse from a kidney complaint that had been troubling him for years. This raised the political stakes as fears that another, perhaps fatal, relapse made the question of the presidential succession extremely acute.'[35]

But it was the involvement of Sukarno with the attempted coup and the PKI in the following bloody months that was to be the British trump card. According to Reddaway: 'The Communist leader, Aidit, went on the run and Sukarno, being a great politician, went to the front of the palace and said that Communist leader Aidit must be hunted down and brought to justice. From the side door of the palace he was dealing with him every day by courier.'

We have established that this information was revealed by the signal intelligence of Britain's GCHQ. The Indonesians did not have a clue about radio silence and this double dealing was picked up by GCHQ. The British had its main eavesdropping base in Hong Kong tuned into events in Indonesia. In addition a special GCHQ unit was operating from Singapore. The GCHQ chief in the area was Brian Tovey later to head the entire eavesdropping organization. According to Reddaway: 'The story of Sukarno's duplicity came out as a traveller's tale by a news agency man, an American, in Hong Kong. And of course, being enormously newsworthy this was put into the plumbing and everybody wanted it all over the world. And it was all over the world in no time flat and back into Indonesia.'[36] Meanwhile MI6 was aiding its contacts in the army and advising them of Sukarno's every move. Eavesdropping and other intelligence was sanitized to keep Soeharto and his colleagues one step ahead of Sukarno.

In 1990 it was revealed by American investigative journalists that as many as 5,000 names of suspected senior members of the PKI had been supplied to the Indonesian army by the CIA. In effect it was a hit-list which helped the army in its bloody task of physically eradicating the PKI: US Embassy officials followed the progress by checking off names as reports arrived of individual murders and arrests. As information came in from Soeharto's headquarters, the officials were able to track the steady elimination of the PKI's political apparatus. Embassy official Robert J. Martens commented: 'They probably killed a lot of people, and I probably have a lot of blood on my hands, but that's not all bad. There's a time when you have to strike hard at a decisive moment.'[37]

Discrediting Sukarno was of fundamental importance. Sukarno remained a respected and popular leader against whom Soeharto could not move openly until the conditions were right. In the spring of 1966 they were. The constant barrage of bad international coverage and Sukarno's plummeting political position fatally undermined him. On 10 March 1966, Sukarno was forced to sign over his powers to General Soeharto. The PKI was eliminated as a significant force and a pro-Western military dictatorship firmly established. It was not long before Soeharto quietly ended the inactive policy of Konfrontasi, resulting in a swift improvement in Anglo-Indonesian relations which continue to be close to this day. Sukarno was allowed to retain his official title of President-for-Life until 1967. He was to die in 1970 under house arrest.

Roland Challis believes that the British played a major role in Sukarno's downfall:

You know, unless you do what the Americans did in Chile – go in and actually murder the boss – leaders are only brought down by their own people. And I think the British played a very major role in encouraging the Indonesian people to bring down Sukarno, to persuade some military leaders that the moment was coming when they were going to have to deal with the post-Sukarno era.

I think the situation was well analysed, it was well managed, in the sense that it didn't look like manipulation and didn't even involve very much in the way of what nowadays we'd call sort of, you know, intervention! It was the manipulation of ideas, it was pure politics. And actually, it was beautifully done in my opinion.[38]

According to Challis, the key figure was the man from IRD, Norman Reddaway: 'I think he was a very key figure, undoubtedly. I mean I don't know who all the other people involved were of course. I am, myself, not conscious of there having been anyone else who was so fully and meticulously, so intelligently engaged with the whole thing.'

CHAPTER TWO

'Lies and Treachery': the Origins of IRD

The origins of Britain's Cold War propaganda lay in the Second World War. It was during this conflict that the British state felt compelled to master the manipulative arts of propaganda. From small beginnings there rapidly grew a huge effort to win the hearts and minds of friends and foes alike. Lessons would be quickly learned and not forgotten. Many of the key figures that were to direct covert propaganda for the forty years of the Cold War were to learn their trade pitted against the Axis powers, themselves no slouches at propaganda. The antecedents were much older. Anti-Sovietism had been a Foreign Office objective since the Revolution. The British were not newcomers to propaganda but the Second World War had introduced a new professionalism and new methods.

The Second World War had started with a propaganda lie. The pretext for the invasion of Poland on 1 September 1939 was an attack by Polish soldiers on a clandestine German radio station over the border at Gleiwitz inside German Silesia. The bodies of the dead Polish soldiers were displayed to the international press and used to justify Hitler's victorious invasion of Poland to Germany and the world, but the Polish soldiers were not what they seemed. In fact they were the unfortunate inmates of German concentration camps who had agreed to take part in a mock attack on the radio station, in the vain hope of preserving their lives. As historian M.R.D. Foot noted, 'by an historic irony, the Nazis started with a subterfuge a war in which subterfuges were to be used with deadly effect against them'.[1]

However, when Britain declared war on Germany following the invasion of Poland, it was ill-prepared for the propaganda war that was about to follow. At the end of the First World War Britain had virtually dismantled the large and effective propaganda machinery that it had built up after 1914. Between the wars, British propaganda had, on the whole, been left in the hands of freelance anti-Communist and anti-labour business organizations, as organized propaganda by the government was largely abandoned.[2] Until 1938, when the BBC began broadcasting in foreign languages – a belated response to the flood of radio propaganda from the European dictatorships[3] – the only organizations active in the propaganda field overseas were the Travel and Industrial Development Association and the British Council, charged with selling the British way of life abroad.[4] This was to change dramatically in 1939. As historian Philip Taylor has written, the Second World War set off 'what was to become the most vociferous war of words yet waged by belligerent powers'.[5] In order to wage that war, allies and enemies alike were to create huge organizations dedicated to maintaining their own morale, undermining and misleading their enemies and articulating their policies

By late spring 1940, Hitler's apparently unstoppable armies were already in the Low Countries and the situation in France was deteriorating. On 27 May the chiefs of staff, in a joint paper on how Britain could take the war to Germany, informed Churchill that 'the only other method of bringing about the downfall of Germany is by stimulating the seeds of revolt within the conquered territories'.[6] On 19 July, the same day as Hitler told the Reichstag that Britain's defeat was at hand, Churchill authorized the creation of a new organization to take the war to the Germans. As historian Ted Cookridge wrote, 'A few strokes of a pen, and a body was created "to coordinate all action by way of subversion and sabotage against the enemy overseas". Or, as the Prime Minister put it, "to set Europe ablaze".'[7] The new organization, named the Special Operations Executive, (SOE), was officially established under the Minister of Economic Warfare, Dr Hugh Dalton.[8] The Ministry of Economic Warfare (MEW) became known in Whitehall as the 'Ministry of Ungentlemanly Warfare', a sobriquet conceived and applied by Winston Churchill.[9] One of Dalton's assistants at MEW was Christopher Mayhew, then a 25-year-old Oxford tutor, who was assigned to help to organize the SOE training schools before serving with Special Forces in North Africa, France and Germany.[10]

The SOE's main concern over the following years, and its *raison d'etre*, was its work with the resistance groups that sprang up across Europe and the Far East. Indeed, as the official historian of the SOE, M.R.D. Foot, wrote, 'SOE was a world-wide body. There was no continent, there was hardly any country, where it did not do something.'[11] Operations included supporting Tito's Partisans in Yugoslavia; supplying, at great cost, the Warsaw uprising;[12] and supporting Malayan and Burmese Resistance to the Japanese. In Poland alone, 600 tons of equipment and some 318 people were dropped into hostile enemy territory.[13] In 1942, the SOE was also responsible for the assassination of SS leader Himmler's deputy, Reinhard Heydrich.[14]

The SOE's propaganda arm was made up of a fusion of recently created departments; a Foreign Office propaganda organization called EH; a research branch of the War Office, the MIR; and Section D of MI6. Section D (for Destruction) had been set up in March 1938 'to investigate every possibility of attacking potential enemies by means other than the operations of military forces'.[15] Like the MIR, Section D had been investigating methods of industrial sabotage and guerrilla warfare.[16] It had also built up a network of agents around the world under the direction of an ex-Fleet Street journalist called Leslie Sheridan. Starting in the Balkans and using his widespread contacts with Fleet Street journalists and foreign correspondents, Sheridan built up a network of agents that, by 1941, covered the principal neutral capitals of the world. Most notably, Sheridan recruited one Kim Philby to MI6 in 1940.

Many of Sheridan's agents were transferred to the SOE, where they came under military orders as commissioned officers. Sheridan, who had the important position of joint personal assistant to the SOE head, Sir Charles Hambro,[17] had the rank of colonel.[18] His agents were usually practising journalists and were required to 'work their cover'. Their first job was to place pro-British and anti-Nazi propaganda in the local press and later, as strategic deception developed into a fine art, to float carefully planned rumours – the so-called 'sibs' – that would eventually reach and mislead the Axis powers. As cover, some of these journalists were placed as foreign correspondents of leading Fleet Street papers, such as the *Daily Mirror* and the *Daily Mail*. Others were accredited to what was ostensibly a commercial news agency, Britanova Ltd, which had offices in Norfolk Street, off the Strand. Registered in October 1940, Britanova – the name of which Sheridan took pride in having invented – was set up by MI6 and soon after came under the control of the SOE.

The first major task for SOE's propaganda arm was in the United States. Until the middle of 1940, the position of the US media was strongly isolationist. The SOE's objective – with Roosevelt's secret agreement – was to bring the US into the war against Germany. In the fourteen months following the establishment of the SOE there was a major shift in America towards support for Britain and intervention, and 'in this turn-about SOE played a hidden but major part.'[19] Churchill's personal representative in the US was William Stephenson ('Intrepid' or the 'Quiet Canadian'),[20] who had direct access to Roosevelt through his American counterpart, William Donovan (later head of the American Office of Strategic Services, the equivalent to the SOE). As a British intelligence representative in New York, Stephenson persuaded the New York-based Overseas News Agency[21] to provide cover for British agents abroad and to cooperate with Britanova's New York office in placing propaganda in the US press.[22]

Originally the SOE was to have had overall control of covert propaganda while overt propaganda remained in the hands of the new Ministry of Information (MOI). However, as a result of attempts by Alfred Duff Cooper – the minister in charge of the MOI, with a remit covering domestic propaganda as well as propaganda aimed at neutral countries to secure control of SO1 (SOE's propaganda wing), it was decided to set up a separate organization for propaganda to enemy and occupied countries. Thus, SO1 was detached from SOE to become an independent entity, the Political Warfare Executive (PWE), run by a director-general under Foreign Office supervision.

In 1941, Robert Bruce Lockhart had been appointed Deputy Under-Secretary of State in the Foreign Office to coordinate the various organizations engaged in propaganda. He later complained that, 'For twelve months the energy of our whole propaganda effort, which should have been directed against the enemy, has largely been dissipated in interdepartmental intrigues and strife.'[23] The result was somewhat confused. As M.R.D. Foot has noted, 'The main contending departments, the FO, MEW, MOI and SOE, were each to be allowed some say in what the policies of PWE were to be; the Foreign Office was allowed overall control.'[24] Nevertheless, despite the messy nature of the arrangements, early in 1942, as Sir Robert Bruce Lockhart later recalled, 'We were given a new charter and two Ministers: Mr Eden for policy and Mr Bracken for administration. I myself was appointed Director-General . . . it was a great improvement and, with some initial creaks, the machine worked.'[25]

The PWE carried the propaganda war to the enemy and neutrals using whatever truths or lies and methods were thought necessary. These included disinformation planted in neutral countries, covert radio stations and the running of disinformation agents. As Bruce Lockhart recalled: 'During the first two years of the War, when we were on the defensive, our activities were confined mainly to broadcasting and the dissemination of leaflets. Broadcasting in every appropriate language went on by night and by day except for the hour or two required for maintenance of the transmitters. Leaflets were distributed by the Royal Air Force and by balloons and, long before the end of the War, reached a high standard of ingenuity and production.'[26]

Intelligence material was provided mainly by the Foreign Office, but eventually a Central Intelligence Directorate was founded. A section was also established to conduct forward planning and to analyse the effect of the propaganda being put out.[27]

Under Bruce Lockhart, Rex Leeper took control of 'country headquarters', the codename for Woburn Abbey where the PWE's most secret activities were organized: by 1941 it was housing some 458 propagandists. Woburn political warriors came mainly from the universities and Fleet Street, and included future Labour Party leaders Patrick Gordon Walker and Richard Crossman.[28]

A highly secret group was set up under Sefton Delmer at Woburn Abbey. Delmer had been a journalist for the *Daily Express* before the Second World War. He had followed Hitler's rise to power and 'was personally acquainted with Göering, Goebbels, Hess, Himmler and many other Nazi leaders'.[29] During the first year of the war Delmer worked for MI6 and the BBC. However, in 1941 he was recruited to run a psychological warfare operation on behalf of the PWE. He set up a series of black propaganda radio stations, including *Soldartensender Calais*. It broadcast its programmes from England while giving the impression that it was, in fact, a German army radio station.

One of Delmer's most famous creations was 'Gustav Siegfried Eins' (GS1). Delmer invented a tough Prussian called 'Der Chef', who posed as a patriot disgusted by the corruption and depravity that apparently existed under the Nazi government and that was described in great, sometimes pornographic, detail. So well was the origin of the broadcasts disguised, that even the American diplomats in Berlin began basing their dispatches on Der Chef's broadcasts, reporting that there had been an appreciable rise in Army hostility to the Nazi Party, evidenced by a new anti-Nazi radio station being run by a mysterious German officer. Evidence of German opposition to the Nazis was in danger of strengthening the Americans' opposition to entry into the war, so Roosevelt was informed of the deception, apparently to his great amusement.[30] The purpose of GS1 was, as author Charles Cruickshank noted, 'purely subversive . . . to stimulate distrust of the Nazis, the SS, and the administration in general. It also sought by rumour and insinuation to stir up friction between the Nazi Party and the *Wehrmacht*.'[31]

The potential success of rumours was startlingly illustrated during the first months of the war. In the winter and spring of 1939/40, the Germans, possibly under Goebbels' direct orders, had spread the rumour that they had large and highly organized 'fifth columns' of secret supporters all over Western Europe. 'Though in fact this fifth column had hardly any real existence, the belief that it was there had a powerful influence, stimulating panic among millions of civilians, and so creating in rear areas a state of confusion ideal for an opposing *Blitzkrieg* attack.'[32] In Britain it was widely believed and had comical side-effects, with the Home Guard arresting anyone of a possibly foreign background.

False rumours, or 'sibs', were a propaganda technique that became widely used by the British secret services, MI6 and the SOE. Sibs – from the Latin *sibillare*, to whisper –

were disseminated widely, relying on the human weakness for passing on bad news. They had to be credible enough to appear true, but alarming enough to excite attention and the need to tell someone else. The effectiveness of rumours was often tested at home before being put into circulation on the continent, tried out in London clubs by enthusiastic propagandists to gauge effect.[33]

Charles Cruickshank recorded that the formation of sibs was a serious business: 'An Underground Propaganda Committee . . . met at Woburn to examine whispers put forward by the Joint Intelligence Committee, the Foreign Office, the Service Departments, and PWE Regional Directors, and to arrange for those which were approved to be put into their final shape.'[34] Once approved, the rumours would be sent on to MI6, SOE and PWE agents for dissemination overseas.

Sometimes sibs were used to provide cover for other operations. G8, or 'Christ the King', was another black radio operation run by Sefton Delmer on which talks were given by one 'Father Andreas'. According to Delmer, the broadcasts opened with a few minutes of contemplative music, followed by a brief service and more music before the talk began. Delmer recalled, 'He denounced the Nazi attack on the German sense of family, the party's contempt for all human and moral law. His material for these talks was factual and accurate. It contained no inventions, no rumours.'[35] What made it a black operation, in Delmer's opinion, was the fact that the source of the broadcasts was disguised. Indeed, according to Delmer, 'I asked my friends in SOE. and OSS to have their rumour agents in the neutral capitals spread it around that this "Christ the King" radio was a "black" station secretly operated by the Vatican radio! That rumour caught on remarkably well, and very soon it was travelling from mouth to mouth, not only in Switzerland, where the Father had a great following, but in Germany and Austria as well. It was superb "evidence" of the Pope's condemnation of the Nazi regime.'[36]

The number of sibs put out during the war ran into the thousands, and the PWE was still being condemned for spreading them by the Vatican as late as 1978.[37] All sibs were filed and numbered for reference. A particularly imaginative example was sib R/669, designed to cause fear and despondency in the German army on the Eastern Front. As The Times reported, this 'attributed to a Swiss doctor the statement that 200 German soldiers had to be castrated due to the severity of the Russian winter. This one found its way into an American news agency's service under the heading "The eunuchs of the Eastern Front".'[38] Other rumours put out to deceive the enemy, governments and public alike included a story that attributed the RAF's Dambusters success to an international organization of foreign saboteurs. According to the rumour, the RAF raids were merely a cover.[39]

According to SOE veteran and later Conservative MP, Sir Douglas Dodds-Parker, sibs were also a highly effective means of combating collaboration. He recalled that, 'If we knew a certain individual had been collaborating, then we would put that out with some source locally who would not say, "I heard it on some radio station over in England." It would appear locally as if from some local source. And that was much better than having it put out on the radio outside. And this worked quite effectively.'[40]

Over the last two years of the Second World War, the bulk of the PWE's work was concerned with the big military operations, the biggest of which was Operation Overlord – the invasion of Europe. Indeed, in the months leading up to D-day, the

PWE had been engaged in a massive campaign of strategic deception. Because the activities of the PWE and the SOE were so closely watched by the Germans, it was confidently believed that they could be used to deceive them. Intensified activity in one area, or country, could be used to mislead the Germans as to where the invasion would take place.[41] For example, Operation Bodyguard was designed to draw attention away from Normandy, to the Pas de Calais (Operation Fortitude) and the Balkans (Operation Zeppelin). Increased activity, such as sabotage and attacks on troops, would suggest a possible landing and tie down German troops away from the actual landing area.[42]

Operations to confuse the enemy continued once the invasion had taken place. For example, during the first weeks of the invasion, *Soldartensender Calais* took advantage of the breakdown in German communications to issue its own situation reports, based on up-to-date information from Supreme Headquarters, Allied Expeditionary Force (SHAEF). As Delmer recalled, 'Our reports were accurate too – ninety-nine times out of a hundred. The hundredth time came when we put in some false information at the request of the tactical deception experts to mislead our trusting clients and send them headlong into a trap.'[43] In fact, they were so accurate that John Kimche, a German-speaking reporter at the *Evening Standard*, who had found out that the reports were based on advance information, used *Soldartensender Calais* as an unattributed source for his articles.[44]

After Overlord, Bruce Lockhart recalled, much of the PWE's work was intended to maintain contact with the populations of the countries to be liberated. 'Our planning began in October 1943 and in preparation we initiated the Voice of SHAEF on the BBC. The broadcasts, which had to be approved by SHAEF, were sent out in French, Flemish, Dutch, Danish and Norwegian to enable General Eisenhower to give his direct instructions to the civil population on the coast of Western Europe and, doubtless, to keep the enemy guessing about his intentions.'[45] As Cruickshank noted, 'It is impossible in a few pages to describe all that PWE did in connection with Operation Overlord.'[46] In the weeks leading up to the invasion of Europe the need to produce propaganda in advance had necessitated the strict isolation of the teams of writers, translators and printers needed to do the job. The work was on an enormous scale. In the days before D-day, two printing presses, under military guard, produced some 32 million leaflets.[47]

The PWE could even claim the distinction of having broadcast the first news of the landings through *Soldartensender Calais*. With advance warning that the invasion was imminent, Sefton Delmer was prepared for when the German news agency put the story out on the air. As soon as the news came through, Delmer explained to Hans Gutmann – the chief news writer – whom they had invited to dinner to keep him on hand, that they needed some broadcasts written, just to be prepared in the event of an Allied invasion. Delmer recalled his conversation with Hans Guttman: 'The object will be to suggest . . . that their line has been breached, that they are cut off and that they might as well give up. We don't want to say that of course. All we do is give them a picture of the situation from which they can draw their own conclusions.' A fully comprehending and, by now, delighted Gutmann set to work. The final reports were written, Delmer wrote later, 'to fit in with the Allied deception plan which was to mislead the Germans into the belief that the invaders were striking at the mouth of the Seine and at Calais'.[48]

Recently released SOE files at the Public Record Office are beginning to show the full extent of black propaganda operations against the Germans. The blackest propaganda, headed 'Adults Only' in the files, was about sexual peccadilloes of the most senior Nazis. SS chief Heinrich Himmler was portrayed as the protector of a group which carried out regular 'cult' orgies. Other leaflets claimed Nazi party leader Christian Weber acted as a croupier at a party where a naked girl was strapped on to a roulette wheel. The girl was then spun and sexually abused by whichever German official she stopped in front of. SOE even put Himmler's head on forged stamps to encourage rumours that he was plotting against Hitler.

The propaganda themes developed by the PWE had one common thread: whatever would bring victory closer by 'weakening the enemy's appetite for war, by hindering his ability to fight, or by sustaining the occupied countries' will to resist.'[49] However, the means to achieve this aim were many and varied. PWE used outright lies and disinformation, but it did not only produce black propaganda. By far the bulk of its material was what are described as white and grey propaganda. As Cruickshank noted, in 1942 a director of production was appointed, 'who was put in charge of the printing of PWE's mass-produced white propaganda – millions of leaflets, miniature periodicals and newspapers, for which the British government could openly accept responsibility.'[50] Part of the PWE's remit was liaising with the BBC's overseas services, which, like the domestic BBC, refused any involvement in black propaganda. Nevertheless, Bruce Lockhart recalled, 'I moved into Bush House in the same block as the BBC. We made a new agreement with the Governors of the BBC, which gave us full political control over our foreign broadcasts.'[51]

The Ministry of Information (MOI) had been set up in 1939 and was responsible for government propaganda into Britain and neutral countries. Initially under Lord Macmillan, effective propaganda policy had been disturbed by the rapid succession of ministers given responsibility, one after the other. Macmillan was followed shortly after by Sir John Reith, founder of the BBC, and Duff Cooper, whose failure to reach agreement with Hugh Dalton, the Minister for Economic Warfare, led to the appointment of Brendan Bracken at Churchill's own instigation. The MOI's principal task was to generate propaganda aimed at the British people. Its mission was to lift and maintain morale and deal with the mass media, including the BBC. Its responsibilities included government information policy, press conferences, publicity campaigns and censorship. The importance of censorship had been recognized in a 1939 Royal Institute of International Affairs enquiry into broadcasting and propaganda considered useful to the planners in the MOI. The RIIA, in a list of general ideas, concluded that, 'The best propaganda is the silent murder of the opposition news – Censorship.'[52]

Other ground rules presented in this document, which helped 'to lay the foundations of the basic principles of Britain's wartime propaganda',[53] included: 'As regards the masses of people, appeal to their instincts and not to their reason . . . Under censorship conditions rumour assumes gigantic proportions. Hence whispering campaigns . . . The highest art in propaganda is to maintain the appearance of impartiality while securing the wholehearted adoption of the view propagated. . . . We must search Hitler's speeches for propaganda points.'[54] Can the postwar popularity of the royal family be traced to recommendation number 31: 'The glorification of the Royal Family is an important matter'?[55]

Initially, the MOI was faced with maintaining that morale in the context of repeated enemy victories by seizing on what few successes there were, and transforming near disaster, like at Dunkirk, into a victory of sorts. When Churchill gave his broadcast to the nation, Dunkirk was transformed into Britain's 'finest hour'.

Arguably, it was the overt side of British propaganda that had the greatest and most lasting effect. During the early squabbles over the control of propaganda, Rex Leeper – in an attack on the MOI's insistence that it should maintain control over all overt propaganda and assertion that this was separate from covert subversive propaganda – wrote in exasperation, 'It is fantastic for the Ministry of Information to interpret subversive propaganda as merely covert or underground propaganda. The most formidable instrument for propaganda today is broadcasting and the facilities offered by the BBC are far and away, our most potent method of employing that instrument.'[56]

The BBC was the principal means of reaching both occupied and neutral Europe with propaganda. During the course of the war, it became an extremely effective weapon of propaganda. The war saw the emergence of a special link between the BBC and the British people – indeed, between the BBC and the peoples of the occupied European Continent.[57] However, despite its nominal independence, during the war the BBC became an instrument of state information policy, 'guided' by the MOI and the PWE in all of its activities. As historian Philip Schlesinger has argued, 'from the point of view of the control of sensitive "material", it mattered little whether the BBC was officially controlled or formally independent. . . . The BBC saw itself as part of the war effort, and hence the question of its pulling in a very different direction from that deemed officially desirable did not arise.' Indeed, such was the understandable identification between the BBC and the propagandists that A.P. Ryan, the top wartime news executive and special adviser to the BBC, was convinced that the BBC 'should supplement the army, navy and the air force as "a fourth arm in this war".'[58]

Under the guidance of the MOI and the PWE, the BBC's objective during the early part of the war, as Germany marched from one victory to the next, was to attract an audience for its broadcasts in Europe through reliable and accurate news, no matter how uncomfortable the facts were. Efforts to shape BBC broadcasts by the propagandists often led to conflict with BBC officials. Richard Crossman, working in the PWE, recalled that, 'meetings between the PWE and the officials of the BBC took the form of long bitter fights. Quite properly, the BBC officials were determined to do nothing beyond reporting the straight news. . . . Our job was to inject the highest percentage of propaganda content we could into the news service of the BBC . . . struggling to corrupt the BBC for the purpose of winning the war!'[59]

Nevertheless, historian M.R.D. Foot recognized that: 'This anxiety always strictly to tell the truth, however unpalatable the truth might be to a patriotic ear, turned out before long to have been a devastatingly effective stroke in psychological warfare. As the BBC always stated the facts, so far as they were known in London, and German- and Italian-controlled broadcasts continued their pre-war habits of boasting, exaggeration, and propaganda, those who were able to hear both sides were quickly able to conclude which was the more reliable.'[60] However, as Cruickshank pointed out, 'Although open broadcasting was confined to the truth, on the ground that honesty is the best policy, it did not necessarily have to be the whole truth. While the white broadcasters were required to promote the current approved propaganda themes no less than were their black brethren, some truths would support them better than others, and some were better left untold.'[61]

Nevertheless, the strength of the BBC was that it inspired trust. For example, with regard to the Corporation's broadcasts to occupied France, 'Britain's military reverses were reported with complete frankness and no effort was made to hide the gravity of her situation. This honesty in adversity much impressed the BBC's French audience, and went some way to restore French confidence in Britain – which had been seriously shaken by Vichy and German propaganda that the British troops had left the French in the lurch at the time of Dunkirk.'[62] Such was its success in establishing a reputation for reliability that, by the end of the war, the BBC 'was regarded by the vast majority of listeners not as an instrument of propaganda but as the purveyor of an objective news service run by people anxious to disseminate the truth. . . . This of course made it a first-class instrument of propaganda.'[63] As George Orwell noted, 'The BBC as far as its news goes has gained enormous prestige since about 1940. . . . "I heard it on the radio" is now almost equivalent to "I know it must be true".'[64]

According to historian Philip Taylor, 'the basic principles of Britain's wartime propaganda [were] encapsulated in Sir John Reith's maxim that "news is the shocktroops of propaganda" and the Ministry's general view that it was more effective to tell the truth, nothing but the truth, and as far as possible, the whole truth.'[65] What the propagandists learned was that propaganda was most effective if it was based on accurate factual information. Spin, to use the modern term, there was, but if outright disinformation was to be used it was most effective when used sparingly, dropped into otherwise accurate and reliable information sources. Bruce Lockhart noted, 'The credit that the propagandist enjoys both with the enemy and in enemy-occupied territory is in direct proportion to the accuracy of his information.'[66] Crossman, for one, was convinced that black propaganda was less effective than its practitioners sometimes claimed. 'Although we found the left-hand activities enormous fun, although a vast amount of talent went into them, although I am sure they entertained the Gestapo, I have grave doubts whether black propaganda had an effect in any way commensurate with that of straightforward propaganda from enemy to enemy.'[67] Dodds-Parker recalled, 'I've always found, as a principle, that truth is much more valuable and effective than trying to concoct a lot of falsities and black propaganda. Sooner or later people find out and they never trust you.'[68]

The lessons learned were to be applied far sooner than anyone expected.

CHAPTER THREE

Origins of the Cold War

In late September 1947, a brooding Stalin was on holiday in Georgia with his deputy, Molotov. During the day they would rest in the sun and drink the robust local wine. In the evening, Stalin would read coded cables sent over a special radio from Szklarska Premba in southern Sudetenland. The names of the correspondents were aliases. The first cable from 'Sergeev and Borisov' was addressed to 'Comrade Filippov', one of Stalin's favoured codenames. The senders were Andrei Zhdanov and Georgi Malenkov, two of Stalin's senior officials, who had been assigned a top-secret task by Stalin. They reported, 'Tonight, September 22, the conference began its work.'

What took place in that six-day conference of the nine Communist powers was the creation of the Informational Bureau of Communist Parties, the Cominform. On the last day they sent 'Comrade Filippov' another message: 'Tomorrow, the morning of the 29th, we will flying to Moscow. On all documents of the conference we will report personally.'[1]

On their arrival, Stalin appointed Zhdanov head of the Cominform and he announced its existence to the world in October 1947. Its creation signalled the beginning of a new and tough policy consolidating the Soviet sphere of influence, especially in Eastern Europe. It sealed the beginning of a period of total Soviet dominance in the countries that it now controlled.[2]

The Cominform was not a debating chamber but a tool of the Soviets. Anybody who misunderstood this was in for a rude shock. According to two modern Russian historians, Vladislav Zubok and Constantine Pleshakov:

> Co-ordination among 'fraternal' parties in the Cominform guaranteed Soviet domination much better than any system of bilateral state treaties, and at the same time dispelled negative associations with traditional imperialist practices, such as the domination of Poland by Czarist Russia in the nineteenth century. But at the same time Stalin did not want the Cominform to be in any way an ideological headquarters of the revolutionary movement. The Yugoslav Communists tried to perceive it as such and were unceremoniously expelled from the Cominform in June 1948.[3]

Stalin had disbanded the Comintern in 1943 under pressure from his new allies, Britain and America. The Comintern coordinated the work of all of the world's Communist parties and was founded by Lenin as the Third International. From its inception the Comintern was the great Communist bogeyman to the West, literally, the global conspiracy made incarnate. Roosevelt demanded its dissolution as a condition of supplying war material during the Second World War. The Comintern had dispensed

'Moscow Gold' to its comrades abroad and dictated their policies. While some of that work was clandestine, it rarely involved itself in espionage, leaving that to other organs of state. This organization had been devoted to spreading the Communist dogma and influence across the world, principally by the use of propaganda and agitation. However, even after dissolution, the key elements of the organization remained intact from the core staff in Moscow, a network of agents and sympathizers linked up with Soviet intelligence and spread over Eurasia.[4] Many were employed in the new Cominform.

The main purpose of the new Cominform was to extend the work of the international Communist parties. It created peace organizations and other Communist 'fronts' to put pressure on the Western powers through public opinion to decolonialize and make 'real' peace with the Soviet bloc on, what were considered to be, Soviet terms. These fronts were designed to be inclusive of traditionally activist groups and included the World Federation of Trade Unions, the International Union of Students, the International Organisation of Journalists and the World Federation of Democratic Lawyers. These organizations were to prove successful, picking up many members and holding many conferences outside the Soviet bloc. The Cominform published a fortnightly journal, *For Lasting Peace, for a People's Democracy*, in numerous languages.

The World Peace Movement was considered to be the most effective of the fronts by both the East and the West. It held large international conferences for a number of years. The Foreign Office argued that the World Peace Movement was, 'in effect . . . merely another instrument of Soviet policy'. Many people felt that the Soviets had hijacked the word 'peace' and used it to imply Soviet fraternity, compared with American and British aggression. Britain was already under increasing pressure to retreat from the Empire and, faced with Communist victories in Western European elections, British officials began to argue that it was time to go onto the offensive. As Denis Healey pointed out in his autobiography, 'Britain, not America, was the first target of Soviet hostility, because it was British troops which stood on the frontiers of Soviet power in Greece, Trieste and Persia, while the United States was trying to disengage from its wartime positions all over the World as fast as possible.' For example, on 8 June 1946, Moscow Radio told its listeners in Norway, 'This little country [Britain] went to war because it and its fascist reactionary leaders love war and thrive on war. The attack on Hitlerite Germany was purely incidental.'[5]

The defeat of the Axis in 1945 left a radically altered political map of the world. Whereas before the war the Soviet Union had been isolated and confined effectively to Eastern Europe, its power now reached beyond Berlin and its influence was more global than ever. The Soviet victory in the 'Great Patriotic War' had made Communism look like it could organize an effective society capable of industrialization on a huge scale. The fact that it had been at the forefront of the war against the fascists, the Communist's mortal enemies, lent Communism an enormous influence and credibility. If it had taken the German invasion of Russia to engage the Soviets in what they had previously called an 'imperialist war', it was the Communist parties across Europe that had often been at the forefront of the resistance to Nazi occupation and, following the end of hostilities, Communist Party membership mushroomed.

The Foreign Office, looking out across a shaken and disturbed Empire, saw a dark horizon. As Lord Mayhew, then a Labour MP and junior minister at the Foreign Office, recalled, 'the Communists were threatening to take power in Paris and Rome, and Berlin, Germany and so on, we were terribly worried even about the influence of Communism in West Germany, and those were the priority countries. Then there was the question of the Commonwealth, we were desperately worried that once they became independent they'd become easy meat for some of these Communists.'[6]

Britain, too, had undergone a radical political transformation. The 1945 election had brought in a Labour government by a landslide on a socialist mandate. A war-weary nation wanted hope through an idealistic and a more egalitarian society. Although Churchill had proved a historic and great war leader, his party had been brushed aside when it came to peace. Initially the Labour government had hopes of a new relationship with the Soviet Union. Quite quickly such hopes were replaced by suspicion. The British State, and even more so, the United States, perceived a Soviet and Communist threat in Europe and the Empire very quickly.

The day the war ended Britain was already confronting Communism. British forces were already six months into intervention against the Left in Greece; the political situations in Italy had been organized for two years to limit the power of the Left; and while everyone thought that the Labour government would move against France, Bevin refused any serious action.

As early as 1946 the British cabinet had been receiving alarming intelligence reports on the dangers of Soviet military intervention in Europe. Western public opinion began to be alerted to the Soviet 'threat' by leading politicians. On 5 March 1946, Winston Churchill made the famous speech at Fulton, Missouri, in which he spoke of an 'Iron Curtain' descending across Europe.

In America, despite the inclination to disengage following the Second World War, the mood towards the Communists was hardening and there was pressure for a more aggressive policy on the Soviet Union. In 1947, after much consultation with the State Department, the US President unveiled 'the Truman Doctrine': the US would assist any nation to deal with internal or external Communist aggression, and would begin by giving aid to Greece and Turkey.

The establishment of Cominform was seen by many commentators in the West as a naked statement of Communist aggressive intent. A more sophisticated analysis may have considered whether it was a reaction to a complex international situation and reflected Stalin's notorious sense of insecurity, which extended from the personal to the international. As relations deteriorated, the Soviets used agitation and propaganda to good effect, particularly railing against Imperial Britain, then trying to control the disintegration of the Empire. Mayhew's then deputy, Norman Reddaway, recalled that, 'the Russians [had] a huge opinion influencing machine, with three members of the Politburo concerned with information and propaganda, beating our Ernest Bevin and Hector McNeil and Mayhew round the head at the UN, [there was a] deluge of propaganda through front organizations, radios and local Communist Parties.'[7]

The Foreign Secretary, the man who set the tone towards the Soviet Union, was Ernest Bevin, one of the few members of Attlee's government who had broken through the class divide. Bevin was the illegitimate son of a Somerset woman who earned her living as a domestic servant and village midwife. She had died when he was only seven years old. He left school at eleven, worked as a farm boy and then went to Bristol, where he worked as a drayman until he was twenty-nine, when he joined the docker's union as an organizer. The 64-year-old Bevin had expected to be made Chancellor instead he found himself at the Foreign Office. According to Denis Healey, 'Though short of stature, he was built like a battle tank, with the rolling gait and thick stumpy fingers typical of a stevedore. Slow and soft of speech in private, he could roar like any sucking dove at a public meeting. He had shown a ruthless ambition in getting to the top of his union and could be brutally arrogant in debate.'[8] Bevin had dealt with Communists in the trade unions for thirty years and was sympathetic to Foreign Office concerns about dangers presented by Soviet Communism. Bevin's anti-Communist scepticism had been reinforced by the Soviet show trials of 1936–8.

The Foreign Office's own inherent anti-Sovietism had had a brief respite during the war, but it soon returned in full flood. In September 1946, Thomas Brimelow, who had been the head of the Consular Service in Moscow from 1942 to 1945 and was afterwards in the Northern Department, wrote on the hard line posture already being taken by the American public against the Soviets:

> In Great Britain a general realisation of the pattern of Soviet policy will come about slowly, and while it is forming every allowance will be made to the Russians and none to the Foreign Office. The result of this will be a split in public opinion between those who blame the Russians and those who blame the Foreign Secretary. If we are to keep this split to the smallest possible proportions – and this we must do if we are to reduce the effectiveness of Communist propaganda inside this country – we shall have to show patience, forbearance and a strict correctness in all our dealings with the Russians. We cannot afford to be in the wrong.[9]

In the climate of increasing tension within the Soviet Union, there grew the belief within the government and the Foreign Office that there was a need to counter Soviet propaganda, especially as the Cominform would undoubtedly professionalize and expand Soviet output. The British had no professional equivalent. The propaganda departments of the Second World War – MOI and the PWE – had been closed down at the end of the war. Although the British government had the Foreign Office's News Department and the successor to the MOI, the Central Office of Information, it had no organized capability for in-depth research for high-impact, overt and covert propaganda. However, Britain's postwar economic and military decline virtually ensured that propaganda would become an important weapon, because it was one of the few means by which the government could respond to the perceived Soviet threat and attempt to maintain Britain's status in the world at minimal expense.

Bevin's two junior ministers were Hector McNeil and Christopher Mayhew. According to Healey, Mayhew was one of the few people on the Left at Oxford in his generation who never joined the Communist Party. 'Chris himself was something of a boy-scout, seeing issues always in black and white. This made him one of the best early television presenters.'[10] It also made him an excellent propagandist. Mayhew was the *eminence grise* behind the formation of the Foreign Office's anti-Communist organization. A tall, thin intellectual with ambition and a cause, Mayhew had been convinced of the need for such a department and strategy by his experiences at the United Nations, where the Russians were conducting a hard-hitting propaganda offensive, aimed in particular against Britain.[11] According to Norman Reddaway, at the time Mayhew's parliamentary Private Secretary,

> It was a reaction to a situation which identified itself sharply at the United Nations in October 1947 where Bevin was belaboured by Molotov and Vishinski with an absolute torrent of well-researched information, misinformation, and disinformation, obviously the product of a very large machine for influencing opinion. When Bevin found himself belaboured, he said he was not going to put up with this and asked Mayhew to do something about it. He [Mayhew] had the wit to realise that, if we were going to stand up to this sort of blast, you had to have some kind of organiza-tion which would do research in depth and then find ways of marketing it.[12]

Like many of the of the Foreign Office mandarins, Mayhew rapidly became a Cold Warrior – profoundly suspicious of the intentions of the Soviet Union. He was firmly on the right of the Labour Party and was unsympathetic to the Soviet Union. Suspicion of the Soviet Union was not universal in Britain. It has to be remembered that, at the end of the Second World War, there was still an admiration in much of the population for 'Uncle Joe' Stalin and the Red Army. Class war was at its height and many British people felt that Communism, for all of its faults, might be better than the brutal capitalism that they had experienced in the years leading up the war. Within the Labour Party, differences in attitude towards the Soviet Union emerged publicly, both in parliament and in the Trade Union Congress. Writing to the Prime Minister on 29 October 1946, a group of Labour MPs argued that British socialist policies could bridge antagonism between the United States and the Soviet Union and encourage Soviet extension. They deplored the 'anti-red' virus, opposed allying Britain with 'American Imperialism' and foresaw the United Nations as the principal future instrument of international security. In November, during a debate on foreign policy, the demand for a 'socialist alternative' to existing policies was popularly made and one of Bevin's fiercest critics, Richard Crossman, made a vigorous attack on the government's 'drift into the American camp'. By the middle of 1947 the risk of a split in the Labour Party and its implications was being seriously discussed.[13]

This mood of antagonism towards American-style capitalism is almost unimaginable today. However, the eminent historian A.J.P. Taylor, for example, considered that nobody in Europe believed in the American way of life – that is in private enterprise. George Orwell, who as we shall see was no Communist, dismissed capitalism as a failed system.[14] Key members of the cabinet, who tended to be more right-wing than many of their backbench comrades, were anxious that all of this left-wing talk would stop the Americans providing more aid. Britain had been financially devastated by the war and the Americans would not be happy about assisting their ally if their aid was going to fund neo-Communist policies like nationalization.

Press and public surveys carried out in the summer of 1947 by the British Embassy in Washington revealed that avowed anti-Communism would be the main issue influencing American support.[15] The Foreign Office had started campaigning early for the control of any government anti-Communist propaganda organization. As early as April 1946, Christopher Warner, an under-secretary at the Foreign Office, was calling for an attack on and exposure of international Communism through a propaganda campaign in response to an apparent Soviet determination to achieve their ends by any means short of war.[16] In the same year, Foreign Office officials persuaded Bevin to agree to offensive propaganda operations against Communism in Iran. The Soviet Union had established a new republic in northern Iran – just about the only actual case of a Kremlin 'land grab' outside its sphere of influence following the Second World War.

The Foreign Office was already making informal use of its media contacts. The Russia Committee noted in late 1946 that a 'considerable amount of material based on official sources' was getting into the press, such as the Canadian blue book on trials of Soviet spies.[17] All heads of the Foreign Office political departments were instructed to find ways to make 'subtler use of our publicity machine', to ensure the publication of anti-Soviet material, to leak information to friendly diplomatic correspondents or to inspire questions that the Foreign Office could pretend that it did not want to answer.[18]

As early as January 1947 the British Foreign Office called its heads of missions in Eastern Europe to a meeting in London, with ministers and leading officials, to develop a concerted response to the Soviet Union.[19] Bevin had resisted a formal organization. His initial reluctance seems to have been, in part, base on the feeling that 'the putting over of positive results of British attitude will be a better corrective'.[20] After holding out against adopting such a policy for some time, Bevin was finally convinced by the linking of the civil servants' plans for a propaganda offensive with Christopher Mayhew's plan for a 'Third Force' campaign. Mayhew had tied up with the Foreign Office behind-the-scenes campaign. While many Foreign Office mandarins felt ill at ease with the Labour Party, they felt comfortable with Mayhew, a natural social democrat, and his boss, Bevin. Bevin was to reject complaints that there were too many public school men at the Foreign Office, saying, 'I am not one of those who decry Eton and Harrow. I was very glad of them in the Battle of Britain.'

Mayhew, in the course of discussions within the Foreign Office during the remainder of the year, drafted a paper that in its final form, was accepted by the cabinet in January 1948 and was to become the genesis of IRD.[21] Mayhew's paper, presented by Bevin, commented, 'If we are to give a moral lead to the forces of anti-Communism in Europe and Asia, we must be prepared to pass over to the offensive and not to leave the initiative to the enemy, but to make them defend themselves.' This would be achieved through a propaganda offensive based on 'the vital ideas of British social democracy and Western civilisation' and could be carried out by a small section in the Foreign Office, established for that purpose, which could undertake the necessary research and dissemination of information and anti-Communist propaganda 'through our Missions and information services abroad.' The cooperation of the BBC would also be sought. In addition, 'Our anti-Communist publicity material should also be available to Ministers for use, when convenient, in their public speeches; and also to British delegations to conferences and – on an informal basis – to Labour Party and Trades Union delegations.'[22]

Mayhew and Bevin believed that a straightforward anti-Communist propaganda operation would not be acceptable to some of the more left-wing members of the cabinet, especially Aneurin Bevan, who were intermittently sympathetic to the Soviet

Union and often more critical of the United States. So Mayhew had added to the purely anti-Communist propaganda campaign suggested by the Foreign Office civil servants the concept of a 'Third Force' propaganda campaign. He had presented the idea to Bevin in a confidential paper in October 1947, stressing that the campaign would attack capitalism as well as Communism and promote the Social Democratic values associated with the Labour government.[23]

The original idea of a 'Third Force' was developed by G.D.H. Cole in 1946 as a left-wing alternative to the close relationship with the United States, to which Britain was drifting in reaction to a deterioration of relations with the USSR. According to Cole, Britain should cast itself as the leader of Western Europe and lead it towards a liberal socialist future independent of both the USSR and the United States – in effect, adopt a neutral position.[24]

However, according to Christopher Mayhew, the purpose of casting the anti-Communist propaganda offensive in terms of the 'Third Force' was purely tactical – a cover designed to undermine any left-wing opposition, should IRD and the nature of its operations come to light. As Mayhew explained:

> I thought it was necessary to present this whole campaign in a positive way, in a way which Dick Crossman and Michael Foot would find hard to oppose. And they were calling for a Third Force . . . so I recommended in the original paper I put to Bevin that we call it a Third Force propaganda campaign. We were going to campaign for Social Democracy, and on that basis Ernest Bevin accepted my first draft. We only dealt with the Third Force idea frankly, or at least I did, because I was parliamentary Under-Secretary and I didn't want Bevin to be defeated and humiliated inside the Labour Party.[25]

The cabinet agreed that the British government would be more forthright in attacking the Soviet Union in public – particularly at the United Nations – and that the ad hoc activities of the previous two years would be combined within a secret Communist Information Department, shortly to be given the anodyne cover title of the Information Research Department. The formation of IRD was approved by the cabinet on 4 January 1948 to 'check the inroads of Communism by taking the offensive against it and to give the lead to our friends abroad and help them in the anti-Communist struggle'. IRD studied 'Communist principles, policy, tactics, and propaganda' and devised 'publicity designed to expose the realities of Communism and the lying Communist propaganda.'[26]

There have been suggestions that the Foreign Office simply hijacked the new anti-Communist organization and that Mayhew's claim that the 'Third Force' concept was a later device to cover his embarrassment. This seems unlikely. A report from Waldemar J. Gallman, minister at the American Embassy in London, to George Marshall in Washington would seem to support Mayhew's claims:

> Foreign Office officials directly charged with Soviet affairs have recently and repeatedly indicated that while there is no change in substance to United Kingdom policy towards Russia, every move must be carefully considered and planned from

the point of view of protecting Bevin from Labour party rebels . . . in light of Labour rebellion, Bevin and Foreign Office now take greater pains to avoid creating impression he is ganging up with the United States against Russia.'[27]

Parliament, which may have rejected an anti-Communist propaganda offensive, was therefore not informed and, as IRD was in part funded through the Secret Vote, by which Parliament votes funds for MI5 and MI6 without scrutiny, nor could it exercise any scrutiny over IRD operations. From the start, IRD had close links with the Secret Intelligence Service (SIS, also known as MI6). IRD also made use of the intelligence coming into MI6, which was sanitized for any form of distribution. In particular, IRD worked closely with the anti-Soviet Section IX of the Secret Service, which had been relaunched in 1944 under the control of Kim Philby.[28]

The economic support provided by Marshall Aid enabled Bevin to initiate an offensive policy against Communism, without which Britain could simply not have been sustained. As Christopher Mayhew commented in a speech at Chatham House in June 1950, 'from the middle of 1947 onwards, decisions were taken towards uniting the free world, at the expense of widening the gap with the Communist world. I would say that the turning point was Mr Marshall's Harvard speech in June 1947. From then on our immediate objective changed, from "one world", "to one free world".' Once given the go-ahead to establish IRD and launch the anti-Communist propaganda campaign, Foreign Office officials were faced with the practical tasks of organizing the new department and developing the methods that it would use. The responsibility of setting up IRD was given to Ivone Kirkpatrick, Assistant Under-Secretary in charge of Foreign Office information, and one of those officials who had been calling for a propaganda offensive since 1946.

CHAPTER FOUR

A Crusade Begins

The new Foreign Office department scored its first major success with a revealing media campaign on Soviet labour camps. Mayhew launched this offensive in October 1948 at the United Nations, already a vital international forum and one that IRD sought to influence. Mayhew said, 'It was decided that Soviet slave labour camps would be the first line of counter-attack. So one of the first jobs of IRD was to collect everything that was known about these camps and when the Russians made a totally irrelevant attack on Britain over our Colonial policies and our undemocratic ways, I retaliated with an attack on their slave labour in a long speech into which was put everything that was then known about the Stalinist tyranny and labour camp system.'[1]

According to Norman Reddaway, Mayhew dug up a great deal of the gulag material himself, 'and he found that Sirov, the head of the KGB, had deported a good many thousand Estonians who didn't like being taken over by the Soviets and had dumped them in Uzbekistan, where a lot of them still are. This sort of thing, Soviet imperialism and what went on in the gulags, what the workers paradise was really about, what was happening in the collectivisation of agriculture with a lot of people starving. All this was very valuable information and much appreciated by the serious journalist.'[2]

The opportunity was taken to compare Soviet labour camps with Nazi concentration camps. Equating Communism with Nazism was to become a key IRD theme. As a memo explained, 'In order to get the idea across to the public it is essential to build up the names of one or two well-known camps until they are as familiar as Dachau or Belsen. Karaganda the remote coal mining region in Central Asia which is worked almost entirely by forced labour, is considered the most promising name to use in this context. It is, moreover, the name most familiar to the Russian public.'

The labour camp theme was given a further boost by the discovery of the text of the Soviet corrective Labour codex outlining the rules by which the labour camps operated. The codex book had been bought by Hugh Lunghi, head of IRD's Soviet Desk, found in a 'commission' – foreign currency bookshop in Moscow – during a visit. Lunghi realized that these totalitarian rules could be utilized to emphasize the iniquities of the Soviet labour camp system. The codex was translated and divulged during the Economic and Social Council (ECOSOC) of the United Nations meeting in Geneva in August 1949. Exposure given to this document in Britain was followed by a successful worldwide publicity campaign. Articles prepared in IRD or drawing on its basic papers were published in some fifty countries, and led to a continuing debate on Soviet labour camps.[3]

Files on the labour codex of the period show that IRD was anxious that they should be seen to be factual, but IRD had already devised methods of placing more sensational material through covert contacts in the media: 'We should not attempt to put out the rough with the smooth. IRD material handled by British Information Services should be closely argued and calm (as usual), and blood curling "building the Siberian pyramids out of human bones" stuff should be put out through subterranean channels.'[4] An IRD assessment was very pleased with the result of the codex publicity: 'Without exception every British national paper gave coverage to this story, three of them (the *Telegraph*, *Herald* and *Mirror*) leading the paper with it and the *Guardian* giving full prominence. . . . The BBC, who made special arrangements, did us proud.' There followed a long list of international media that picked the story up.[5] At the Public Record Office these are four files packed full of cuttings on the codex from regional newspapers collected by British Embassy officials around the world.[6]

The new department had been given offices at Carlton House Terrace at the Admiralty Arch end of the Mall. Built in around 1830 by John Nash, these are two sumptuous terraces; Gladstone, Lord Curzon and Palmerston once lived there. One of the terrace buildings was well known to generations of recruits to the intelligence services as the place where they were interviewed for their suitability for 'government service'. It had suffered considerable bomb damage during the Second World War and had just been patched up as IRD moved in. The offices of the new 'hush-hush' Foreign Office department were at numbers 12 and 17 Carlton House Terrace. They had been requisitioned during the war. A member of the IRD staff, the Honourable Barbara Miller, daughter of the Liberal politician Lord Buckmaster, remembered as a girl going to dances at number 18, which then belonged to Lord Astor; IRD also took it over later. Internal communication between the two parts of the department was rather like a catwalk in an airship, which traversed the intervening upper regions of what later became Crockford's gambling club. Up until the end of Foreign Office occupation, the minuscule lift in one house bore a small plate indicating 'Her Ladyship's Bedroom' and number 18 retained some fine malachite panels as well as a spacious, if somewhat seedy, bathroom.[7] Although lacking longed-for amenities such as reliable heating, there was hot water, a facility that was made full use of by some of the poorly paid typists, one of whom recalled that 'They kept lots of files in the bathrooms, but the baths were still there and there was hot water so you . . . just used to sort of lock the door and have a bath amongst the files. Because you couldn't really afford hot water.'[8] Another member of staff, Hugh Lunghi, recalled the building: 'Terrible conditions – garrets, and we had to bring in our own kettles – but the views were nice, looking across to Admiralty Arch and Horse Guards Parade. We saw the funeral of George V from this advantageous position.'[9]

★★★★★

By late February 1948, IRD's first head, Mr (later Sir) Ralph (pronounced Räf) Murray, an assistant and one expert had been appointed, and a starting budget had been agreed with the Treasury.[10] Murray was also in charge of the other Foreign Office publicity departments, including the Information Policy Department (IPD). The difference between the two departments was set out as follows: IRD was responsible for 'negative' anti-Communist covert propaganda and the IPD for 'positive' propaganda about the British way of life.

According to the Foreign Office history of the origins of IRD, 'The need to recruit specialist staff, free from the limitations of civil service pay and conditions, was one of the considerations which led Murray to suggest, in September 1948, that part of the costs of the unit should be transferred to the Secret Vote. In addition, the move to the Secret Vote would enable a more flexible use of money, and avoid the unwelcome scrutiny of operations which might require covert or semi-covert means of execution.'[11] Conveniently, this hidden funding would help to avoid parliamentary scrutiny. By the end of 1948 it had been agreed that £100,000 would be allocated from the 1949–50 Secret Vote to cover the operational costs of the unit. By 1950, funds from the Secret Vote for just one of the 'operations which could not possibly be acknowledged by H.M.G.' were estimated to be in the region of £20,000 for the coming year.[12]

A vicar's son, Ralph Murray had left Oxford and joined the BBC in the 1930s. In 1939 he joined the Foreign Office 'by the back door' and was later assigned to the PWE. Many of the techniques used by IRD were inherited from the PWE/SOE, as were a number of the first recruits. Murray was, according to an admiring deputy, 'A man of great drive, with an almost Churchillian technique of bombarding his heads of department with minutes on every imaginable subject about, as the expert, he usually knew a good deal more than his subordinates. I found that under his direction all the Information Departments in the Foreign Office were working at high pitch and with a new sense of purpose.'[13]

One of the first people whom Murray recruited to IRD was Col Leslie Sheridan, the former SOE psychological warrior, known to all as 'Sherry'. He was to be the dynamic force of IRD for fifteen years. Sheridan was, according to those who knew him, 'a real behind the scenes operator – but with more enthusiasm than intellect'.[14] He was always inventing some new scheme or firing off letters in the office. He would gather up his coat and hat and dart out for the continuous succession of meetings and discrete lunches with journalists and opinion makers at their London clubs. The real power behind the throne, though, was Sheridan's wife. During the war, Sheridan married the remarkable SOE secretary, Adelaide Maturin. Professionally she had proved highly capable, and on the SOE's demise she had became an MI6 officer whose duties dovetailed into IRD. Highly intelligent, attractive and taciturn, Adelaide had natural authority. Capable of great attention to detail, she was considered to be a natural manager of MI6's large, delicate long-term 'front' operations.

In the hiatus that followed the Second World War, Sheridan also remained attached to MI6. According to Colin Wintle, another former SOE man, he and Sheridan started a new business as public relations consultants from an office at 47 Essex Street off the Strand in 1946.[15] With the rapid onset of the Cold War, Sheridan found MI6 calling on more and more of his time to set up covert media operations. When Murray brought Sheridan into IRD, he gave him a free rein, described him as 'our import from the world of professional publicity', and put him in charge of the editorial section with Colin MacLaren as his deputy. Sheridan used as a 'cover' his work as public relations consultant.

John Cloake arrived in the department only months after it had started to function. Cloake, who would later become British Ambassador to Bulgaria, recalled: 'It was my very first job. I started in August 1948 and I was sent along to this curious department, which had been, by that time, going for a few months. When I arrived, Ralph Murray . . . greeted me and said he'd have to rush off to a meeting, took me in to meet the Assistant, who at that time was Milo Talbot, who said "Well for the moment, in fact you're going to be sharing this office with me." Sat me down at the desk opposite him and started to teach me everything he knew.'[16] In the summer of 1948, IRD was still a small department and at an early stage in its organizational development. Cloake remembered that, when he arrived:

> There was Ralph Murray and the Assistant. Myself as – quote – the third room, which meant that all the incoming papers came to me and I farmed them out as nec-essary. There was an intelligence section of four, of which Cecil Parrott was the senior, and he was dealing with Eastern Europe, there was Robert Conquest, also dealing with Eastern Europe, Jack Brimmell, on the Soviet Union and Catherine Illingsworth on South East Asia and the Far East. There was what was called an edi-torial section, which was putting out material, and that was two – Colin MacLaren and Rosemary Allott. We had . . . a reference section with a card index and newspa-per archive and . . . our usual Foreign Office registry, which actually looked after our departmental papers, Two shorthand typists and that was the entire strength of the department when I first joined it.[17]

The daily routine, as Cloake recalled, began with 'a morning meeting'. Murray would gather together a group to plan the day's work. With the department so small at the beginning, more or less everybody would attend, 'but after that at least heads of sections; discussing work and what we would do. And if it was agreed that some paper should be written or article should be written, or whatever, then probably the raw material, as it were, would come across from the intelligence people, who would also be digging stuff out from the reference section, and then it would go to editorial who would write it up and put it out.'[18]

Unlike Cloake, who had served with the Royal Engineers at the end of the war before reading history at Cambridge, a number of the early staff already had experience of information work. Both Murray and Leslie Sheridan had backgrounds in journalism and propaganda. The head of the intelligence section, Cecil Parrott, later British Ambassador to Prague, had also served several years as an information officer. Parrott was Information Officer and First Secretary in Prague from 1945, setting up and running the information service from scratch. His experience highlighted the importance given to information work following the war. Parrott recalled that: 'My Information Department rapidly expanded. I came with one assistant and soon had three female secretaries and a language expert who translated the newspapers for the Ambassador and the senior staff. A good while later I acquired several higher-powered helpers: an Assistant Information Officer and Press, Film and Broadcasting Officers.'[19] Parrott joined IRD in 1948 but, in his autobiography, he discreetly limits his comment on the one year period he spent there to a reference to 'a preliminary run in one of the Information Departments of the Foreign Office'.[20]

It was decided by committee that the new department was to disseminate two categories of information. Murray described it in a memo: 'Category A is secret and confidential objective studies re Soviet policies and machinations which are designed for high-level consumption by heads of states, Cabinet members, etcetera. None of this material publishable or quotable for obvious reasons.' Category A material was 'derived from diplomatic and intelligence sources. It is entirely distinct from that which might be utilised in the secret propaganda campaign'. 'Category B is less highly-classified information suitable for careful dissemination by staff of British missions to suitable contacts (e.g. editors, professors, scientists, labour leaders etcetera) who can use it as factual background material in their general work without attribution. Successful category B operations depend upon activity British representatives in various countries.'[21]

One of the first tasks of Murray and the senior Foreign Office mandarins was to set out the ideological message that the Foreign Office should disseminate. In keeping with the politics of the government in power, the Foreign Office was allowed to advocate the merits of socialism. Bevin indicated his preferred approach in a cabinet meeting: 'We cannot hope successfully to repel Communism only by disparaging it on material grounds, and must add a positive to Democratic and Christian principles, remembering the strength of Christian sentiment in Europe. We must put forward a positive rival ideology. We must stand on the broad principle of Social Democracy which, in fact, has its basis in the value of civil liberty and human rights.'

Foreign Office officials no more seriously promoted Socialism as an alternative to Communism than they were to prompt a 'Third Force' agenda. Historian Dianne Kirby suggested that 'by virtue of their background, upbringing and education, Foreign Office officials were poor publicists for socialist ideals which is why successive Labour Party conferences between 1946 and 1948 witnessed resolutions for the democratisation of the Foreign Service and the replacement of those in high diplomatic posts.'[22] The landslide Labour victory had changed the political landscape and IRD was to employ a number of left-of-centre journalists as well as propagate anti-Communist writings by famous left-wingers. On the occasions when a comparison with the Soviet way of life was needed, it was the virtues of the British way of life that were emphasized. IRD, particularly, picked up on religious themes, taking every opportunity to contrast the West and its religious tolerance with the atheist Communism – ' religion without a God.' Bevin and IRD enlisted the help of many leading religious figures in their campaigns, even Catholics.[23]

High-level conferences were held at the Foreign Office to develop the themes that were to underpin its propaganda. The first big idea was the equation that Communism = Red Fascism. The files show that a whole list of equivalents were worked up – for example Stalin = Hitler, Beria = Himmler and, of course, Soviet Labour Camp = Nazi Concentration Camp. At one point, Murray suggested popularizing the expression 'communazi', but it never took off.[24]

Mayhew was in overall political charge of the operation. At that time the Foreign Office, Colonial Office and Commonwealth Relations Office were still separate. With regard to the colonies, the directing arm of British propaganda was the Colonial Official Information Policy Committee, headed by Mayhew and Patrick Gordon-Walker, the Commonwealth Secretary. Gordon-Walker had risen in the Labour Party after campaigning against the 1936 Munich agreement as a young Oxford don. During the war he had been a member of the PWE. Besides overseeing much of IRD's output, the committee worked up another theme that was to dominate IRD's output, equating any anti-British sentiment in the colonies with Moscow-inspired Communism. This was developed in documents like 'Stalin on Marxism and the National and Colonial Questions', which were distributed to British posts in the colonies and also to 'emerging countries' like Indonesia.

According to the Foreign Office's IRD history, 'Both the Colonial and Commonwealth Relations Offices had an interest in countering Soviet propaganda, which consistently attacked Britain's colonial record, misrepresenting both policy and conditions within British controlled territories, while distracting attention from Soviet behaviour in the backward areas of the former Tsarist empire.'[25] It did not point out that at this time Britain was tenaciously hanging on to whatever parts of the Empire it could, or at least trying to hand the countries over to those deemed suitable. Furthermore, it was a gift to the Soviets who were able to highlight British excesses in the colonies in their propaganda.

There is a defining moment that reveals the ascendancy of the Cold War propagandists of IRD over the more considered views of other Foreign Office officials. Early on, Mayhew and Murray asked for a paper on Anglo-Soviet relations since 1939. This was to be an IRD briefing paper. The paper was written by the Foreign Office Research Department in a rather scholarly style.[26] It concluded that Soviet policy could be understood as a search for security. Both this conclusion and the non-journalistic style incurred Mayhew's derision. It was sent back with strict instructions for revision, and the second version appears to be in an entirely different hand. The second paper, thirty-five pages long, took almost the opposite view of the first. It began, 'The Soviet Union is not merely a State among other States. It is the vehicle of an aggressive ideology. It was dedicated by Lenin and has been repeatedly rededicated by his successors to its task of reshaping the world to a Marxist pattern.' The second paper specifically repudiated the analysis of the original: 'Apologists for the Soviet Union attempt to explain her expansionist tendencies as a "search for security", a natural desire to convert a former sphere of Western influence into a Russian cordon sanitaire against the West. The superficiality of this view is obvious to all who have read the basic works of Marxist-Leninist ideology.'[27] The paper continued to outline a Soviet Union that only cooperated with other nations if it might further the triumph of Communism on a world scale. It stated that the wartime alliance with the West was a necessary evil to Soviet leaders; that the Cominform had been the ceremonial reinstatement of the Comintern, and that the dominant feature of Soviet domestic and foreign policy since the end of the war had been the vehement reassertion of uncompromising Marxist-Leninist orthodoxy. Murray made a surprisingly apposite, if waspish, comment in the covering note: 'I take it that scholarship goes ahead and issues, and propaganda does a rehash: but that scholarship's version does not get sent to MPs etc, and propaganda's does. I have taken the liberty of detaching Mr Mayhew's requirements so we may work to them.'[28]

The Foreign Office Research Department was not geared, either ideologically or practically, to supply the new department, and IRD realized that it needed its own research team. By 1949 'It had become quickly evident that a department confined to the administrative role of servicing and distributing material produced by other people would achieve nothing and, further that IRD would have to do most of its own research, the main aim being to rely on Communist sources to provide proof of what was happening in countries under Communist control.'[29] An intelligence section was set up and, as John Cloake says, its founder members included Cecil Parrott, Jack Brimmell, Robert Conquest, former Information Secretary in Sofia, and Harold Machen, formerly Vice-Consul in Seoul. Their job was to collate information from all sources and to fill in the gaps.

Much of IRD initial output concerned the workings of Communism in the Soviet sphere of influence. Important to this work was the Foreign Office's assessment of Soviet capabilities and intentions. Foreign Office sovietologists like R. Carew Hunt, like their American counterparts, believed that the Soviet Union was bent on world domination, and this became an underlying theme. Carew Hunt and his colleagues pointed to Marxist first principles. The sovietologist believed that the essence of Marxism's original foreign policy doctrine was very simple: world revolution. Marx and Engels' *Communist Manifesto* (1848) had announced that:

> The working men have no country. . . . National differences and antagonisms between peoples are daily more and more vanishing, owing to the development of the bourgeoisie, to freedom of commerce, to the world market, to uniformity in the model of production and in the conditions of life thereto. . . . The supremacy of the proletariat will cause them to vanish still faster. United action, of the leading civilised countries as least, is one of the first conditions of the emancipation of the proletariat.

These beliefs were further hardened by the Soviet-engineered takeover of the Czechoslovakian government in February 1948, one of the first of a number of actions reflecting a new harder line policy in Moscow. IRD's Cecil Parrott, a fluent Czech speaker, had been stationed in the Prague Embassy during the coup. Returning to Britain to join IRD, he brought back a chilling account of the episode.

Regardless of any evidence to the contrary, the idea that the Soviet and Communist systems' hidden agenda was world revolution was the abiding gospel of IRD throughout its life. Without that premise, IRD had no legitimate *raison d'être*. The mounting tension gave IRD a busy first year, recruiting many East European émigrés to its ranks. In 1948 it produced twenty-two briefing papers on different aspects of Stalinism which were circulated not only to British diplomats abroad but also to selected journalists, politicians and trade unionists at home.[30] Much of the British media were becoming increasingly anti-Soviet in stance.

In his analysis of the influence of IRD on the British media's attitude to the Cold War, historian Tony Shaw said that Czechoslovakia was a turning point for many British newspapers, including the *Daily Mail*, the *News of the World* and the *Sunday Graphic*, bringing them four square against the Soviet Union:

> If the roots of the press's reaction to the Czech coup are to be found in individual editorial offices, government propaganda also played its part by framing how the crisis was perceived by newspapers. This worked in a variety of ways. Foreign Office informa-

tion officials briefed journalists on the many analogies between 'Hitlerite' and Communist systems, and used Czechoslovakia as evidence of the imperialist nature of Russian Foreign Policy. The IRD issued material of a more hard-hitting nature documenting the many real shortcomings in Soviet and east European society, with a particular focus on the Stalinist Terror. The department also highlighted the increasingly prevalent fear of subversion in Britain, of trade unions being captured by anti-democratic conspirators who would use industrial power to undermine the state.[31]

Former IRD officials maintain that they dealt with only accurate, factual material and that the department's reputation was based on its accuracy. This was certainly the way that IRD was presented: 'No other government except that of the United States of America – and they less intensively – and probably no unofficial organization supplies a constant stream of carefully checked factual anti-Communist material. As a consequence, journalists, writers, speakers and organizations all over the world welcome this material and use it freely'.

Norman Reddaway said that an IRD slogan was, 'Anything but the truth is too hot to handle'.[32] British propaganda in the Second World War was effective because – apart from a relatively minor area of black propaganda – it consciously tried to adhere to the truth. Based on sound practical considerations, former IRD insiders say that their emphasis on the mobilization of truth – grey, rather than black propaganda – was more effective as a means of influencing public opinion. Not only was it likely to be far more effective in the long term, but the concentration on factual reports and in-depth research eased access to the 'free' media and enhanced IRD's credibility with its clients. Factual evidence would be mobilized in order to back the argument that the briefing or publication was attempting to make, 'grey' propaganda or 'the truth imparted with a certain spin'.[33]

When asked what he believed to be the most important ingredient of effective propaganda, Lord Mayhew explained that he thought it was the selection of facts: 'It's quite extraordinary how if you select the facts you want, you can make a very powerful case, and certainly, all the propaganda I've done has not been distorting facts or inventing them but selecting them. The policy of IRD was not to lie or distort facts, but to select the facts that proved our case that Bolshevism was no good and plug them.'[34]

One of the formats in which IRD presented its factual material was in a series of pamphlets. The themes of these *Information Reports* were, at least in the first few years, all anti-Communist and examined such topics as *Forced Labour in the USSR: the Facts*, *The Communist Peace Offensive* and *Russian Imperialism and Asian Nationalism*. *Sabotage of Peace*, dated August 1949, illustrates how the USSR had systematically refused to work in harmony with other nations following the end of the Second World War, despite 'the great concessions made by Allied statesmen in the interests of co-operation for world peace'. An attached note marked 'Confidential' indicated that the material was primarily for the use of 'His Majesty's Missions and Information Officers in particular' and explained how the material could be used:

The information contained in this paper is, as far as it is possible to ascertain, factual and objective. The paper may, therefore, be used freely as a reference paper, but neither copies of it nor the material contained in it should be distributed officially without the sanction of the Head of Mission. It and/or the material in the paper, however, may be distributed unofficially in whatever quarters seem useful so long as it can be assured that there will be no public attribution of material or of the paper to a British source.

In the first year, attempts to obtain specialized anti-Communist articles through existing channels, mainly the Central Office of Information (COI), did not prove particularly fruitful. Outside the Foreign Office other means of finding contributors were advanced. George Orwell was approached and, as we shall see, suggested the names of a number of journalists. IRD approached and obtained articles from writers, including Harold Laski (a comparison of British and Russian Trade Unionism), Leonard Schapiro ('Communists' Utopian vision fades') and Richard Crossman (a reassessment of the Hitler-Stalin Pact of 1939).

Documents also show that the left-wing magazine *Tribune*, published by members of the Labour Party, was supplied to Foreign Office posts abroad for use in anti-Communist propaganda. Ralph Murray defined the goal of the department as 'Work in weaning people away from Communism.' By exporting the *Tribune*, Murray saw an opportunity to release propaganda discreetly. He hoped to turn many of its left-of-centre articles to 'this department's purposes' by the 'resolute exposure of Communism'.

IRD supplied briefs to ministers, British delegates to the United Nations and Members of Parliament, sent material to the COI for distribution through its news agency, the London Press Service, and sent propaganda articles to foreign posts. With such a variety of means, and a global network of targets, IRD was both highly ambitious and considered a highly successful department.

In the first year, France and Italy were identified as priority targets, in view of the possible Communist success in the elections of April 1948. Italy was considered a success for IRD, which had placed a great deal of material in the Italian press. France was quite another matter. The French 'mindset' had always proved problematic for the British, and IRD had little success. Meanwhile, the Middle Eastern effort was concentrated in Egypt, and, in South-East Asia, in Malaya and Burma. By the end of the year, Mayhew was pleased: 'There is no doubt that this work has achieved a remarkable measure of success. The material based on our output appears in the press of anti-Communist countries all over the world.' Ten months later, by October 1949, Mayhew concluded that 'IRD has had an impact out of all proportion to its size and cost'.[35]

If IRD was a 'hush-hush' department, the Soviets had a total picture of its operation within weeks of its inception. Guy Burgess, one of the Cambridge ring of Soviet spies, had been working as private secretary for Foreign Office minister Hector McNeil. Burgess's infamous behaviour as a drunk and degenerate had once again got him into trouble but according to 'old boys rules' he was not to be fired. His bosses looked for somewhere to put him and assigned him to IRD. His trial period there lasted only three months, because his behaviour deteriorated rather than improved. Reluctantly, Mayhew fired him. However, unknown to Mayhew, the damage had already been done. Burgess had gone to the Middle East on holiday in January making detours in order to brief officials in various British embassies about the new department's work. But his real objectives were to evade the English winter and to confer with his co-conspirator, Kim Philby, who was in Istanbul. Burgess passed documentary evidence to his Soviet control, showing what the new department did and who ran it.[36] Moscow knew about IRD within a matter of weeks. However, it was to remain a secret from the British public for another thirty years.

CHAPTER FIVE

Korea: a Hot War in a Cold War

In the years immediately after the Second World War, South-East Asia underwent massive change. India and Pakistan had bloodily divided and achieved their independence. China had fallen into the hands of Mao Zhedong's Communists, displacing the corrupt Kuomintang to the island of Formosa. Many other countries in the area found burgeoning Communist parties in their midst. Britain, desperately short of revenue after the war, was trying to hang on to its remaining colonies for as long as possible, or, as in the case of Malaya, to make sure that control was handed over to pro-Western leaders. South-East Asia was the most important and immediate target for IRD's propaganda outside Europe.

It was in this region that Anglo-American cooperation in combating Communism was to undergo its first trial by fire. The British, through IRD, were the first to go on the propaganda offensive against the 'red menace'; when it came to undercover work, they were still more experienced than their American partners. During the Second World War, and for at least the first five years after, both in psychological warfare and in covert operations, the Americans learned everything from the British. As the Cold War emerged, the Americans took a little longer to get their act together. As elsewhere, the 'special relationship' was operating and the British kept the Americans reasonably well informed of their activities.

In November 1948 the State Department circulated its missions abroad, allowing them to cooperate with British 'information services' provided that this was kept secret and that nothing was done that would give a public impression of joint activity. It also asked missions to report on British information activities locally, and to state what steps they had taken towards joint liaison.[1] The replies received, which can be seen at the US National Archives, document growing cooperation all round the world. The reports from India are particularly revealing.[2] Loy Henderson, US Ambassador in New Delhi, reported that the British High Commission was 'about to launch [a] highly confidential anti-Communist propaganda program in India and has been instructed by London to work closely with us'. J.S.H. Shattock of the British High Commission had reported on the 'anti-Communist propaganda' being prepared by a 'special research committee' in London, which would be distributed in two main ways. Referring to IRD's Category A material: 'In the first place a certain amount of this high grade material can be slipped into the otherwise innocuous . . . British Information Service material disseminated . . . throughout India. A good deal of material would probably be published in this way without attracting undesirable attention to the UK Government.' With regard to Category B material: 'In the second place and much more importantly the UK office felt that a very carefully selected group of completely reliable and trustworthy contacts could be built up over a period of time. These could be drawn from various groups, reliable correspondents and editors, British and Indian merchant missionaries and others. Information given to them could then be used at their discretion and of course with full Protection to the Government.'[3]

The report continued that considerable time and effort had gone into planning the programme and that, in addition to New Delhi, personnel had been selected in UK branch offices in 'Madras, Calcutta and Bombay who will work with the initial group of 24 contacts.' It was also suggested that contacts in All India Radio were being developed. The Americans conceded that the British programme went much further than anything that they had started, and rather naively they asked the British if they intended to tell the government of India what they were doing: to this inquiry they were given an ambiguous reply.[4] On receiving a copy of this report in London, US Ambassador Lewis Douglas asked the Foreign Office for more information on IRD. Under-Secretary Dening, responsible for South-East Asia, told Douglas that IRD: 'originated last December when Bevin submitted British Cabinet memo re: effect on SEA of Communist successes China . . . recommended SEA countries should get together to combat Soviet menace. View was expressed that with due caution the UK might usefully attempt be coordinating factor in stimulating in each country creation adequate police forces, intelligence agencies, and legal powers to deal with Communists.' Dening said that there was nothing sinister about IRD material, which was purely factual but that it had, 'proved surprisingly popular among western union governments as anti-Communist source material . . . Idea using local contacts is based on theory that only Easterner can convince Easterner. Contacts selected are men of standing and influence known to be already well-disposed towards West and anti-Communist.'[5]

On 9 May 1948, Ambassador Henderson in New Delhi received the following personal cable from George Kennan, the State Department's chief Cold War strategist and head of its Policy Planning Staff (PPS):

> Top Secret . . . No Stencil – No Distribution. UR 469, Apr 27, of deep interest. You will recall discussion possible special projects you had shortly before your departure with two AMER officials one of whom saw you off Union Station. Most helpful if you would pursue this matter with appropriate BRIT REPS New Delhi with view obtaining complete info and submit . . . report addressed me indicating how best US GOVT might tie in with BRIT Plans or arrange parallel program.[6]

About a year earlier the US National Security Council had accepted a proposal that unvouchered funds should be used by the State Department to support the covert utilization of native anti-Communist elements in Eurasia, in countries still outside the Iron Curtain.[7] This was an early step towards the massive 'covert action', which was soon to be taken over, expanded and funded by the CIA.

A later dispatch from Ambassador Henderson to Washington confirmed that Sir Archibald Nye, British Ambassador, was proposing to show some Category A material to Nehru to see how he reacted.[8] Indian relations with the Soviets were initially lukewarm after partition because of Soviet hostility towards Asian nationalism, which had been all too apparent at the nineteen-nation conference in Delhi to consider the Indonesian question. Nye reported that he discussed an exchange of information and comment on the realities of Communism with Pandit Nehru, and had met with 'a very friendly response', although Nehru felt that India's reciprocation would be on a limited scale owing to the smallness and inexperience of its Central Intelligence Bureau.[9]

For the British, the Malaya emergency was turning South-East Asia into a priority area and an IRD satellite office was to be set up. In January 1949 the US Embassy in Singapore sent Washington the following extract from a letter by Ralph Murray, to the British Embassy in Singapore:

> As you know we are proposing to set up a Regional Information Office there, cover- ing all South-East Asia, which will take care of our material: re-writing it for local consumption and putting it through the various media such as the press, broadcasting, etc. The Commissioner General attaches considerable importance to the project, which has become even more necessary now that the Communists look like becom- ing the masters of at least most of China. Could you perhaps find out informally what sort of Information Research Department work the United States authorities propose to do in Singapore? We shall keep them in the picture locally about our own activi- ties and we shall hope to be able to arrange that our respective operations comple- ment one another.[10]

IRD became an important part of the organization built up by the British at Phoenix Park in Singapore to counter Communist insurgency in the area.[11] J.B. Smith, a CIA liaison officer at Phoenix Park in the early 1950s, reported that IRD was running a joint operation with MI6, represented at that time by Maurice Oldfield assisted by Fergie Dempster. Oldfield was later to become director of the Secret Service.[12]

IRD's Singapore office was already in place when, on 25 June 1950, the Communist Army of North Korea launched an invasion of South Korea. Kim Il Sung's troops crossed the 38th Parallel and swept deep into the south, the start of a gruelling conflict that was to last for more than three years. The Korean War was to be the major hot war of the Cold War. Foreign Office documents from the period show that officials did not really believe that this was Stalin's first step towards war with the West. However, the underlying tone of IRD's output was in line with its Cold Warrior role and raised suspicions that the Kremlin's aim was world domination.

Korea was in the American sphere of influence. The Japanese had occupied Korea throughout the Second World War until it was liberated by American forces in 1945. As part of the three-power postwar agreements, the country was divided into two at the 38th Parallel. The Soviet Union took control of the north and the United States control of the south. By further agreement, both sides withdrew militarily in 1948, leaving effectively puppet regimes in place. Domestic tensions between the north and south grew and it was only a matter of time before one side began a civil war. However, the north's invasion took the south and the United States by surprise. The State

Department's expert on Korea, U. Alexis Johnson, for example, was holidaying on Sky Ridge, 100 miles from Washington, with his children, when the invasion took place. A park ranger was sent out to find him and ask him to return to Washington immediately.[13]

The Americans then reacted very swiftly in condemning the invasion and in gathering a rag and tail unit of US military reinforcements from the Japan garrison. The British government fell in behind the Truman administration. In a hastily convened session, the United Nations condemned the invasion and began to assemble a task force to assist beleaguered South Korea. While the major constituent of the UN task force was American, some thirty-two other countries sent troops to fight against the north. The British were to send soldiers, aircraft and ships as their contribution.

Only recently has the part the secret British propaganda operation played in pulling the world behind the West begun to be appreciated. The perception that this was a Kremlin-instigated invasion by a puppet regime permeated Western thinking. The British Joint Intelligence Committee informed the chiefs of staff: 'If the forces of the UN were to fail to stem the drive of militant Communism in Korea it would be a major defeat for the Western Powers, and would shatter the faith of the free countries of the Far East and South-East Asia in the ability of the Western Powers and United Nations to defend them from Russian domination. Repercussions would, in fact, be felt in other parts of the world, notably Western Germany.'

The British government, however, took a more measured tone than the United States. It had the Truman administration remove from the June 1950 UN resolution, the attribution of the North Korean invasion to 'centrally directed Communist imperialism', on the grounds that it presented an inflammatory challenge to Moscow.

IRD, too, reacted quickly and began an extensive campaign on the Korean War, both at home and abroad. On 4 July 1950, head of IRD Ralph Murray warned the Lord President's office, responsible for the coordination of the government's information services, of 'the considerable danger' in allowing 'the great efforts [already being] made by Soviet and Communist Propaganda about Korea' to go unanswered. Murray suggested counterattack against Communist claims. The Communists had claimed that the north had merely responded to an attack from the south. Murray saw this as 'the wolf accusing the lamb as usual'. The Communists also claimed that the UN's intervention on behalf of South Korea was invalidated because of the corrupt and unpopular regime of Syngman Rhee's government.[14]

Fifty years on, we can now be certain that the north did instigate the invasion. However, Rhee's regime was undoubtedly corrupt, repressive and unpopular. It was not as unpopular, though, as Kim Il Sung's regime. More the wolf accusing the fox than the lamb. According to journalist Andy Roth, who was in Korea in 1949, the members of the South Korean government made no bones about their desire to attack the north when they were militarily stronger.[15] At the time Murray said that allegations against the south should be seen as a 'particularly dangerous red herring', and suggested that they should be refuted by reference to the 750,000 Korean refugees who had fled south of the 38th Parallel since 1948. IRD material proselytizing these themes was passed on to the BBC and used.[16] Public opinion in Britain was in favour of the government's intervention in the summer of 1950, but it was by no means unanimous. In a recent paper, historian Tony Shaw noted that: 'From August 1950 onwards, Attlee's cabinet found itself on the sharp end of a steady stream of criticism from trade unions fearful of an American induced third world war and demanding withdrawal of all British forces. In the run up to the Labour Party conference in October 1950, Denis Healey, the party's International Secretary and main link with IRD, received fifty-one resolutions from local associations relating to Korea, only six of which fully supported the leadership's policy.'[17]

The International Department sought to quell such criticism and bring the Labour movement behind the government. It dealt with the Korean War in the *Labour Party Talking Points*, a regular factual booklet given or sold to many people and groups in the Labour movement. These provided simple, supportive explanations of Britain's involvement in the war. On 22 July, under the heading 'Who Stands for Peace?' it took to task the British Peace Committee's petition against UN intervention. It said, 'The British Peace Committee is stepping up its campaign. People everywhere are being asked to sign the "Peace Petition". But what is behind the petition? . . . right from the beginning the "Peace Campaign" was a fraud, run on Russian instructions.' This denouncement of *Talking Points* incurred the wrath of the British Communist Party's *Daily Worker*, which sent a list of nit-picking factual inaccuracies in the article.

IRD helped the Labour Party's International Department to counter criticism and gather support for the UN line. As Tony Shaw observed:

> The material focused on four themes: Kim Il Sung's preparations for aggression against South Korea; the lawful status of the South Korean government, based on elections; Moscow's involvement in the NKPA invasion and North Korea's growing satellite status; and how the collectivisation of land captured by the invading forces in the South was disadvantageous to the peasantry. The IRD also passed onto the Labour Party pamphlets produced by the Central Office of Information and the United States Information Services (USIS) detailing, amongst other things, the humanitarian aspects of the UN's activities in Korea. These were combined with information designed to deter industrial sabotage, much of which formed part of a broadcast on strikes delivered by George Isaacs, Minister of Labour in late September 1950.[18]

On 21 August, the assistant head of IRD, Peter Wilkinson, sent a large dossier. 'Here is the material on Korea which Adam Watson promised to Denis Healey.' The dossier contains a collection of statements monitored from the North Korean radio, press and political decrees showing that 'Preparations for aggression on North Korea against the Republic of South Korea can effectively be traced back to the formation of the National Front in June 1949.' It also cited 'evidence of Russian assistance'. For example, 'Pyongyang on the 7th January 1950, gave details of the successful results achieved by the agricultural research stations in cross breeding indigenous Korean seed with Russian varieties donated by the Soviet Union.' The material may have been accurate, but in classic IRD 'spin doctor' style, it makes no reference to the South Korean government actions and policies.[19]

Rhee's regime was not easy to defend, and those suggesting that the Korean War might become more complicated than just a fight between good and evil gave IRD a major headache. In August 1950, Alan Winnington, a correspondent of the Communist *Daily Worker* who was covering the war with the North Korean Army, reported the discovery of mass graves near Taejon containing the corpses of more than 700 men and women executed by the South Korean Police. Further stories of atrocities committed by Rhee's forces began to emerge in the media. Moscow's English language *Soviet Weekly* published photographs of alleged victims of atrocities. In November 1950, these allegations were to turn into one of the nastiest confrontations in the British media, raising profound questions of whether the duty of press was jingoistic support of the government or reporting the truth as it found it. James Cameron, the leftist reporter, filed a story for the *Picture Post*, reporting Rhee's dictatorial ways and implying that the Americans were condoning the regime's excesses. The proprietor of the *Picture Post* banned the article and the magazine's legendary and long-standing editor Tom Hopkinson was fired. The *Daily Worker* then printed a leaked copy of Cameron's banned piece over its front page.[20] The cabinet considered prosecuting the *Daily Worker* for treason and introducing press laws banning journalism that gave 'aid and comfort to the enemy'. Ministers discussed the matter. They dropped these proposals when it became clear that many of the allegations were true and that taking the reporters to court would just make matters worse.

The government was anxious to nip any further criticism in the bud in case such allegations were to undermine popular support from the public. IRD provided confidential briefing notes for MPs' speeches, explaining that South Korean atrocities were just revenge for northern ones, and making it clear that one had to understand that the peoples of the Far East had a historical tendency to barbarity. Straying some way from its claims of the 'truth will prevail', IRD ordered the redubbing of a Chinese propaganda film showing alleged American brutality in Korea, so that it instead appeared to show the barbarity of Kim Il Sung's soldiers.[21] The Foreign Office's News Department showed a number of newspapers in confidence a report written for the UN Commission for the Unification and Rehabilitation of Korea (UNCURK), which emphasized that the war enabled the resolution of personal feuds. Overall, as Tony Shaw has pointed out, 'Editors tended to accept the Government line that the real issue was not the nature of the Rhee regime, but the need to resist aggression.'[22]

The British government found itself trying to calm the wilder inclination of the Americans. Indeed, the Truman administration was itself trying to suppress the even wilder aspirations of the American military. General MacArthur had put into place plans to use atomic weapons against the Communists. Nine 'silver-plated' B-29s capable of carrying atomic bombs were moved to a base within striking range of North Korea and China. One plan was to use A-bombs to create a 10 mile 'radioactive' cordon sanitaire across the north. Truman's ructions with MacArthur were to lead to the general's dismissal. The decision to push beyond the 38th Parallel was to prove controversial. MacArthur's success and desire to teach the Communists a lesson seem to have overwhelmed the UN's political sense. It was one thing to restore the status quo, but to push on towards the Chinese border was quite another. China shared key hydroelectric stations inside North Korea. It was also worried about a possible American-backed

mainland landing from the defeated Nationalist Chinese who had retreated to the island
of Taiwan. The Chinese issued warnings through the Indian Ambassador that they
would have to react if MacArthur drove on towards their borders. The warnings were
ignored and the Chinese reacted by sending in their army. What had started essentially
as a civil war was teetering on the brink of the Third World War. Forty years later
Healey was to say in his autobiography that 'Washington ignored China's warnings that
it would not stand idly by if MacArthur crossed the thirty-eighth parallel. He did cross
it, and the Chinese then entered Korea. So a war that might have ended with the
successful landing at In'chon, six months after it began, lasted four more disastrous
years.'[23]

Throughout these years, Korea was a propaganda battlefield. The north's ill-treatment
of POWs became a *cause célèbre*. In fact, issues surrounding POWs came to dominate the
war, being central to many of the key controversies. Disagreements about the
repatriation of Communist POWs probably delayed the end of the conflict by a year or
more. In the first few months of hostilities the North Koreans treated POWs from the
Republic of Korea (ROK) and the United Nations appallingly. 'Pak's Palace' in
Pyongyang, an interrogation centre run by a particularly vicious North Korean officer,
became notorious. Many died on forced marches to POW camps near the Yalu. As the
UN forces pursued the northern forces, photographs began to flood the press of UN
POWs shot on the roadside with their wrists tied behind their backs. The Chinese and
Soviets were alarmed by this, not least because a dead POW was of no intelligence or
positive propaganda value. By the end of 1950 the Chinese took over the running of
most POW camps. They conducted interrogations of POWs and passed any intelligence
on to Soviet advisers. The Chinese treatment was far better than that meted out by the
North Koreans. Unless an individual tried to escape or breached disciplinary rules, the
Chinese were rarely brutal. However, stories of systematic oriental brutality were to
continue past the end of the war to the extent that they became a popular myth.

The battle over POWs became ideological and was fought with propaganda weapons.
The Chinese set up education sessions to explain the evils of capitalism. They had some
success. Many British POWs were conscripts and had Socialist leanings. American
troops captured early on were noted for their low morale. A number became involved
in Communist peace initiatives, signing petitions for peace, writing home about their
good treatment and condemning the West's role in the war. At the end of the war,
some twenty-one American and one British soldier declined to be repatriated. Hundreds
of others who had sympathy with their captors did return. To explain this 'treason', the
idea of brainwashing was seized upon and used to excuse the POWs' behaviour. The
term brainwashing is usually attributed to an American journalist, and alleged CIA
agent, Edward Hunter, in 1950. An article, originally published in the *Miami News*
headlined '"Brainwashing" Tactics Force Chinese into Ranks of Communist Party.'
The idea that UN POWs were brainwashed into becoming Communist stooges thus
became commonplace.[24] At its most populist, it was taken up by Hollywood and used in
chilling Cold War films like *The Manchurian Candidate*.

The Communist propagandists also stole the march on the West with their concerted
germ warfare allegations. In spring 1952 they began to allege that the United States was
dropping germ warfare bombs in North Korea and China. Worse still a number of US

Air Force POWs confessed to being involved in germ warfare attacks; these included two senior officers, Col Frank Schwable and Col Bud Mahurin. The Chinese published twenty-two confessions in the English language magazine the *People's Daily*. All of those who confessed retracted their allegations after repatriation, stating that they had been made under duress. A committee of international observers was invited by the Chinese to conduct an investigation. This included a highly regarded Cambridge scientist. It concluded that germ warfare had taken place.

Communist claims and American denials became yet another battle in the propaganda war.[25] These issues became primarily US versus Communist in tone. The returning British POWs roused less curiosity in England. The Minister of Defence's 1955 White Paper on the Treatment of British Prisoners of War in Korea concluded that, of 979 British returnee POWs, the officers and senior NCOs 'remained almost completely unaffected by Communist propaganda'. Among the other ranks two-thirds 'remained virtually unaffected' but most of the remainder 'absorbed sufficient indoctrination to be classed as Communist sympathisers . . . A small minority – about 40 altogether – returned home as convinced Communists.'[26] There is a set of interesting documents in the Public Record Office which comprises the assessments of AI9 (Army intelligence unit) of the returning POWs, giving each a shade of grey between white and black to represent their Communist sympathy and their level of collaboration with their captors.[27]

IRD's main concern was the representation of the Communist threat throughout the world. For the Korean War, IRD reinforced its contingent in the Regional Information Office in Singapore. Its task was to get as much pro-Western propaganda into the local media as possible, not least because the Korean situation was making Britain's anti-insurgency campaign in Malaya much more difficult.[28] IRD also worked hard alongside the Americans in India. The Indians, under Jeherwalal Nehru, had, from IRD's point of view, taken an increasingly unhelpful neutral stance in the Cold War, so much so that senior Indian generals were able to act as neutral intermediaries over difficult POW questions during the Korean War.

Such was the anxiety about the situation that the British and Americans met in late July 1950 about the coordination of propaganda to avoid different presentation. IRD official Adam Watson, who had already gained experience in the British presentation of the Malayan emergency, was sent to liaise with Washington. The British benefited from this arrangement. Tony Shaw has shown that IRD published a range of unattributed American material, including some based on US Army Military Intelligence, outlining, for instance, the discovery of Communist intelligence schools in occupied north Korea (complete with interrogation tools) and the existence of serious divisions within Kim Il Sung's cabinet. An extensive report produced by the State Department's Office of Intelligence Research, 'North Korea: a Case Study of a Soviet Satellite,' was put out by IRD 'as part of series designed to impress upon the educated sections of Asian opinion the seductive yet repressive nature of Moscow's "own brand of imperialism"'.[29]

With such close cooperation with the Americans, IRD found itself involved in the germ warfare allegations. It had begun to pick up Peking TASS reports of the US poisoning of wells and spreading of typhus and smallpox bacteria in North Korea in March 1951. Then, in spring 1952, the Communists launched their allegations of a germ warfare campaign by the United States. IRD counterattacked by implying that disease was rife because of the Communist's poor system of government and that their poor sanitation and medical facilities were responsible for infection. More effective was the publicizing of the UN's requests for an impartial investigation of biological and chemical warfare claims. The Communists refused, instead inviting an international group of scientists to investigate. The members of the International Scientific Commission, while having some respectable figures including Dr Joseph Needham of Cambridge University, was flawed by the inclusion of Soviet placemen.

The success of the Communist media in setting the agenda shook the West and, in particular, the American information specialists. A period of reassessment followed and a new policy document was issued that was to apply to all anti-Communist propaganda and not just that involved in the Korean War. Adam Watson, IRD's man in Washington, telegrammed back to the Foreign Office the key points of the new campaign in which the Americans hoped the British would participate. The 'Campaign of Truth' would consist of four elements:

1. exposing to the world, directly and indirectly, the truly reactionary, vicious and phony nature of Kremlin Communism;
2. building up a spirit of unity, spunk, determination and confidence in all nations of the free world;
3. inculcating in other peoples a readiness and desire to cooperate with America by disproving Soviet lies about us and by making clear that we are a resolute, strong and honest nation whose moral strength and physical strength can be counted on;
4. building, behind the Iron Curtain, psychological obstacles to further Kremlin aggression.[30]

Adam Watson confirmed IRD's involvement in the Korean War, but questioned the effectiveness of the campaign. 'I never thought our operations in Asia were as good as they should have been. But the slogan was, "Communism is the enemy of Asian nationalism" – that was one of Ralph Murray's. He insisted in getting that phrase everywhere. All over Asia.'[31] The wider implications were significant. According to historian Susan L. Carruthers, 'The Korean War, more broadly, also reinforced a growing belief especially in America, that the Cold War was uniquely a psychological contest. Winning meant not only keeping one's own side absolutely convinced of its moral and material superiority but also attracting converts for a "campaign of truth".'[32]

Korea had been the spur to massive rearmament in both the US and the UK. To keep a positive tone of any media coverage of such massive expenditure, IRD coordinated a special briefing group on rearmament chaired by the Russia Committee's head, Sir Pierson Dixon. The committee's documents show that IRD was concerned to get the public behind the '£4,700m 3-year defence programme' before it started to bite into the pockets of the taxpayer.[33] As Shaw has observed, it was part of IRD's job to convert a general awareness of the Russian menace into 'a more acute fear'. An example of IRD material in this regard was a sixty-nine-page pamphlet drafted by John Peck. Entitled 'The British Defence Programme', it was distributed to 'educated' opinion formers like the BBC. 'In measured but powerful tones, the pamphlet portrayed the free world under siege, with Korea the latest in a series of examples of Soviet attempts to expand its client base. However, the reader was left in no doubt about the innate weaknesses within the Soviet system.'[34] As Tony Shaw has commented:

> Korea certainly bore out the value to the British government of a propaganda depart-
> ment whose priority was anti-Communism. The IRD's ability to devise and dissemi-
> nate material demonising the monolithic Soviet bloc in various forms to suit different
> audiences showed subtlety and imagination. (It also contrasted with the Communists'
> overly crude and ultimately counter-productive tendencies). The non-attributable (or
> 'grey') nature of its output added to the public's impression that politicians were
> reflecting opinion rather than seeking to lead it.[35]

If Britain's smaller military contribution to the Korean War brought criticism from the United States, which constituted the bulk of the UN forces, the British propaganda services were considered to have performed exceptionally.

Armistice negotiations stuck on the question of the repatriation of Communist POWs. It transpired that many of the North Koreans did not want to return to a homeland run by a man who was to prove to be the world's longest-standing Stalinist leader.[36] The Communists insisted that they should be returned. Stalin had no interest in a swift resolution to the war, as it was Chinese casualties that were sapping Western military strength. It was not until Stalin's death in March 1953 that the matter could be resolved in a ceasefire.

CHAPTER SIX

Offensive: into the 1950s

By the early 1950s the IRD's London headquarters staff had grown to more than fifty. The department in Carlton House Terrace had been reorganized on the Second World War Political Warfare Executive (PWE) model into a series of geographical 'desks'. One member of staff, Fay Weldon, recalled that on each desk, 'There were probably about six of us. The "desks" just meant it was a couple of rooms. One would have the boss in it, files and a secretary, and the other one would have about three girls, one of which would be me.'[1] Hugh Lunghi, a Russian speaker who, as a wartime Army officer, had served with the Military Mission in Moscow was an early recruit: 'I went in and set up Soviet and East European Desk. I recruited several Russian speakers I knew from Oxford – they applied for jobs and I took them on. Fred Stacey took over the East European desk.'[2]

In 1952, Fay Weldon, later a novelist and dramatist, was a fresh-faced and by her own account, somewhat naïve 21-year-old. Despite the fact that her uncle was the Labour MP Michael Stewart (later Foreign Secretary), Weldon's knowledge of international politics was almost non-existent. She was one of a group of well-bred, well-educated girls recruited into Whitehall. As Weldon recalled:

> There we were, fresh out of various universities, landed in London, no jobs other than waitressing in cafés. It was so unusual for girls to have degrees in those days. But in the employment exchange in Great Marlborough Street there was one really remarkable woman who took it upon herself to filter us through into various jobs in which we would be able to use our intelligence and an ability to get things out of our heads onto bits of paper, which was really all we had.[3]

One of the employers that was able to offer qualified women the opportunity to put things down on paper was IRD, where Weldon soon found herself. 'A group of us were taken on by IRD, by the Foreign Office as temporary assistant clerks. And we were paid six pounds a week. And we were put into various desks. I was put on the Polish desk. My friends did rather better than me and got put on the Soviet desk, which was always much more fun.'[4]

By this time many of the desks had their own room, with facilities for the storage of sensitive material. As Weldon recalled:

> In every room there was a Top Secret cupboard and a Secret cupboard. And our Top Secret cupboard was usually empty and so we never locked it. Anything Top Secret we put in next door's cupboard. And we used to keep our hats and umbrellas in the

Top Secret cupboard. But one night security made a spot check and we came back and this metal cupboard, this wardrobe thing, was sealed up with red ribbon and sealing wax. A terrible sort of draconian punishment. And we all had to go down and admit our contrition and our sin and be threatened with expulsion, but it never happened in the end. It was sort of very mysterious.[5]

New members of staff were vetted, although the loyalty of English girls from public schools appeared to be assumed. And, although not ordered not to talk about the work, staff were told to be discreet.

By the time Weldon arrived at Carlton House Terrace the need for staff proficient in foreign languages and with detailed local knowledge of Eastern Europe, in particular, had led Murray to bring in a number of émigrés, often dispossessed by the Soviet occupation of their countries. Owing to their lack of British nationality, and because it would have been inappropriate to make them sit the Foreign Office entry exam, they were paid for on the Secret Vote. Thus the staff of IRD became, according to Weldon, 'a mixture of . . . straight Foreign Office people who were very good and of émigrés who had been called in to run the desks, partly out of politeness I imagine, and partly because they knew the country.'[6] Lunghi also recalled these often larger-than-life characters: 'We had lots of émigrés. There was one, Mrs Tcherniavina, a remarkable Russian woman. I was in touch with her for years. She had been a curator at the Hermitage. She had escaped from Russia with her husband in the late 1930s. She was left with a young son. She was great character – invited us to her home – in Collet Gardens, Barons Court. She was a translator. You used these people to advise one about their country.' Lunghi said that the editor of IRD regular newsletter to their diverse outlets, *The Interpreter*, was also an émigré, Zina Korentchevskaya.

The émigré influx gave IRD a different tone from the rest of the Foreign Office, bringing a more emotional anti-Communist set of values into play. Weldon recalled, 'There was a lot of anti-Communist paranoia and the people who were in charge of the desks usually . . . were the sort of Polish who ought really to be riding white horses into battle. But then somehow there they were, washed up in this very strange place. And they were always out drinking and we girls, as we learnt the way of the world, you did all the work, kept the place running and got none of the credit.'[7]

IRD staff, though, felt a sense of urgency about their work. Lunghi said, 'You have to realise the extent of Communist propaganda at the time. The *Soviet Weekly* in the English Language was in every common room in the country. My desk had a lot to do then. There were masses of anti-Western propaganda in the Soviet press. The Cominform was putting out a lot of material.' These were the years of perceived 'maximum danger' where the West was convinced that a Soviet attack was imminent.

New information from the archive of the former Soviet Union shows that the threat at the time was limited. The international situation was exacerbated by the West's support for rebuilding an independent Germany. With Hitler fresh in minds, the USSR saw this as a threat. But the Foreign Office's, and for that matter the British government's, warnings of an imminent Soviet threat were based on a major underestimation of the true extent of war damage and casualties in the Soviet Union.

The Cold Warrior and IRD associate Denis Healey admitted in his autobiography that he got it wrong: 'Like most Western observers at this time, I believed that Stalin's behaviour showed he was bent on the military conquest of Western Europe. I now think we were all mistaken, We took seriously some of the Leninist rhetoric pouring out from Moscow, as the Russians took too seriously some of the anti-Communist rhetoric favoured by American politicians.' This may be an avuncular admission, but it is cold comfort for the major policy errors that followed those misjudgements. Healey was plugged into the intelligence and IRD machinery that poured out the minutiae of everyday life under Russian Communism, yet they did not find out the true extent of Soviet destruction during the Second World War. We now know that the Soviet Union lost more than 27 million people and at least a quarter of its industry.

The main activity on the various desks at Carlton House Terrace was the production of briefing papers, most of which, in the early 1950s, dealt with the Eastern bloc and the myriad failures of the Communist system. Weldon recalled, 'I remember writing a report on housing, Polish housing. And you knew what your function was, which was to tell the bad news; they didn't want to know the good news. The good news, it seemed to me, was that there was the most amazing lot of stuff going on in Poland as they tried to rebuild it, open schools, build factories, all the rest of it.' To achieve this enormous reconstruction, Polish carpenters had to use fresh, unseasoned wood. This in itself became a propaganda point. 'All you were meant to talk about was the way the door frames didn't fit the doors, which they probably didn't. Which was why I started writing fiction in the end, because it seemed so much more accurate than anything written by someone like me.'[8] Or as Lunghi put it; 'We were responsible for getting facts with a twist – a twist in the best sense.'[9]

Once the background papers had gone out, the writers at IRD would sometimes notice their pieces surface in the press. Lunghi recalled, 'We didn't mind if our stuff appeared word for word in the papers. We thought at least we were getting it in.'[10] Weldon also recalled identifying IRD material in the press: 'Little bits of what you'd said would appear . . . except that they would have the spin on it . . . in which everything that came out of those worlds was bad. There was no room for ambiguity.'[11]

Slanted as it was, the material was factual and detailed, and it often provided journalists with information that they might otherwise have been unable to acquire. For example, IRD produced a loose-leaf folder of continually updated biographical sketches – a kind of *Who's Who* in the Eastern bloc – which journalists found extremely useful. It detailed the subject's career up to date, but also often included a little extra. For example, an IRD paper written in December 1955, reporting on the second Congress of the Romanian Workers Party, included brief biographies of the four main speakers. These included one 'N. Ceausescu', who was later to become Rumania's iron-fisted and megalomaniac dictator for three decades. IRD characterized Ceausescu in the following (perhaps in retrospect too mild) terms: 'Ceausescu is reportedly a short, fat young man with black crinkly hair and unpleasant features, a pushing, ruthless and objectionable type, who is said to be thoroughly disliked by everybody, including his fellow Communists. A major-general (political) and a member of the Central Committee at 30, he is obviously a rising star of the youngest generation of Communists.'[12]

The scale of IRD's operation is reflected in files at the Public Record Office which show its activity reaching just about every country in the world by one method or another. In themselves the contents of the files are sometimes dull reading, but what they indicate is the placing of IRD material in the media of hundreds of countries: the reports came from regional information officers in every country in Latin America, Scandinavia, the Far East and the Commonwealth. Topics dealt with ranged from material on Poland's preparation for its first post-Stalinist election in 1957 to papers on Soviet 'Proletarian Internationalism', an assessment which concluded that: 'Any hopes harboured abroad that the Soviet Union was ceasing to direct the work of foreign Communist Parties have been dashed. As under Stalin, interference in the internal affairs of other countries is known by the euphemism of "proletarian internationalism." '13

Each desk was charged with conducting in-depth research and the compilation of material for distribution under the direction of 'political officers'. While eventually the research desks would cover Africa, China and Latin America as well as the Soviet Union and Europe a notable exception was the United States, confirming that a 'Third Force' exposé of the evils of *laissez-faire* capitalism was never a factor under consideration on a practical level. The size of the desks varied over time in response to political developments and the demands of those for whom the propaganda was being produced. In addition there was a desk dealing specifically with Soviet fronts and organizations, owing to the international nature of their activities. It was known as the English desk because many of these fronts operated in Britain itself.

Most of the sources used for the compilation of IRD material were open. One extremely important fund of information was the BBC monitoring service at Caversham, near Reading. Weldon recalled, 'Our business was to monitor the radio broadcasts and newspapers. And they would all be translated for us, and we would put them in files and every now and then write reports.' Other sources included the diplomatic correspondence, which could sometimes be passed on directly to interested journalists, and anyone who had recent and direct knowledge of the Eastern bloc. Weldon recalled: 'I went through the statements of all the people who had escaped from behind the Iron Curtain, as it was then called, and who jumped ship or who sought sanctuary. And they would all be brought in to make statements, give accounts of everything they knew. Any defectors were just interrogated, everything they said was all marked down.'

Material gathered from all sources would be stored in a massive card index system. 'We had a sort of card index so if there was a change of government or if anything happened, you know. Everybody we knew had a card and you knew who they were, where they were coming from, all about it. . . . And probably it was very effective in fact.'14

MI6 officers around the world fed information into IRD via their headquarters at Century House. In addition, local MI6 officers kept IRD regional officers informed. Mayhew's Category A material, to be fed to high-level opinion makers, was often sanitized material from MI6, and this is what made IRD so valuable to selected journalists in the media. When the Iron Curtain came down, the West had few ways of getting information from within the Soviet Union. Travel was restricted for foreigners, and the Soviets were very effective at identifying and breaking up spy rings. The main source of information was discreet operations run by both British and American intelligence. The technique was simple: debrief all returning refugees and POWs. It was this military programme, known to the Americans as PROJECT WRINGER, that provided the bulk of intelligence for strategic planning. WRINGER employed 1,300 specially trained military and civilian personnel in Germany, Austria and Japan who questioned thousands of repatriated prisoners from the Soviet Union. Begun by the joint service Far East Command in December 1946, it had so expanded its scope by 1951 that the US gleaned most of its strategic intelligence from it.

Refugees could tell a great deal about conditions in the Soviet Union and behind the Iron Curtain. Indeed, arrangements were made by IRD for access to defectors from the Eastern bloc being held by military intelligence. On 18 January 1951, Murray was informed that there was no objection to a small IRD team operating under the Chief of Intelligence Division in West Germany.[15] Interviews would be granted on condition that they were subjected for clearance and 'In no circumstances will any facilities to interview a defector in the care of Intelligence Division be granted to any journalist etc. who is not sponsored by the Information Research Department of the Foreign Office.'[16]

In addition, the Foreign Office already operated as a huge collator of intelligence from many different sources – MI6, their own diplomats, newspapers and periodicals from the country in question, and radio transmissions picked up with the BBC/FO monitoring unit at Caversham.

Masses of material from ordinary diplomats was also fed into IRD. One early IRD file shows a request to field diplomats for examples of standard text books used in elementary and secondary schools in/under Communist domination. On 11 January 1949, IRD sent the following telegram to posts in Prague, Belgrade, Bucharest, Warsaw, Budapest and Sofia: 'We are making a study (for publicity purposes) of standard text books used in elementary and secondary schools in countries under Communist domination. Can you procure as many examples as possible?'

Sir Oliver Wright, who says his Foreign Office career was otherwise conventional, worked for IRD in Berlin between 1954 and 1956 screening refugees from Eastern Europe for information and running a small research section on behalf of IRD. He would also search for material that might interest IRD while stationed in Bucharest and Berlin.

The Soviet invasion of Hungary in 1956 damaged the international image of Communism more than any other event in that decade. It provided anti-Communist propagandists with a golden opportunity to deride Soviet pretensions of being the bringers of peace to the world. On 26 October 1956, Krushchev informed the Soviet presidium that disturbing reports were arriving from Budapest and that 'the situation in Hungary is extremely serious.'[17] Eight months earlier, at the Party Congress of the Communist Party of the Soviet Union, Krushchev had made his secret speech denouncing Stalin and had postulated three new ideological points, offering, so it seemed, an entirely new Soviet approach to the Cold War. First, he had accepted, through his criticisms of Stalin, that the Communist system was fallible. Second, he advanced the theory that Communism's victory didn't need to come about through inevitable conflict with capitalism and that it could be secured through peaceful coexistence with capitalism. Last, he suggested that there was not only one path to

Communism and that national Communist parties could adapt themselves to local conditions. This last point was particularly important as it suggested that the Soviet Union would accept a measure of independence in the countries in the Eastern bloc. In a background paper on the subject, IRD dismissed the announcement's significance and pointed out that 'The phrase "different roads to Socialism" does not in any circumstances mean that the Communist Party will not be in command' and concluded that 'it is difficult to take seriously the Soviet leaders' affirmed belief in the principle that "questions . . . of difference in concrete forms of Socialist development are the exclusive concern of the peoples of the respective countries."'[18]

Nevertheless, the new principle was soon put to the test in Poland, where the death of the Communist Party leader, Boleslaw Beirut, had led to the release of political prisoners and the removal of Stalinists from the Communist government. The Poles also made sure that the contents of Krushchev's secret speech reached the West, apparently in an attempt to prevent Soviet intervention. Then, during a wave of strikes and anti-Soviet riots in Poznan, the Poles set about electing Wladyslav Gomulka, a victim of Stalin's anti-Titoist purges, and in Soviet eyes an unreliable ally. However, despite flying to Warsaw, attempting to bully Gomulka and being refused entry to the Polish party plenum electing Gomulka, which he demanded, Krushchev backed down. As historian John Lewis Gaddis noted in his recent reassessment of the Cold War, 'However graceless the process may have been, a Kremlin leader had for the first time compromised with another state on who its leader was to be.'[19]

Developments in Hungary took a far more serious turn and elicited a far more serious response. In July, Krushchev had already authorized the replacement of the unpopular Communist leader of Hungary, Mathias Rakosi. As had been the case in Poland, Rakosi was identified with past injustices. In October the IRD reported that 'The Hungarian press, no longer stopping short at condemning the "era of Rakosi", is beginning to attack Rakosi directly and opinion, even in some Communist circles, will not be convinced that the regime intends to remedy past abuses unless those responsible for them are punished.'[20]

The situation in Hungary swiftly deteriorated and Krushchev reluctantly ordered the Red Army into Budapest to 'restore order'. But this intervention inflamed the situation further and the Red Army was met by a population armed with stones, grenades and Molotov cocktails, plus Hungarian security forces that looked increasingly unreliable. As a result, the new Hungarian leader, Imre Nagy, who led the liberalizing wing of the Communist party, was reappointed in an attempt to bring into government the main opposition figure. Nagy was able to negotiate the withdrawal of Soviet troops form Budapest on 28 October.

However, as historian W. Scott Lucas noted, 'When the protesters, encouraged by broadcasts from the CIA's Radio Free Europe, made new demands, including Hungary's withdrawal from the Warsaw Pact, the Soviet leadership ordered Soviet tanks to crush the uprising in Budapest.'[21] Krushchev, facing the disintegration of Soviet control over Eastern Europe and Soviet pre-eminence in the international Communist movement, which China was challenging, had decided to act.

'At 12.13 a.m. on Sunday, November 4, 1956, Moscow Radio made the following announcement: "The Hungarian counter-revolution has been crushed."' So started an

IRD paper brought out immediately after the invasion, which made the historical link with Czar Nicholas's crushing of the Hungarian revolution of 1848. A further paper by IRD, which kept the news agencies informed with news from Hungary throughout the crisis, analysed the situation in the following terms, confirming IRD's reading of the twentieth Party Congress:

> Faced with the prospect of part of their empire choosing freedom and independence, the Soviet leaders have abandoned the principles of coexistence and all pretence of legality. . . . It is now clear that in repudiating Stalinism, Krushchev has not abandoned the primacy of the Soviet *raison d'état*. The basic contradictions between the international pretensions of Communism and the national and imperialist self-interest of the Soviet Union has not been resolved. Communism as an ideology capable of attracting by its superior merits, on which Krushchev based the doctrine of coexistence, is patently bankrupt. . . . The Soviet leaders have lost the battle of ideas. Their eventual retreat is certain.[22]

CHAPTER SEVEN

Nothing but the Truth: IRD and the BBC

The airwaves were to prove perhaps the most important battleground of the Cold War. Throughout those forty years, the West broadcast consistently into Communist bloc countries using powerful radio transmitters. The Soviet leadership was painfully aware that such a different perspective on world events could potentially undermine its credibility. Radio was the only media that could not be banned or intercepted at the border and the Soviets had to jam Western broadcasts, a strategy that was both expensive and only partially successful. Historian Michael Nelson, a former Reuters correspondent and executive, has said, 'I believe that Western broadcasting to the Soviet Union and Eastern Europe, in which the BBC External Services played one of the leading roles, was one of the most important developments of the Cold War. It was important because of its role in bringing down the most pervasive political movement of the century.' He added, 'The weapons used in the propaganda war were the same on both sides, with one difference. Both broadcast to the world; but the Communist had few listeners. The difference was that the weapon of defense the Russians used was jamming; the weapon of defense the West used was free communication.'[1]

The three principal Western broadcasters into the Communist bloc were the BBC, Radio Free Europe/Radio Liberty (RFE/RL) and the Voice of America (VOA). The RFE and the RL were founded by the CIA as surrogate domestic broadcasters, with a similar tone to that of local radio stations in the targeted countries. The RFE was aimed at Eastern European countries and the RL at Russia. The VOA was funded by the State Department. Other important Western broadcasters to the Communist bloc included Vatican Radio, Radio Canada International, Radio France Internationale, Deutsche Welle and Radio in the American Sector (RIAS) Berlin.

Given that American propaganda was funded and run directly by the US government, why did the British government not set up a separate propaganda broadcasting service? The answer is that it neither needed nor wanted to, because the BBC performed this mission so well. The BBC depended on the government to set its licence fee and the External Services were funded directly by the Foreign Office.

During this period the BBC and the government presented publicly an arms-length relationship, but behind closed doors they often worked hand in hand. When in 1946 the BBC showed signs of editorial freedom, a number of politicians suggested that it might need more direction.[2] The resulting inquiry and White Paper publicly emphasized the BBC's independence and Bevin expressed this view to the cabinet on

30 April. This was seen as particularly important owing to the BBC's international reputation for honesty and accuracy built up during the Second World War, when it had been allowed to maintain notional, if not real, independence from government control. Less widely noted is the fact that the White Paper also required the external services to accept information from the Foreign Office regarding conditions in, and official policies towards, targeted areas: 'the Foreign Office is also able to determine the languages the BBC broadcasts, which geographical areas they will broadcast to, and for how long'.[3] In a crisis, or when broadcasting about a sensitive issue, the Overseas Service was obliged under a formula drawn up by Cabinet Secretary Norman Brook to consult the Foreign Office.[4] Norman Reddaway said:

> Well the Norman Brook formula was a very wise one – Norman Brook was a very wise man and he said that the Overseas Services should consult the Foreign Office on matters of foreign affairs so that their programmes could be drawn up in the national interest. Well that is a jolly good phrase. That was the Norman Brook formula, and what it said in fact was that if the Overseas Services wanted to be talking about – say the Soviet Union and the Communist offensive and so on – then they should consult the research people in the Foreign Office. And they did.[5]

Exactly how close the BBC and the Foreign Office were can best be seen from recently released documents. In September 1946 the head of the BBC's European Service, Gen Sir Ian Jacob, approached the Foreign Office for guidance on the attitude to be adopted to Russia and Communism. The response was an invitation to attend the Russia Committee, which set the agenda on dealing with the Soviet Union and Communism. They even changed the meeting day from Tuesdays to Thursdays to suit Jacob's diary. The active participation of Jacob, a senior ex-military man, who had recently turned down the job as head of MI6, in the Russia Committee ensured that he was fully briefed on government policy. The MI6 representative on the committee was Kim Philby.[6]

Jacob was, by all accounts, a shy, scholarly man who could show independence on occasion. Often, as revealed by the Russia Committee minutes, he was more aggressive in his desire to use anti-Communist propaganda than his Foreign Office colleagues. One minute noted: 'General Jacob had raised the question of the general line our relations with the Soviet Union which was being taken in the European Service of the BBC. He had inquired whether we were not being too indulgent, and whether we should not make a more vigorous reply in out broadcasts to Russian propaganda against us, by carrying more anti-Communist material.'[7] In early 1947 it was Jacob who wrote to the head of the Foreign Office's Northern Department, the Hon. Robin Hankey, suggesting fortnightly meetings between 'Winther, the head of my Scandinavian Region, and his opposite number in the Foreign Office.' Jacob noted, 'We have this arrangement in all our other regions and it is very valuable.'[8]

Strictures over the independence of journalism in the BBC had understandably been eroded during wartime and were slow to recover during the Cold War. The closeness between the Foreign Office and the BBC was as informal as it was formal. Many of the executives of the BBC had gone to the same public schools, and inevitably Oxbridge, with their Foreign Office colleagues. Both were part of the establishment, attending the same gentlemen's clubs and having an implicit understanding of what constituted the national interest. Like IRD head, Ralph Murray, some had worked for the BBC before joining the Foreign Office. When the head of IRD's Soviet Desk, Hugh Lunghi, left in 1954, he went to the 'Communist affairs' desk at the BBC's External Services in Bush House, where he worked with Denis Healey's protégé, Walter Kolarz.

One has to remember that this was the BBC that had MI5 vet its staff for 'subversives' from the 1930s until the practice was revealed in 1985. This eliminated some of the more interesting thinkers from the airwaves. Sometimes MI5 just cocked up on its vetting, seriously damaging individuals lives and careers without the victims knowing why. To show how erratic the process could be, it is worth noting that Hugh Carleton Greene, later Director General of the BBC, had failed his vetting when joining as head of their German Service. 'I was vetted in 1940. MI5 thought I was a Communist, but it turned out to be a mistake.'[9] Greene was fortunate in being well connected and his friends cleared up the misunderstanding.[10] By and large, during the Second World War the vetting rules were relaxed and left-wing broadcasters were employed for the duration. But during the Cold War, vetting expanded. Hugh Greene recalled one victim in the External Services while he was controller of Broadcasting in the German Zone: 'He wasn't a security risk at all. It turned out that he had worked for MI6, the rival secret service, and there had been an internal quarrel.' Gen Sir Ian Jacob later confirmed, 'I was shown lists of Communists in the BBC. It was handled by the controller of Administration. A relative of mine was actually on the list because he had a Communist wife.'[11] Hundreds were kept out of the BBC in this underhand way.

According to the Foreign Office's own history of IRD, 'high-level links' were quickly established between the new IRD and the BBC, recognized as the pre-eminent channel for publicizing HMG's policies to the Soviet satellite countries. In February 1948, IRD's head, Ralph Murray, declared his belief that 'the BBC might be geared into the new policy much more than it is at present', and then listed a scale of broadcasting 'target priorities'. This was, he admitted, 'very thorny ground', but the new publicity policy none the less required IRD to induce the BBC, by persuasion if possible, to undertake 'such programme development that might help us'.[12] Murray was correct in his optimism. His priority list was approved at a meeting on 27 February between him, his boss (Christopher Warner) and the BBC's Sir Ian Jacob.

Reading through the correspondence between the Foreign Office and the BBC held at the BBC archive at Caversham, near Reading, the authors were forcibly struck by the intimacy and frequency of contact at the most senior level. The Overseas Service, in particular, was bombarded with information and suggestions, and instructed as to the needs of British foreign policy and the desired content of programming on a regular basis. Despite frequent and vocal defences of theoretical independence and whatever junior BBC staff might have believed, programming was developed in close consultation with the Foreign Office and its information departments. It would take a major schism – Suez – within the political class, the BBC itself, and the wider public to provoke a significant challenge to the cosy relationship.

To prevent dangerous deviations, IRD kept a close watch on the BBC's political content and was not afraid to intervene behind the scenes in that peculiarly English way.

On 17 February 1948, Sir Maurice Peterson, the British Ambassador in Moscow, wrote a memo to IRD's supervising Under-Secretary, Christopher Warner, complaining of a broadcast by a Mrs Watts that was 'Communist inspired drivel'. Mrs Watts was, apparently, 'Olga Schwartz, who is a British subject, resident in the USSR since 1936, teaching at the Moscow Institute of Foreign Languages. We know very little about her. . . . However, her talk as reported here is so phoney that one wonders how to the BBC allowed themselves to be led up the garden path by her.' Further correspondence then took place between IRD and Jacob's office. Warner suggested that the BBC 'should in future get their Russian experts to check their reliability of speakers on Russia before they are allowed to come on the air.' On 10 March, Warner received a letter from the director of spoken programmes concerned, a Mr G.R. Barnes who said, 'Jacob has shown me your letter of the 6th March. We have received a protest about this talk and we can only say we regret that it was broadcast.'[13]

A similar complaint was made regarding a news item broadcast on the Eastern European Service in 1952. On 21 May, the Foreign Office's R.H.K. Marett wrote to R. McCall at the BBC regarding a news item on 25 April: 'It was not, we understand, considered to be of sufficient news value to be broadcast on the Home Service of the BBC. We are a bit puzzled by the use of this item – so favourable to the Communists and discouraging to our friends'. The item in question, which had been aired again on the same day, was a news report on an Italian Jesuit Priest who had left his order to join the Italian Communist Party. An interview with Father Tondi had appeared in the Communist paper *Il Paese*. In the second broadcast, the BBC reported that 'A Vatican semi-official source said today that Father Tondi had been under medical care for some time.' According to a written note on Marett's letter, the issue was 'Dealt with verbally.'[14]

It would not be fair to suggest that the BBC never exercised editorial control against the wishes of the Foreign Office. However, this episode reveals the constant tensions existed between the BBC and government in all forms. The BBC's external broadcasting staff knew that the Foreign Office was watching for the slightest slip and the Foreign Office monitoring of the BBC output was to continue. In April 1948, embassies in Communist and satellite countries were commissioned to monitor BBC broadcasts in local languages. One of the main conclusions of the exercise was that news emanating from Communist sources, 'often found to be inaccurate', should not be broadcast without explanatory or corrective comment unless there was no danger of misunderstanding.[15] According to the Foreign Office History Notes on IRD, 'The results of the survey were discussed with Sir Ian Jacob by Mayhew and Warner, and Posts informed.' Agreement was reached on a number of improvements, such as that programmes including press summaries should make clear when these represented minority views, as in the case of the *Daily Worker*. On the other hand, the BBC rejected that more time should be spent correcting misrepresentations of the HMG's policies, on the grounds that this would surrender the initiative to the Communists.[16]

Through Jacob it was arranged for the controller of Overseas Services to be supplied with IRD Category A confidential briefs, along with the editor of European Services. Jacob thought that they would find these papers 'very useful as background information for speakers, and as private material for drawing for comparisons and the refutation of glaring mis-statements.'[17]

The BBC assisted IRD by monitoring foreign broadcasts, for example in Uzbek, in which the department was interested. In return, much of the work of British diplomatic information officers, particularly in Eastern Europe, appears to have been the supply of material for the BBC Overseas Service, as well as for the Foreign Office. In correspondence with the Minister of State at the Foreign Office, Maj Kenneth Younger MP, the head of the British Legation in Budapest, Sir G.A. Wallinger, noted that 'More than half the work of the Information Officer during this quarter has consisted of briefing the Hungarian Service of the BBC and collecting information for Chancery volunteered by visitors to the Information Office.'[18]

IRD provided stories for the BBC and brought publications such as ex-Communist Ruth Fischer's *Stalin and the German Communist Party* to the BBC's notice.[19] At the end of the first year of IRD's existence, Jacob gave wholehearted support for the department's work. Advising on tactics at the United Nations he said that IRD's task was to whittle away the effect of Soviet tactics by the constant exposure of the fallacy of Soviet theory.[20]

Over the next three decades, IRD material poured into the BBC, and was directed to news desks, talks writers and different specialist correspondents. IRD provided background briefings, analysis, articles and suggested speakers. In addition, IRD specialists were available for consultation. Significantly, IRD soon boasted of its influence: 'the British Broadcasting Corporation Overseas Service is obviously a most important vehicle for anti-Communist publicity. We have the most cordial relations and daily contacts with those running this service at all levels and supply them with guidance and material which they make excellent use in their news bulletins, talks and commentaries'.

The material supplied by IRD was not, however, without its problems. In a memorandum to the controller of BBC European Services, Tangye Lean, the Russian Programme Organiser, Mr D.M. Graham, while noting the usefulness of an IRD paper on the 1939 Nazi-Soviet Pact, noted that, 'Its usefulness would be still further increased if experience had not shown that it is necessary to verify all dates and quotations.' Having given a number of examples, Graham concluded with some encouraging word for the IRD researchers, 'If the Information Research Department could establish a reputation for super-human reliability, much more of their work would be brought to the attention of our audience.'[21]

The main target of IRD activity remained the Communist bloc. It is worth remembering that, at this time, the BBC was largely a radio broadcaster. Television, which was suspended during the Second World War, was still in its infancy. The ideological war translated to a radio war. In 1949 the BBC broadcast for 687 hours per week compared with the USSR's 434 and the US's 214. In 1950 the BBC was broadcasting for 643, the USSR was up to 533 and the US was up to 497.[22] The Russians were very sensitive to the power of broadcasting. From 3 February 1948 they started a massive jamming operation against foreign broadcasts.

The radio battle was to continue for the length of the Cold War. Historian Michael Nelson told a remarkable story of Soviet incompetence: 'Despite the billions of dollars spent on jamming, it was the Soviet state that saw to it that its citizens had cheap short-wave radios which they could use to listen to Western Propaganda.'

Shortly before Stalin's death, on 17 February 1953, the USSR Council of Ministers proposed that the Ministry of Communications and Industry should stop from 1954 the production of receivers capable of picking up western broadcasts. However, by 1954 the production of such short-wave receivers had dramatically increased to 4 million a year. The ministry had simply forgotten to effect the order. 'Thus our technical measures directed against hostile radio broadcast were brought to nothing by the mass production of short-wave receivers', said a later report in the Central Committee archives. 'It is enough to point out that at present, up to 85 per cent of short-wave receivers are located in the European part of the USSR, where our own short-wave broadcast cannot be heard and where it possible to listen only to hostile radio.'[23]

The BBC was to be one of IRD's best customers. It was quite willing to go to what, according to Hugh Greene, was known to many as an anti-Communist propaganda department for its background information on highly sensitive issues.[24] Lord Mayhew confirmed this: 'I should think they were our best customer, very likely. Because, you see, they were not inhibited by the thought of using taxpayers money to change political opinion in Britain, this was the Overseas Service. I don't think they used it at home, I'm not sure they ought to have used it at home, but they used it abroad and that was fine.'[25]

The BBC was able to acquire sensitive material through IRD, including GCHQ material when it was capable of being sanitized to disguise its origin. Charles Wheeler, the veteran BBC correspondent, was appointed to BBC External Services in Berlin in 1949. He was regularly visited by an IRD man based in the city who would turn up at his office armed with cyclostyled sheets of information. Wheeler was not allowed to look at them, but the IRD man paraphrased the contents. They were mostly 'gossipy new items' about East Germany, which Wheeler sent to the German Service of the BBC. 'I used to get regular visits from the Information Research Department. Peter Seckleman used to come and see me with snippets which I think were taken from intercepts from the Berlin Tunnel,' said Wheeler. This was the 600-yard tunnel dug by MI6 and the CIA beneath the city's Soviet zone. It connected with the tunnel through which the Soviet's main telephone lines ran. GCHQ experts monitored the telephone lines and reported any interesting material. 'I would pass anything interesting back to the German Service in London. It was all done on the old boy's basis. There was a quid pro quo: I handed material over to IRD and they gave me stuff back. . . . Remember this was the height of the Cold War.'[26]

Hugh Greene, head of the Eastern European Services between 1949 and 1950, said that he regarded IRD as 'just another source of factual information from which one could select'.[27] Anatole Goldberg, chief commentator for the East European Services of the BBC, knew about IRD from the beginning. He recalled that his contacts with the department were personal and that he maintained very good relations with various IRD representatives, particularly Mr Heath-Mason. He found the department helpful in that it had 'documentary facts, and the Government's view on a particular issue – it was useful with sensible people.' His contacts with IRD were in the 1950s.[28] Throughout the IRD years, the Foreign Office placed its disguised material and brought pressure to bear on the BBC when its people broadcast items that the government objected to. In 1956, this close and effective relationship was to be sorely tested.

The Suez Crisis was to cause a rocky patch in many establishment relationships, and the common law marriage of the BBC and the government came under serious strain. At the time the BBC was broadcasting only one-and-half hours a week in Arabic, but Britain's declining relationship with Egypt permeated the Corporation's broadcasts both at home and to the rest of world.

British troops had first occupied Egypt in 1882. The canal, which was built a few years before, had rapidly become a major strategic asset for maintaining the Empire and the British moved in to protect this vital lifeline to the far-flung colonies. The canal had dominated British defence strategy in the Middle East during the Second World War. After 1945 the occupying forces remained, and this caused increasing resentment in an Egypt that was immersed in major domestic political upheavals. In July 1952 a group of officers, including Gamel Abdul Nasser, overthrew King Farouk. British relations with the Egyptian people went rapidly downhill and the British found their presence challenged by the new nationalist and assertive President Nasser, who felt they should not be in Suez.

Nasser found the West generally suspicious, at best unhelpful and often hostile. However, he was not to be intimidated, and with popular support he placed increasing pressure on the British until they agreed to withdraw their troops from the canal zone in June 1956. Tensions between the West and Nasser mounted. Nasser was refused the Western arms that Egypt felt it needed to defend itself against the growing power of the Israelis. This pushed Nasser into the arms of the Soviets, who were ever anxious to exploit these kinds of diplomatic splits. In early 1956, Krushchev agreed to supply arms to the Egyptians (using the Czechs as the conduit) and to help to build the Aswan Dam in a deal worth $1,200 million.

In July 1956, Nasser nationalized the Suez Canal Company, much to fury of the British and the French, who began to threaten the Egyptian government. Nasser remained defiant. Without American support, the British and French hatched a plot. In November 1956 the Israeli Army launched an attack on Egypt as a pretext for the British and French to intervene to 'separate the combatants'. Their forces invaded the canal area. The result was worldwide condemnation and even dissent within the ruling Tory Party. Eventually, Eden resigned and his place was taken by Harold Macmillan. The British withdrew from Egypt in one of the last great fiascos of the empire.

IRD was once again at the centre of events and the BBC was expected to follow suit. Foreign Office officials clearly expected government policy to be explicitly supported. As early as March 1951, Christopher 'Kit' Barclay, then in the Foreign Office's Information Policy Department,[29] wrote to the BBC's Gordon Waterfield, expressing Bevin's concern that 'what we, the British, are doing for under-developed countries in the economic and social sphere, and particularly in the Middle East, is not sufficiently known'.[30] The letter was copied to the Deputy Director of Overseas Service, J.H. Clark, by R. Scrivenor at 17 Carlton House Terrace, indicating IRD's interest. In reply, Clark told Scrivenor, 'we shall be glad to ensure that appropriate attention is given in all our External Services to British encouragement of development in the Middle East'.[31] Later that year, Barclay wrote again to Waterfield, this time with a more specific suggestion: 'We have decided that we should now start taking a rather more direct publicity line for the benefit of the Sudanese about Independence with a view to discouraging them from thinking that any form of link with Egypt would be in their interests.' Barclay discreetly suggested that 'You may like to consider whether you can help with a general talk or two about independence on the Arabic Service, without of course indicating that these lectures are in any way directed at the Sudan. . . . The so-called autonomous republics in the USSR and the satellite countries should provide examples.'[32]

One example of how material was passed to and used by the BBC in the build up to the crisis was given by Norman Reddaway: 'The BBC Domestic Service talks person, a very bright lady called Grace Wyndham Goldie,[33] rang me up and said "We don't really know very much about this fellow Nasser. Who is he and didn't he write a book? Do you have anybody who could do me a quick summary of this?" We had some extremely able ex-journalists and a perfectly honest summary went off the next day.'[34]

Nasser, too, was aware of the advantages of radio services that broadcast in accordance with government policy. He had initiated a very efficient Arabic radio service, Voice of the Arabs, in the early 1950s, broadcasting to a range of Arab and African countries. This service contained a great deal of anti-British and anti-Western commentary. According to Gordon Waterfield, then head of the Eastern Service, the BBC was encouraged to respond with anti-Nasser propaganda as early as 1953. 'The BBC was attacked by the Foreign Office for not answering in the same terms. The BBC refused as it would have lost trust in our accuracy. All the Arab staff came to see me at the start of the intervention and said they would only stay if the BBC continued with objective reporting'.[35]

In the months leading up to Suez, the BBC found itself under increasing pressure to place the situation firmly in a Cold War context. The IRD line was run that Nasser was becoming a Soviet dupe – the favoured all-purpose propaganda line for anti-colonial leaders. This was increasingly hard for the BBC's Middle East specialists to take as they were only too aware of the complexities of Nasser's position and that much of the politics involved was local or Arab rather than Cold War. Nevertheless, senior BBC officials were still standing shoulder to shoulder with the government's increasingly difficult position. In 1956, Hugh Greene, by then the controller of Overseas Services of the BBC, joined the secret Egypt Committee, formed to determine anti-Nasser propaganda.[36] The pre-meeting briefing papers for 12 October 1956 set out the objectives: 'In the long term, we aim to get rid of Colonel Nasser. In the short-term, we must prepare the Arab World, the rest of the World, for negotiations with him – the result which must be presented as a success for us.'[37] A minute from a later meeting of the committee, with Greene's successor Donald Stephenson, shows cracks beginning to appear in the party line: 'The BBC would always work on the assumption that the Government was right; but it needed to give a fair reflection of public opinion and to be believed by its listeners.'[38]

When the British and French military finally intervened, the cracks widened into a split. Senior BBC editors tried to keep the output pro-British government, but many BBC commentators and journalists were appalled by Eden's intervention and refused to toe the government line in their broadcasts. This in turn led to a backlash against the BBC. One of the sorest wounds came when Labour leader Hugh Gaitskell's response to Eden's speech of 3 November was broadcast. He accused British troops of being the aggressors, called for the Prime Minister's resignation and offered support to any

Conservative successor who complied with UN resolutions. The broadcast aroused controversy at home and in the Mediterranean, where servicemen listened to the BBC World Service. Eden thought that the BBC should never have broadcast the speech and the government renewed its pressure on the Corporation.

An ad hoc committee on overseas broadcasting, with Lord Privy Seal Butler as chairman, had already recommended that a Foreign Office liaison officer should work with the BBC because 'the views of HMG on specific issues of major importance often receive insufficient emphasis in broadcasts to other countries'. It was an elegant Foreign Office euphemism for censorship. Press Secretary William Clark claimed that Eden 'instructed the Lord Chancellor to prepare an instrument which would take over the BBC (Overseas Service) altogether and subject it wholly to the will of the Government'. This assertion cannot be corroborated. Nevertheless, government intervention can be seen. IRD's supervising Under-Secretary, Peter Grey, told the BBC: 'it was not the national interest to include in the Arabic Services news bulletins virtually identical with those now appearing in the Home Service'. The Corporation was instructed not to broadcast news bulletins on the Arabic Service in the near future.[39]

Following the fiasco, a liaison officer from the Foreign Office to the BBC was appointed to re-establish government ascendancy and control over the Corporation. This was J.L.B. Titchener, better known as 'Titchener of Tartoum'. Titchener was able to demonstrate within a year that the BBC was back under government control and IRD was setting the line; he wrote, that 'much of the material and a great deal of the background for the BBC's broadcasts to the Soviet Union, the satellites and China reaches the BBC from this department. The liaison in this respect is both close and constant.'[40]

The BBC's painful involvement in Suez was only part of the anti-Nasser propaganda story. The British government had carefully placed other media weapons to attack Nasser, albeit again with mixed results.

CHAPTER EIGHT

The Medium is the Message: IRD and MI6

According to Fay Weldon, the arrival of mysterious MI6 visitors to the IRD's Carlton House Terrace offices would generate a thrill of excitement, particularly among some of the younger female staff. 'Every now and then the spies would come by and would come down the corridor and there would be a sort of *frisson* of excitement. There were glass doors and we were told to turn our backs. Somebody would come along the corridor and say "Turn your backs. To the wall" and you would turn so this person could walk down these corridors unseen. Except we always peeked! Kind of good looking they were. But that was the sort of Bondish bit.'[1]

The relationship between IRD and the intelligence services MI5, MI6 and GCHQ is perhaps the most controversial area in the history of IRD. Unlike Fay Weldon, many, if not all, old IRD hands play down contact with the secret services. Close involvement with a proactive intelligence service implies IRD's engagement in darker activities than the Foreign Office has so far cared to admit publicly. However, throughout IRD's life élite officers had very close relations with MI6 and MI5, and the department was, in part, a secret service itself.

One of the best kept IRD secrets was the existence of a special unit – the action desk – which coordinated IRD's 'dirty tricks' operations. Only senior staff and those involved were in the 'need to know'. The existence of covert activity blurring the distinction between IRD and MI6 was confirmed by several insiders including Lord Owen, the former Labour Foreign Secretary (1976–8).[2] 'This unit also planted sanitised espionage information gained by MI6 into the media,' said one MI6 source. In addition, various ad hoc arrangements were made for specific countries and operations, in coordination with MI5 or MI6, as needed. In the compartmentalized IRD, these arrangements were not known to the majority of low-level staff, who spent their time merely monitoring the foreign media and preparing briefing papers. A sense of the 'spooky' side of IRD was revealed by a former CIA officer from the period, who said that IRD was represented at meetings between MI6 and the CIA for most of its life.[3] IRD was also frequently represented on high-level Foreign Office and intelligence committees.

The closeness of these links is also demonstrated by the fact that many IRD staff were, at one time or another, also MI6 or MI5 officers. John Ogilvy Rennie, the IRD head during Suez, was later to head MI6.[4] IRD's head in the late 1960s, Nigel Clive, had been a senior MI6 man from the time of the Second World War but most notably was MI6's political officer during Suez. Former IRD employee Brian Crozier, a well-known commentator on Western intelligence services, has also spoken of the interchangeability of IRD and MI6 people. In addition IRD also took on a number of MI5 people. The legendary and glamorous MI5 officer, Ann Elwell, was married to another MI5 officer, Charles Elwell. She joined IRD in 1955 and made several trips to the Middle East, her allotted territory. She stayed with IRD for twenty years.[5]

Initially IRD's terms of reference forbade subversive propaganda in or to the Communist-controlled countries, especially anything that would instigate military acts or sabotage. Wartime operations had shown that it was dangerous and wasteful to encourage any premature resistance against occupying forces.[6] The British cabinet did not want provoke anti-Communists inside the Soviet bloc into futile acts of resistance that the British would not realistically be able to support. However, as the Cold War progressed, the cabinet began to support very specific acts to undermine Communist regimes. The restrictions on exciting subversion were lifted at a cabinet meeting of 19 December 1949, provided that such operations were approved by a minister.[7] These changes left IRD free to help MI6 with its work, most immediately in aiding the landing of Albanian guerrillas to overthrow the Communist regime.

The policies of 'containment' advocated by the Western powers actually involved a covert roll-back policy. What neither IRD nor anyone else in the West mentioned (although it was extensively covered in the Communist newspapers so avidly poured over by IRD researchers) was that from 1949, the West began supporting the non-Communist partisan armies still operating against the Soviet Union. Arms and agents were poured in behind the East European borders by unmarked planes and boats run by the CIA, MI6 and French intelligence. The Soviets were engaged in full-scale engagements with these units in the Ukraine and Baltic States, and also experienced constant sabotage and attacks from smaller units across a wider area.

In late 1946, MI6 had set up the Special Operations Branch and Political Action Group. These were revamped, SOE-style units that were aided by the Royal Navy and Royal Air Force in operations in the Baltic, Ukraine and other countries. They put hundreds of agents into the Eastern bloc and supported the anti-Communist partisans who fought small-scale wars with the Soviets until they were eventually suppressed one by one. Agent drops in support of these partisans, many of which resulted in capture, continued until 1954. The Soviets knew that the British had been behind the abortive landing of Albanian partisans to attempt a coup in 1949. The British public did not. Withholding this kind of information gave a deliberately lop-sided view of the Cold War and Soviet claims of Western aggression.

Like IRD, MI6 was under Foreign Office control, although in its case the tightness of that control waxed and waned over the years. From 1950 the now unchained IRD was able to complement MI6's SOE-style operations as a smaller version of the old PWE.[8] The details of IRD's support of MI6's operation against Albania, and then the overthrow of President Mossadeq's government in Iran in 1953, remain secret. However, the Suez Crisis provides a textbook case of IRD involvement in covert operations. While the files are not yet publicly released, a great deal of information has become available. Suez revealed how IRD's media assets could be used in a British intervention, even if the result in this case, and the actual handling of the affair, was a débâcle that severely damaged British prestige across the world.

The British had retained a formidable covert propaganda presence in the Middle East after the Second World War and were conscious of the strategic importance of the region especially in terms of oil and the canal. The radio station, *Sharq al Adna*, was the primary British propaganda weapon in the region during the Suez Crisis. A wartime asset taken over by MI6, in 1948 it had transferred from war-torn Palestine to the relative safety of Cyprus. The station was based in a collection of Nissen huts on a scrubby slope near the village of Polymedia. It boasted the most powerful medium-wave transmitter in the Middle East. After a visit to the region in 1949 to establish the extent of pro-British news, IRD's supervising Under-Secretary, Christopher Warner, wrote, 'Our posts agree that the BBC are good and on political material *Sharq al Adna* still better. It is the general view that the Sharq transmitter is the most listened to after local broadcasts. The sets are in cafes and therefore broadcasting penetrates to the villages.'[9] Warner may have been overestimating *Sharq al Adna*'s appeal. At any rate, by late 1951 IRD's Christopher Barclay was informing Gordon Waterfield that the BBC had overtaken *Sharq al Adna* in popularity.[10] Nevertheless, *Sharq al Adna* was a major regional broadcaster and during the mid-1950s, the station – also known by the British name Near East Arab Broadcasting Station – had become a major medium for the dissemination of IRD's subtle pro-British propaganda. For this role it was, at least initially, extremely valuable. In 1951, Barclay could report that 'in critical times when people believe that the Egyptian Government is censoring news, practically everyone listens in to either the BBC or *Sharq al Adna* or both.'[11]

The director of the radio station was Ralph Poston, who had previously been the editor of the Royal Institute for International Affairs magazine, the *World Today*, which he made a conduit for IRD material. Richard Beeston, a British journalist, worked for the station in the mid-1950s. The station's success, he said, was 'due in part to a first-class drama and music programme supplied by the station's largely Palestinian Arab staff'. It was a considerable enterprise and something of a sinecure for the British staff. 'The 150 or so Arabs on the staff were respectable, sober, hard-working group, mostly married with children. The small expatriate staff of administrators, technicians and journalists were a racier lot altogether, whose goings on constantly amazed their Arab colleagues.'[12] On the face of it, *Sharq al Adna* appeared to be a normal commercial station and made money. According to Beeston, this was something of a headache for MI6 as it did not have an administrative mechanism for dealing with profits.

Documents also show that IRD, following in the footprints of the SOE, had made the Middle East a priority for covert propaganda operations. Besides radio, other techniques were used, such as putting out 'sibs' to sow the seeds of distrust against the Russians, who were emerging as rivals in the region. Internal Foreign Office correspondence from 1949 shows some of the suggestions, including blaming the Russians for forging currency. Information Officer Mr T.E. Evans in Beirut liked the idea, 'There's are always a lot of forged currency round here,' he observed. Anthony Haigh, regional information officer in Cairo, suggested spreading a rumour that 'The Russians . . . are using Zionists to create international disorder in the Middle East.' John Cloake in London advised, 'Each post must decide on the advisability of rumours in its own territory.'[13]

As the Suez Crisis worsened during 1956, the British government put into place a number of covert operations against Nasser and his regime. Many centred on the

British-owned company the Arab News Agency (ANA). From its head office on the first floor of the Immoblia Building in Sharia Sherif Pasha in the heart of Cairo, the ANA serviced a vast section of the media in the region. The agency was run by journalist Tom Little, a Middle East specialist who had joined during the war.[14] Jan Morris, later a famous travel writer, had worked for the ANA after the Second World War: 'This was never boring. The news was full of drama. The war in Palestine was at its height, affairs within Egypt were rich in intrigue, menace and corruption, and our correspondents in the remoter Arab parts flooded us with piquant intelligence – marvellous cameos of desert crime, court conspiracy, religious polemic or family feud.'[15]

The ANA provided a convenient base for British anti-Nasser undercover operations during Suez. The memoirs of Selwyn Lloyd, the former Conservative Foreign Secretary, record that, as the Suez Crisis worsened in the summer of 1956, the British cabinet's plan for toppling Nasser called for several months of psychological warfare to be followed by military intervention if this did not work.[16] In Cairo, temporary additions to the large staff at the ANA office included Sefton Delmer, who had been in charge of British black propaganda during the Second World War, and William Stevenson, biographer of 'Intrepid', whose assistant he had been in the SOE. Delmer was now working for the *Daily Express* which supported his secondment back into 'secret government work'. Delmer and Stevenson's propaganda objective was to equate Nasser with Hitler, which was Eden's view. In this they had more success in London – notably with Delmer's own paper, the *Daily Express* – than in the Middle East.

These and other activities resulted in the arrest by the Egyptian authorities in August 1956 of thirty people including four Britons. All were accused of being members of a spy ring, of which James Swinburn, secretary of the ANA, was said to be the head.[17] Two officials of the British Embassy were expelled. At the time of the arrests, Sefton Delmer, William Stevenson, Ann Sharpley of the *Evening Standard* and Eileen Travis, an American working for the *Daily Mail*, were also expelled.[18] According to Reuters reports of the later trial, Swinburn confessed, for which he received a lighter five-year sentence. Another Briton was sentenced in his absence to ten years, and a Maltese businessman, James Zarb, who had served with the SOE in Yugoslavia during the war, was also given ten years by the court. One Egyptian was executed, his son, an Army captain, was given a life sentence and a number of other Egyptians were given long sentences. Several other Britons were acquitted.

The ANA spy ring was part of a much larger MI6 operation. From March 1956, British intelligence, through Julian Amery, the Conservative MP and former wartime SOE officer, had made contact with a group of rebel Egyptian officers outside Egypt. If the British government overthrew Nasser, these officers were prepared to take power. George Young, the deputy director of MI6 responsible for Middle East operations, and his colleagues were discussing the destablization of Nasser with various dissident groups. They even discussed the possibility of assassinating him, an idea that would have appalled calmer heads at the Foreign Office had they known. The Foreign Office consensus was that Nasser was popular and an attempt to remove him could misfire, especially as there was no obvious pro-Western successor with sufficient presence. As the crisis mounted through September, MI6 developed further assassination schemes. One was a plan to inject nerve gas into the Egyptian leader's office. The scheme was allegedly approved by Eden before he suspended it in preference for military intervention.

With the decision taken for a British and French military campaign the principal direct 'psychwar' tools available to the British for anti-Nasser propaganda were powerful radio stations, including *Sharq al Adna*. Newer and more powerful transmitters were considered for British stations in Libya, Aden and Kuwait. The Iraqis, after persistent efforts by the Foreign Office, erected a transmitter in September 1956, which was more powerful than any Egyptian station. A British network of radio stations in the Middle East broadcast 'factual stories' supporting Britain's case over Suez. British and French 'black' stations started broadcasting disinformation into Egypt from 28 July. A 'Free Egyptian' station, transmitted from France and operated at a frequency close to Egypt's Voice of the Arabs radio, while the British conducted radio operations from Libya, Cyprus and Aden. The Israelis detected a mobile station, with an Iraqi announcer, calling for the assassination of Nasser and transmitting coded messages.[19]

Disinformation was not limited to the radio. In another British 'psychwar' operation, a forged pamphlet was attributed to the 'Government of Egypt Information Department' and sent to oil companies in Egypt. The document suggested that Nasser would effectively take over Middle Eastern oil.[20] The 'psychwar' operations were run by Lt Col Bernard Fergusson, a man with no previous experience in psychological warfare. A Black Watch officer, he had been a highly regarded Chindit leader in Burma during the Second World War. Afterwards he had been sent to Palestine as part of the counter-insurgency operation, which went awfully wrong when a former SOE officer was arrested as part of a British team charged with killing Zionist guerrillas. At Suez it started going wrong, too. The RAF flew operations to drop propaganda leaflets on the Egyptian population. The problem was that the 'leaflet bombs' were designed to explode at 1,000 ft, using an altitude fuse, and scatter paper over a wide area. However, because of barometric differences in Egypt, the bombs exploded at just 6 ft causing death or injury to any Egyptian in the vicinity – a real own goal.

The main British anti-Nasser propaganda war was fought, both in the Middle East and across the world, by IRD working closely in conjunction with MI6. IRD was involved in every stage of the crisis. The political adviser to the British Supreme Commander, Gen Sir Charles Keighley, was Ralph Murray, the former head of IRD. IRD's current boss, John Rennie, and his deputy, Norman Reddaway, told Eden's press secretary, William Clark, of their desire for more 'black' propaganda from British radio stations.[21]

Another figure who was to later head IRD was Nigel Clive, a secret service career officer who was MI6's political adviser during the crisis. Clive and the deputy director of MI6, George Young, had convinced Eden of the serious threat that Nasser posed to British interests. In April 1956 they set out to do the same with the Americans. According to a CIA cable from London, they were told that:

Nasser's aims are total destruction of Israel; Egyptian domination of all Arab governments and elimination of all Western positions in the Arab area; material extension of Egyptian influence in North Africa, particularly Libya. In order to realise his ambitions, Nasser has accepted full-scale collaboration with the Soviets, and is prepared to allow the Soviets whatever role in the area they desire in order to assure himself of their support. Nasser is now taking the initiative for extension of Soviet influence in Syria, Libya, and French North Africa. Egypt must therefore be regarded as an out-and-out Soviet instrument.

Young and Clive proposed the overthrow of the Syrian government and King Saud of Saudi Arabia, plus operations against Egypt.[22]

Peter Grey, IRD's supervising Under-Secretary, was closely involved in setting the Foreign Office public position on Suez. In March 1956 IRD's Sydney Hebblethwaite, part of the British Psychological Warfare Committee set up for Suez, urged British Information officers in the Middle East to use 'their best endeavours to cultivate the appropriate key personalities of small broadcast stations in their countries so as to ensure that through such friendly contacts, anti-British criticism is reduced and a little more space be given to objective news about Britain'. During the crisis, IRD's Middle East desk became the centre for coordinating pro-British propaganda to a range of media outlets. This desk also serviced a variety of internal and external committees hastily brought together to support government policy.[23]

The Arab News Agency, which was so convenient for MI6 operations, was in fact secretly funded by the British government. It was the first of a string of secret British government new agency fronts. On 23 January 1945, the United States Office of Strategic Services (OSS) filed a revealing source report on the ANA:

> This is a 100 per cent British Agency which is Arab in name only, is a direct offshoot of the short-lived and now defunct Balkans News Agency, which was set up shortly after the present war, was started by the London *Daily Telegraph* organization.
>
> When the Germans successfully invaded the Balkans the whole staff and outfit were evacuated to Egypt and formed the nucleus of the Arab News Agency. It started very modestly but soon mushroomed into a very elaborate organization, with extensive offices in Cairo, contiguous to the Military Censor's offices where Abd El-Rahman Nasr, a journalist on the staff of *Al-Ahram*, was sumptuously enthroned in the managerial chair. Mr Mallet, who later took up the post of Director of the Publicity Section of the British Embassy in Cairo, was however the real backstage string puller. After his departure he was replaced by a Mr Barnes.
>
> Abd El-Rahman Nasr, was successively sent to Jerusalem, Beirut, Damascus, Baghdad, and Djeddah to open branches for the agency. His name and services were also used to interview Arab personalities in the middle East, in order to give Arab colour to the news and agency.[24]

The ANA continued after the Second World War and was one of a global network of news agencies run by MI6, aided by IRD. Its purpose was to keep a British voice in many parts of the world during the Cold War, to disseminate IRD grey propaganda and, if necessary, to support a range of MI6 operations from black propaganda to giving working cover to MI6 agents. The ANA had initially built up a good reputation with the Middle East media for its news and feature reports. In an early form of information technology, it provided the Middle East's first ever Arabic language teletype service.

According to Gordon Waterfield, BBC executive and friend of Little's, in the years leading up to Suez, 'ANA was influential trying to do what the BBC did – give factual information – and succeeded. Arabs had been misgoverned for so long that they had ceased to trust their own people.'[25] Again it was a considerable enterprise. 'There are 35 ANA staff members in Egypt and 59 in other countries. Of the 76 stationed in Arab world, 5 are British and 71 Arabs, of whom 65 are Moslems. The registered office of ANA is in London.'[26] Richard Fletcher, the investigative journalist who first publicly revealed these news agency 'fronts', said, 'ANA operated the most comprehensive service in English and Arabic available in the Middle East with branch offices in Damascus, Beirut, Baghdad, Jerusalem and Amman, and representatives in some 15 other cities, including Paris and New York. It was taken by nearly every Arabic newspaper, as well as Sharq al Adna, All-India Radio and the BBC.' Tom McFadden, an American diplomat writing in *Journalism Quarterly* in 1953, said that the ANA charged very little for its service and frequently gave it away without charge.

It employed local staff, and some were full-time and long-standing. During the long build-up to Suez ANA avoided blatant anti-Nasser material, which would have resulted in its closure. Nevertheless, among other news, a stream of IRD Cold War articles were channelled through the ANA. These were mainly designed to provoke suspicions about the growing Soviet involvement in the Middle East.

Like the rest of the British government's Suez operations, not everything went quite to plan at the ANA. According to Bob Petty, one of the ANA staff, Tom Little and his Cairo team were not in favour of Anthony Eden's military intervention and thought that the British cabinet was misreading Nasser. This stance must have been pretty clear to the Egyptians as Little managed to retain a friendship with Nasser throughout these difficult times. This was, at least in part, so that Nasser had a sympathetic ear to convey his views back to Whitehall. The ANA did not provide quite the service that the Foreign Office had hoped: 'Hadden Knight was in charge of news from the London side. He was very pro the Foreign Office during Suez. Tom Little spiked his attempts to plant news. Little sent him a telegram saying we weren't children.'[27]

Things did not go well at *Sharq al Adna* either. Arabic propaganda has its own distinct problems. Gordon Waterfield remarked, 'Once a foreign station starts to abuse anything Arab, they close their ranks.' As the crisis developed, the station's British director was told to shift his white propaganda into the realms of grey through to black propaganda.[28] Then, as D-Day for Operation Musketeer arrived, he was told to change the name of the station to The Voice of Britain. Grasping exactly what was about to happen, the director of the station went on air and warned the Egyptian audience that it would shortly be hearing lies and might experience bombing. It was not to believe the lies and must endure the bombs; these acts were not those of Englishmen who knew Arabia and cared for Arab people. He was promptly arrested by the British military for his trouble.[29] The director was brought back to England and removed from any public platform. Several of *Sharq al Adna*'s staff joined Nasser's Cairo Radio. After Suez, Sir Donald Maitland was brought in from the Foreign Office to run the station until it was finally closed down. But IRD operations against Nasser did not stop with the failures of 1956. In 1964, IRD set up, in liaison with major oil companies, a radio station called The Voice of the Coast. This was situated in the compound of the Trucial Oman Scouts in Dubai.[30]

Suez also made it much harder to capitalize on the Soviet invasion of Hungary. The invasion revealed the contradiction between Communism's international pretensions and nationalist and imperialist self-interest, but much the same could have been said of Britain and its Suez adventure. Indeed, although the brutal suppression of the democracy movement in Hungary offered the perfect opportunity for a propaganda offensive against the USSR and Communists in general, the ultimately disastrous attempt by Eden's government to regain control of the Suez Canal and remove Nasser seriously undermined British attempts to claim the moral high ground. Denis Healey said in the House of Commons:

> On the morning of 30th October the Soviet Government made an official statement of its readiness to withdraw its troops from Hungary and to seek in conversations with the Governments of the East European States a new basis for the relationship between them and the Soviet Union. Twenty-four hours later Soviet policy changed. Did anything happen between the first event and the second which influenced that change in Soviet policy? I put it no higher than to say that it is impossible for any Hon. or Right Hon. Member to maintain that there is no connection between the somersault in Soviet policy between Tuesday and Wednesday morning and the action of Her Majesty's Government.[31]

In a speech at the Albert Hall on 6 November, Hugh Gaitskell made a similar point: 'If what happened on Tuesday last, if the ultimatum and invasion of Egypt, the resort to the law of the jungle, had the slightest influence on the Russian decision to send in tanks and bombers to crush the movement for democracy in Hungary, then it is something for which we should never forgive ourselves.' He went on to state that Britain had no moral right to condemn Russian aggression 'because we have been guilty of aggression too.[32] The head of the CIA, Allen Dulles, saw it in a similar light. 'How can anything be done about the Russians,' he asked his brother, Secretary of State John Foster Dulles, 'when our own allies are guilty of exactly similar acts of aggression?'[33] The Suez Crisis was an ill-considered venture that tore apart the consensus of the British establishment. Nevertheless, it illustrates the propaganda resources that Britain could at that stage muster in a full-scale military operation. However, it also reveals that no amount of propaganda can change opinion on a foolhardy venture.

Suez remains a small glimpse of IRD's wider operations in support of MI6 during the Cold War. It is hard to discover the mechanisms by which IRD, MI6 and other psychological warfare departments worked in support of covert operations like the attempt to overthrow Enver Hoxha in Albania in 1950 or the successful overthrow of Mossadeq in Iran in 1953. Even with the gradual release of IRD files, it is unlikely that those that cover the MI6/IRD interface will be made public in the foreseeable future. To estimate British covert media capabilities in these dark areas, one has to piece together information from not always reliable sources. One example comes from Kim Philby's interview in the Estonian periodical *Kodumaa*, long after his defection. In 1946, MI6 had set up a Special Political Actions department to organize covert operations. Philby said that in 1953 a cabinet committee, 'the Committee to Fight against Communism', was set up under Gladwyn Jebb to wage the Cold War. This was later replaced by the Psychological Warfare Consultations Committee, known as the Dodds-Parker Committee. Col Douglas Dodds-Parker, then parliamentary Under-Secretary at the Foreign Office, was responsible for liaison with MI6.[34] There must have been a liaison and policy body. Dodds-Parker denies such a role, but he is still covered by the Official Secrets Act.

Philby goes on to assert that MI6 had penetrated the 'English mass media on a wide scale. . . . Paid British agents work in scores with editorial staffs of provincial and London newspapers. These papers include such widely read publications as the *Daily Telegraph*, the *Sunday Times*, *Daily Mirror*, *Financial Times*, the *Observer* and many others.' Philby made no mention of IRD, and it is not clear whether he included IRD 'assets' in the media or he was just referring to (but perhaps exaggerating) the number of journalists that were close to MI6.[35] If large numbers of British journalists were also on MI6's payroll, this would be one of the last great secrets of the Cold War.

MI6 remains the most glamorous intelligence service, with its aura of 'cloak-and-dagger' activity. What is not generally appreciated is the importance of covert propaganda and cultural activities to the intelligence services. As we will see, during the Cold War the CIA organized a secret and vast anti-Communist operation in the media, trade unions, education, military and many other institutions in foreign countries throughout the world. The difference with the British was that they had two separate agencies: MI6 to handle the 'cloak-and-dagger' stuff and IRD to do the propaganda work. As we have seen, they frequently shared resources and personnel.

CHAPTER NINE

Agencies of Change: the News Agency Network

IRD's relationship with MI6 extended far into a shadowy world of media ownership and manipulation. MI6 built a global network of news agencies, which were used to disseminate IRD Cold War output alongside routine news. In the late 1990s there are now just a handful of vast international computerized news agencies dominating the world media; with the instantaneous nature of television communications, it is hard to remember that there was once a plethora of such agencies competing to bring news across the world. Then a string of apparently independent agencies could supply hundreds of newspapers, periodicals, radio stations and a growing number of TV outlets, especially if their prices were set artificially low. The importance of these agencies to an organization like IRD is explained by Norman Reddaway: 'A news agency man will get hold of the facts from a source he regards as reliable and will put it into the plumbing of the news machine, and it will be all over the world in no time flat.'[1] As we have seen, these media assets, secretly owned by the British government, also enabled IRD to be called in to assist psychological warfare operations in times of crisis or in support of British undercover operations. According to former IRD sources, the agencies were used as cover for MI6 spies working undercover across the world. For much of the Cold War, the news agencies discreetly did their work in routine manner. Much of the news they covered was obtained by local staff and was unremarkable, except that it tended to reflect a British view of events. The hidden agenda was for them to feed a steady stream of IRD-generated articles and Cold War propaganda into their output. They shared a London office so that IRD material could be fed centrally and discreetly into all of the agencies.

The original Second World War agencies included Britanova Ltd, and the Arab News Agency (ANA) and Globe News Agency in Calcutta, which were set up by Leslie Sheridan on behalf of the SOE between 1940 and 1943. From the war until well into the 1950s, these agencies were generally thought by outsiders to be independent, run by the London-based Hulton Press, a large Fleet Street media empire owned by Edward Hulton. Hulton had merely allowed himself and his company to provide cover for MI6. Annual reports at Companies House, London, show that, in 1948, Hulton and the other wartime directors resigned from Britanova and the ANA to be replaced by a new set of figureheads. Over the next thirty years a host of journalists and major establishment figures, many with Foreign Office connections, appeared as directors. These included Tom Clarke, a journalist;[2] Maurice Macmillan, the publisher, Conservative MP and son of the British Prime Minister; and the Hon. Alan V. Hare, son of the Earl of Listowel, who worked for the Foreign Office (1947–61) and was later chairman of the *Financial Times*.

It is clear from the company returns, interlocking directorships and personnel, office addresses and entries in press directories at the time, that all of these firms were run, behind the scenes as a single operation, together with a number of companies registered overseas: Globe Agency Ltd (India), Star News Agency Ltd (Pakistan) and later Africa Features (Kenya). Some of these companies acted as local bureaux for the London agencies; Globe was an Indian-based company of which Tom Clarke was a director; Star was registered in Pakistan. Thus it can be seen that, with one director in the Foreign Office, a company secretary from the Secret Service together with ample funds, and the journalistic experience of Tom Clarke and the colleagues he had recruited, this group of companies was in an ideal position to assist the secret propaganda campaign.

The agency operation was adapted for the Cold War by the holy trio of Col Leslie Sheridan, Adelaide Maturin and Victor Cannon Brookes. With the new directors, in 1948 Victor Cannon Brookes took over responsibility for filing the companies' annual returns and Adelaide Maturin continued as the registered secretary of both agencies. Victor Cannon Brookes had been in the SOE during the Second World War as private secretary to Lord Selbourne. After the war he set up in private practice as a solicitor, where he was to run the legal side of a network of MI6/IRD front companies for more than thirty years. At the end of the war, nearly all of the SOE's office workers had returned to civilian life, but Adelaide Maturin remained in government service and was appointed a career officer in the Secret Service, a post in which she continued until her retirement in 1970.[3] According to former ANA staffer Bob Petty, Maturin was in charge of the money, spent time in the agency's London office and had to be consulted over any expenditure.[4] As we will see she in effect became the managing director of a chain of new agencies that at their height employed some 600 staff located across the world. Between 1948 and 1952, Cannon Brookes, on behalf of his secret employers, launched three further news agencies: Near and Far East News Ltd (NAFEN), NAFEN (Asia) Ltd and Arab News Agency (Cairo) Ltd. Adelaide Maturin was registered as company secretary in each case.[5] The 'footprint' of these agencies corresponded with the areas that the Foreign Office felt were at most risk of succumbing to Communist influence. The Near and Far East News Agency was based in Istanbul. Contemporary annual reports state, 'the main activity of the company is the purchase of news and feature articles for resale throughout the world'. That a sizeable staff was employed is indicated by a substantial wage bill, for which provision was made in the balance sheets.

The MI6 front news agency presence in Asia was enormous. NAFEN (Asia) Ltd, the successor to the Globe News Agency Ltd, was based in Calcutta, with bureaux in New Delhi, Bombay, Calcutta and Madras, with correspondents and stringers throughout India and the principal cities of South-East Asia, the Far East, Middle East and Africa.[6] It had 100 employees and issued news in English, Urdu, Hindi, Marathi, Tamil and Malaysian. It was a main supplier of news to All India Radio. The Star News Agency had been set up in Pakistan in 1948 after partition and was 'mainly concerned with the distribution of foreign news and news of Moslem interest'. It supplied Pakistan Radio and published in English and Urdu. It was based in the Hassanali Mamooji Building in Karachi with sub-offices in other major cities. The secret subsidies of these agencies made it hard for competitors and enabled them to get their material placed extensively in media across the world.

There were problems. After the British/French invasion of Suez, in 1956, the ANA's Cairo office was closed down and much of its former coverage taken over by Nasser's Middle East News Agency (MENA).[7] The ANA, however, moved to Beirut and continued in existence, with staff in London, Cairo, Amman, Damascus and other Middle East capitals.[8] Various British news operations worked out of the same Beirut building, including the *Observer*, whose correspondent and former KGB mole in MI6, Kim Philby, worked there until he fled to the Soviet Union in 1963. It is hard to believe that he did not keep his Soviet masters up to date on this aspect of British activities. The ANA operated in the Gulf, well into the 1960s.

The operations of these subsidized fronts made business extremely difficult for the genuine British-based news agency, Reuters. Now one of the biggest business and information providers in the world, it has always claimed to be entirely independent of the British government, but behind the scenes Reuters has always had an important role in advancing British interests. In the last century it had a near monopoly – in association with Havas (French) and Wolff (German) – of the production and flow of international news. Britain owned most of the world's telegraph cable network, which was laid and maintained under the protection of the Royal Navy. After the Second World War, Christopher Chancellor, then general manager, travelled the world, proclaiming Reuters' independence from the British government. In reality, Reuters had got into bed with the British government in return for payment on a number of occasions. Up against the subsidized ANA, Reuters had made heavy losses in the Middle East until it negotiated a secret agreement with the Foreign Office. However, Chancellor allowed its regional service in the Middle East to be resold by what the CIA would call a 'proprietary' of the British government. Under this agreement, Reuters was paid an initial £28,000 per year and the ANA became sole distributor for Reuters in the Middle East from 1954. Reuters was also able to use ANA staff for the collection of news and was effectively given free distribution in the region. In the mid-1950s, press directories recorded that the ANA 'supplies a news and feature service to newspapers in the Arab Middle East and distributes a Reuter Service throughout this area'.

The MI6-subsidized agencies and Reuters were to snuggle up close. In the mid-1960s, all of the agencies had as their London office, St Brides House, 10–11 Salisbury Square, then largely occupied by Reuters and backing onto the Reuters building at 85 Fleet Street. At this time there appeared to be a new burst of IRD-orchestrated activity, with three new companies being launched by Cannon Brookes: Regional News Services (Mid East) Ltd and the RNS (Latin America) Ltd (St Bride's House, Capital £50,000 and £40,000) and International News Rights and Royalties Ltd (118 Fleet Street, capital £40,000). Alongside Tom Little,[9] Gordon Waterfield head of the BBC's Arabic Service, joined the RNS (Mid-East).[10] RNS (Mid East) took over the functions and coverage of ANA, including the Reuters service in both English and Arabic. By 1964 this had expanded to include broadcasting and TV, with coverage extended to Iran and Somalia.[11]

IRD was also subsidizing Reuters to distribute news with its inherent anglophile perspective in Latin America. The accounts of the RNS (Latin America) showed payments of £25,000 for both 1966 and 1967 for 'News Agency Subscription'. Reuters was under considerable pressure from the Foreign Office to increase its Latin American coverage, yet it was losing about £80,000 per annum on the regional service. The RNS (Latin America) was just a means to launder Secret Vote money to Reuters.

In the late 1960s in a cost-cutting exercise, the Foreign Office paid Reuters to take over RNS (Mid East) operations. Tom Little opposed the deal. Gordon Waterfield said that, as a result, Little was excluded from the negotiations: 'the FO got a bad deal. Tom Little did not trust Reuters to keep up the excellent network he had built up.'[12] This takeover was negotiated for Reuters by executive Gerald Long. When he became general manager of Reuters in 1963, he decided to terminate the agreement and by July 1969 Reuters had resumed its independent Middle East operations. He was aware of the use of the agencies to subsidize Reuters. 'I wouldn't pretend that I liked the original arrangement. I didn't. But business is business,' he said. In 1969, Long negotiated the deal where the Foreign Office paid Reuters to take some of the news agencies over. He said that it was to save the Foreign Office money: 'I think these activities are extremely dangerous, although I don't say that of these particular people. I think that everything that government does it should do openly.'[13] In a similar but much smaller-scale move, IRD also attempted to buy the *Observer*'s Foreign News Service for redistribution on a similar basis.[14] Former overseas correspondents now in London say that it was common knowledge that IRD would subsidize Third World newspapers that wished to subscribe to British news agencies.[15]

Meanwhile the IRD agencies had kept up their work, changing titles from time to time. Tom Clarke became majority shareholder in Britanova in 1955, taking over the 4,500 £1 shares of the then Foreign Office official, the Hon. Alan Hare : Britanova was dissolved in 1965. In the 1950s, chairman and London editor of the group of companies (including Star of Pakistan) were Tom Clarke and Peter Hadden Knight respectively. Clarke died in 1957 and was replaced by Tom Little, the former ANA journalist.

The two Near and Far East News companies continued in existence. NAFEN increased its capital in 1970, bringing to 21,500 the shareholdings of both Maurice Macmillan and Lord Hillingdon. Hillingdon (C.H. Mills) was a member of the family that had long been associated with Glyn Mills, the bankers. Other directors were journalists Norman Morris and William Loving; Conservative MP and former MI6 officer Cranley Onslow,[16] noted for 'His fiery anti-Communism, which sometimes smacks of McCarthyism',[17] and R.P.T. Gibson, now Lord Gibson, chairman of the huge publishing group Pearson Longman Ltd from 1967. Labour MP and *News of the World*'s 'The Voice of Reason' Woodrow Wyatt, was a shareholder from 1952. As about the time of the split with Reuters, all of the news agencies changed their registered address to Buchanan House, 24/30 Holborn WC1, a tall austere Victorian building, just yards from the home of Mirror Newspapers. In 1972 the solicitors firm of Cannon Brookes and Odgers also moved to Buchanan House.

In the late 1960s, International News Rights and Royalties (INRAR) then became the central operating company.[18] Its first directors were the Hon. Alan Hare, now at the *Financial Times*, and Tom Little (chairman),[19] with 1,000 shares each. Controlling shares, however, were held by nominee companies, which prevent the real source of funds from being publicly identified.[20] In March 1969, Alan Hare resigned as director and shareholder and his place was taken by James Holburn to whom 3,500 shares were transferred. Holburn, had joined *The Times* in 1934 and was chief correspondent, Middle East (1952–5), returning to his native Scotland as editor of the *Glasgow Herald* (1955–65). He later said that his directorship was purely nominal, having been arranged by Tom Little, whom he understood 'liaised with a department of the Foreign Office'. He seemed to be unaware that 3,500 shares had been registered in his name and stated categorically that he had never put up the money to purchase them.[21] Some of those involved with the news agencies were fully aware of their task as MI6 frontmen. Others say that they had no idea. After the closure of IRD, Alan Hare was asked about his involvement. Hare, a reserved Etonian who had served with the SOE in the Balkans, said that he did not know that there was Foreign Office backing for the agencies and that he joined them as an ordinary commercial director and paid for his own sizeable shareholdings. Another co-director, Maurice Macmillan, a friend of Hare, said, 'I was fully aware that what we were doing was consonant with government policy, I didn't expect to make money: it was a do-gooder purpose. Putting across the British point of view – that was the purpose of the operation.' He said that he could not remember whether he paid for any of the shares that he held as director. Another shareholder, Lord Gibson, said that he did not wish to comment about his role in the new agencies.[22]

In the last wave of IRD fronts in 1971, Victor Cannon Brookes registered a new company called World Feature Services Ltd (WFS) with the same address (Buchanan House) and personnel as the other agencies. At about the same time, INRAR ceased trading. The new agency moved to offices in Lambeth,[23] with shareholders listed as Derek Charles, a journalist; and Tom Neil, chairman, a former colonial civil servant who rose to be chief British official in Kenya at the time of independence in 1963.[24] He then became director of the Thomson Foundation. In 1968 INRAR had bought thirty-five out of ninety £1 shares in a Kenya company called Africa Features, of which James Holburn was a director. Three years later, Africa Features was registered as a British company by Victor Cannon Brookes at the same address as WFS. Its first directors were Holburn; Sir Kenneth Granville Bradley, a Colonial civil servant; and John Collier, a British journalist in Kenya. Collier, the managing director of Africa Features, was an assistant editor with Visnews, 'the world's leading supplier of TV news film' (from the BBC, NBC and the Japanese NHK network), before he returned to Nairobi in 1966 'to start Africa Features service'.[25] Majority shareholder in Africa Features was Seventh Nominees Ltd, a nominee company controlled by Cannon Brookes. Holburn and Bradley resigned in July 1975 and were replaced by Derek Charles and Tom Neil. Africa Features and WFS were then housed in the same office with shared staff, and with Neil as chairman of both companies.

By the end of the 1970s the end was nigh for smaller news agencies. A few international agencies geared up to provide financial material for the burgeoning global markets. This cash subsidized the news side of the operations. Even with a Secret Vote subsidy, small agencies could not compete. By the early 1980s they had all gone. How much did the British taxpayer subsidize these agencies? Losses after the 1966 Companies Act came into force amount to more than £100,000 for the extant British-registered agencies. However, these accounts also reveal that much larger sums were spent – on occasion up to nearly £50,000 in one year – suggesting that direct annual subventions could have been made to help these companies balance their books. This, together with the fact that the agencies' activities seemed to have begun to run down by 1967 while their period of operation spanned more than thirty years, suggests that total expenditure must have been enormous. Who put up this large sum of money? They must have been subsidized by MI6's part of the Secret Vote.

The domination of news agencies was important in the kind of news the rest of the world received. In his book *The Media are American*,[26] Jeremy Tunstall described the continuing control of the flow of news between the countries of the world by a handful of Anglo-American institutions. He set the current situation in the context of social, economic, political and technological developments over the last century. D.R. Mankekar, the chairman of the Non-Aligned News Agencies Pool, a former editor of the *Times of India* and ex-employee of the Western news agencies in India, described the result of Western power over international news flow as 'One-Way Free Flow'.[27] This involved non-aligned countries of Africa, the Middle East, Asia and Latin America receiving news about the rest of the world through agencies of the advanced Western countries, which are not, to put it mildly, primarily concerned in furthering the interests of the mass of Third World people.[28]

CHAPTER TEN

Imperial Adventures: IRD and the Colonies

In 1955, Greek Cypriot guerrillas, led by a neo-fascist Greek called Col George Grivas, started a violent campaign to force Britain to grant its colony, Cyprus, the right to self-determination and union with Greece – Enosis. A year after the campaign had begun, in June 1956, John Peck, ex-head of IRD, was in Washington working as the head of British Information Services. In a confidential communication with the British Embassy in Nicosia, Cyprus, Peck made a request for information. He demanded 'Anything on Communism and its power, motives in supporting Enosis and future prospects.'[1] Peck was facing a debate in the United Nations on the question of Cyprus's right to self-determination and Enosis, or unification, with Greece. The debate had been agreed at the behest of the Greek government and against trenchant British opposition. An old IRD hand, Peck wanted to play the 'red' card – to imply the loss of Cyprus to Greece through Enosis would be a victory for the Communist bloc. In the zero-sum game and two-dimensional framework of relations that the Cold War had become, a victory for anything that one side in theory supported could only be a loss for the other side. Peck conceded that, in view of the right-wing anti-Communist government in Greece, the Communists had everything to lose from unification with Greece. In spite of that, he had been making the argument that the Communists stood to gain as a result. Among other things, he had been suggesting that, 'if Cyprus went on the Greek economy, its prosperity would promptly vanish and the Communists could then become so strong that they could successfully control the island against the interests of Greece and NATO'.

If the arguments that Peck was propagating in the US on behalf of a British government intent on preventing Cypriot independence or Enosis with Greece, seemed a little far-fetched, he recognized it. In the same communication he wrote, 'On rereading the above, it occurs to me that you may feel that some of the arguments for which I am seeking supporting evidence go a little far for a Government Information Service. In fact, of course, we usually conform strictly to our policy directives in our official material, but in informal arguments and off-the-record discussions one can achieve a great deal by unofficial comment and suggestion.'[2]

As far as the unofficial element of British propaganda is concerned, the way IRD attempted to shape international and domestic perceptions of Britain's colonial struggles during the Cold War vividly illustrates how facts were mobilized in support of British foreign policy. Evidence of Communist involvement was presented to great effect by

IRD, but this was nevertheless often criticized as being a distortion of reality, even within Whitehall.

*****

If one theme can characterize the period of British history in which IRD existed, apart from the Cold War – IRD's *raison d'etre*, it was the British withdrawal from the empire.[3] The Second World War had left the British empire in a radically changed international context. Not only was it fast becoming clear that the war had brought about a radical shift in the balance of international power to the detriment of Britain, but Britain also, for the first time, found itself committed to the dismantling of its empire.[4] Although it had imperial possessions stretching around the globe from Hong Kong to the Falkland Islands, Britain was, bankrupt and in desperate need of the resources that many of its colonial holdings could provide. Following the Second World War the colonies were exploited by Britain on an unprecedented scale. According to historian David Fieldhouse, between 1946 and 1951, 'one way or another, the colonies were lent or given some £40 million by Britain but were forced to lend or tie up in London about £250 million. This was disinvestment on the grand scale'.[5] And as historians P.J. Hopkins and A.G. Cain have pointed out, 'Far from being abandoned after 1947, the empire was repositioned in Africa, Malaya, and, informally, the Middle East. These regions were sources of vital supplies; they contributed to the hard currency pool through dollar earnings; and they were all directly or indirectly under British control.'[6] Consequently, once elected, the Labour Party took up the burden of the empire with the enthusiasm of the converted evangelist, despite its often and long-proclaimed opposition to imperialism.[7]

Given the economic plight in which Britain found itself at the end of the Second World War, it was no coincidence that the areas of the empire with the greatest economic value were those where Britain's determination to maintain control was most obvious. Two such areas were Malaya and Kenya, where, as Cain and Hopkins noted, 'coercion tended to be the first resort of policy. The bogey of Communism was invoked, where it was not already present, and this surfaced in the early stages of the Cold War to legitimise the use of force.'[8] Almost immediately after the department's establishment, IRD became involved in the Malayan Emergency, where a largely Chinese Communist guerrilla army was present, having initiated a guerrilla war for independence from the British in 1948. IRD's job was to ensure that this was understood in the correct framework, as a battle against the worldwide Communism and an attempt by the Chinese Communist minority (40 per cent of the population) to impose Communism on the Malay majority.

The Chinese community had originally been encouraged by the British to settle on the Malay peninsula owing to the lack of native labour. Its numbers had swollen during the nineteenth century after the discovery of tin in the inhospitable Malay interior, and it grew to even greater numbers with the development of the rubber plantations in the late nineteenth and early twentieth centuries. By the end of the Second World War, the immigrant community almost equalled the Malay population. Indeed, as Brian Lapping wrote in his history, *End of Empire*, 'A Malay walking down the main street of Kuala

Lumpur, the administrative centre of the Federated States, or any other Malay town, saw shops and banks entirely dominated by Chinese. The same was true of tin mines, of the few factories and even some of the rubber estates.'[9]

During the Second World War, resistance to the Japanese occupation of Malaya had been spearheaded by the largely Chinese and Communist Malayan People's Anti-Japanese Army (MPAJA), with the support of the British. Following the end of the war, the MPAJA expected to play a significant role in the development of postwar Malaya. Although an insurrectionary strategy was considered at the end of the war, the MPAJA was disbanded and the Malayan Communist Party (MCP) reverted to its pre-war policy of building its strength and authority through front organizations. In hindsight, any chance that the MCP might have had for a successful insurrection was missed.[10] But when the MCP's strategy failed in the face of British determination to hold on to the colony, a disillusioned MCP embarked on its badly organized and poorly judged rebellion. As historian Michael Stenson noted:

> The essential factor in the growing support for revolt . . . was the manifest failure of the main open fronts to obtain significant concessions or to extend their support after March 1947. And in addition, the British refused demands for any form of democratic representation (upon which the whole logic of the MCP's postwar united-front-from-above policy was based) and extended evermore restrictive control over trade union activity and eventually completely destroyed the Pan-Malayan Federation of Trade Unions.'[11]

The Malayan emergency was Britain's longest colonial conflict after the Second World War. At its core was the vast wealth provided to Britain from Malaya's natural resources, especially rubber plantations – mainly run by British owners. The prolonged conflict with the MCP started in 1948 and lasted until 1960 and it was one of the first major challenges to face IRD. The MCP was to prove to be a dangerous and ruthless enemy, emerging from the jungle to kill rubber plantation and tin mine managers and policemen. In 1951 MCP guerrillas killed 504 members of the security forces and some 533 civilians. For some time the future of Malaya seemed to hang in the balance. By the time of Gen Sir Gerald Templer's arrival in 1952 as the new High Commissioner, 5,000 guerrillas were tying down a huge force of British and Commonwealth troops, which reached a peak of a quarter of a million.[12]

The emergency, combined with the threat posed by Nationalist and Communist agitation elsewhere in South-East Asia, led to the establishment of IRD regional office at Phoenix Park in Singapore in 1949, as part of the Office of the Commissioner-General for Britain in South-East Asia. A secret briefing on the work, carried out by the Regional Information Officer described its main areas of interest as 'Singapore, the Federation of Malaya, Hong Kong, British possessions in Borneo, Indonesia, the former Indo-Chinese States, Burma, Thailand and the Philippines.'[13] The same paper stated that 'the Regional Information Officer's duties are to plan the production of positive and IRD material, produce it and supply it to the information officers of all the territories concerned. In practice, however, the spread and influence of Chinese Communism in the region has greatly increased the importance of the IRD work.'[14] Such was the importance of the work of the RIO that, when, in 1951, economy cuts were made to the Singapore office, IRD drew on the Secret Vote money to make up the difference.[15]

In this early period, IRD's role was not limited to persuading the public, but often included convincing other parts of the British government to take the Communist threat seriously. John Cloake, who was responsible for liaison with the Colonial Office, recalled that 'One exercise I do remember was trying to wake the Colonial Office up, who were aware that there were some Communists in Malaya, but at that time . . . it was hard enough to get them to concentrate on that, let alone anyone else in the colonial world. . . . That was one exercise we did.'[16]

By 1950, events and IRD had apparently succeeded and the Colonial Office was eager to perceive the MCP as 'part of the Kremlin's world-wide campaign against the Western powers'. In 1950 a paper on colonial problems and policies outlined the view from the CO:

> All available evidence shows that the MCP though small, is a well organised and orthodox Communist party implementing an impeccably Stalinist policy. Evidence of direct links with Moscow and Peking is, not surprisingly, lacking; but unnamed delegates from Malaya attended the Conference of the World Federation of Trade Unions held in Peking last November. These delegates undoubtedly brought back to Malaya advice and instructions based on the war experience of the People's Liberation Army of China.[17]

The importance of presenting the emergency as part of worldwide Communist aggression was clearly recognized by IRD official Adam Watson, not least for the purpose of ensuring US support for British policy:

> It seems very dangerous to pretend that the troubles in Malaya are not caused by Communism but only by a kind of local banditry. As we saw in Greece, where the Greek Government were for long anxious to describe the Communists only as banditry, international public opinion in the United States . . . and elsewhere is inclined to that the line that when wholesale military operations are required to suppress mere internal unrest, it is in some way due to bad government. This is especially so in a colony; and instead of receiving sympathy and support from American public opinion in our praiseworthy struggle to combat the well-known international Communist menace, we shall merely be regarded as a bad colonial power coping with rebellions.'[18]

Another target of IRD's pro-colonial anti-Communist propaganda was the Labour Party, many members of which were inclined to object to their government's apparently imperial policy. As early as August 1948, Bevin and the Secretary of State at the Colonial Office, Arthur Creech Jones, were alarmed enough to demand material for a counterattack on Communist propaganda in Britain.[19] Material to counter hostile complaints from trade unions and labour groups and to rebutt Communist propaganda was passed to Denis Healey at the Labour Party's International Department.

While Britain's economic dependence on the empire had increased, colonial exploitation could not be easily squared with support for the United States's new world order, or the Labour Party's committment to decolonization. However, with the beginning of the Cold War, American attitudes softened towards British colonialism and the British Empire was transformed into 'a bulwark against the Communist menace.'[20] Indeed, according to Cain and Hopkins, 'Washington was persuaded, by a mixture of self-induced anxiety and skilful British diplomacy, that a friendly empire spanning the globe would be a useful ally in containing the threat to what was becoming known as the Free World. . . . Liquidation was not on the agenda: the empire was to be given a shot in the arm rather than a shot in the head.'[21]

Not least to ensure the support of the United States, it became essential that challenges to British colonial rule should be understood within the right framework – that of a substantial Soviet and Communist threat rather than legitimate nationalist demands for an end to colonial rule. It is clear that IRD made a substantial contribution to the fact that the long retreat from the empire was largely understood within that Cold War framework of Soviet intrigue and expansion. In some respects this was not too difficult. Not only did the Soviet Union profess its support for movements of national liberation, but many Nationalist movements seemed at best neutral and at worse penetrated by Communists. Brian Lapping, in *End of Empire*, noted:

> Throughout the British Empire's declining years the great threat to its survival was widely thought to be the international Communist movement. White settlers on their farms in Kenya and Rhodesia, Nayasaland and Tanganyika, white officials in Cyprus and Aden, the Gold Coast and British Guiana, declared whenever things went badly wrong that there was a red under the bed. A nationalist leader had only to show a mild interest in Marx or Moscow to be at once branded a Communist. British newspapers like the *Daily Express* and the *Daily Telegraph* continued to declare, year in year out, that the Empire was under siege by Communists.[22]

However, presenting colonial problems in the context of the Cold War, or playing the 'red' card, sometimes met with objections. The Mau Mau insurgency in Kenya raised just such problems and caused difficult questions to be asked. In the summer of 1952, reports of an African underground organization called the Mau Mau began to reach Britain. After the emergency was declared in October, the question of how to present the colonial insurgency through propaganda was raised and led to an ongoing dispute between IRD and the Colonial Office. Although IRD searched for a Communist angle on the Mau Mau, the evidence was not promising. Indeed, press articles claiming a Communist connection had prompted the Foreign Office Information Policy Department and Colonial Office to assert publicly, in a press release put out through the British Information Service, that 'there is no evidence that either Mau Mau or its policy is in any way inspired or directed by Communists'.[23] In fact as the press release indicated, the Mau Mau insurgency was entirely indigenous. Nevertheless, IRD vigorously pursued attempts to have an intel, or intelligence briefing, on the Communist connection with the Mau Mau. This met with stiff resistance from the Colonial Office. While IRD argued that the attributable briefing paper should contain 'possibilities and presumptions,' officials at the Colonial Office were less eager to wander into the realms of the unknown. In 1953, in response to an IRD attempt to base an intel on an unsubstantiated article in *Life*, Dixon Barton of the Colonial Office complained, 'I am afraid I cannot force myself into proving what I do not believe . . . and I thought all this had been thrashed out with the FO's IRD some time ago. As I have said, that FO Department gets the summary of Intelligence every month; they can be reminded of that and be, yet again, told that when we have anything approaching "evidence" of Communism being behind Mau Mau we will make a point of telling them.'[24]

Historian Susan Carruthers, who has studied the limited papers available that cast light on the role played by IRD in colonial conflicts, found that the case of Kenya suggested 'that the IRD was rather keener to detect the hidden hand of Communism than many of its Colonial Office opposite numbers.'[25] Carruthers argues that, while the Colonial Office took the possibility of Communist involvement seriously, without tangible evidence it was not eager to postulate the Kremlin conspiracy theory. However, as Carruthers noted:

Such scruples exercised the Foreign Office Information Research Department rather less. . . . The IRD's very *raison d'être* . . . predisposed it towards regarding Communism as more pervasive than did other departments. Moreover, the nature of its work, and the unattributable character of much of its output, doubtless inclined the IRD to be more creative with the facts than colleagues in the Colonial Office. Consequently friction arose between members of the CO Information Department and the IRD over how to handle the question of Communism and Mau Mau.[26]

An even more intractable problem than the Mau Mau in the 1950s was the guerrilla war waged against the British in the last European colony, Cyprus. Like Malaya and Kenya, Cyprus was an asset that British governments were reluctant to relinquish. As in the two former cases, IRD was required to play its part in the propaganda war.

The international importance of Cyprus for thousands of years has rested on its perceived strategic value. Set in the eastern Mediterranean, at a great trading crossroads and on the edge of the Middle East, Cyprus has consistently been seen as a vital stronghold. Occupied at various times by the Egyptians, Rome, Venice and the Ottoman Empire, the island was obtained by Benjamin Disraeli in 1878 in exchange for security from Britain for the crumbling Ottoman Empire against Russian encroachments. Despite its rulers of various nationalities, Cyprus had consistently maintained a Greek identity over the centuries. Cypriot fighters supported the Greek revolution against the Ottomans in 1821, and the island's incorporation into Greece had been a long-term aspiration for both mainland Greeks and the majority of Greek Cypriots, who made up roughly 80 per cent of the Cypriot population. Despite the occupation by Britain, the Greek Cypriots had good reason to believe that Enosis was no idle fantasy. Again and again they could point to British promises that Cyprus would join Greece rather than revert to Turkish rule.[27] During the First World War, Sir Edward Grey, the British Foreign Secretary, went as far as to offer Cyprus to Greece in order to pursue that very objective, the dissolution of the Ottoman Empire against which Britain was now at war. Were it not for the Greek king's belief, in 1915, that the

Axis would win and that more was to be gained through friendship with Germany, Cyprus may have passed into Greek hands. However, when Greece did join the British in 1917, the offer was not repeated.

During the Second World War, when Britain and Greece, alone in Europe, resisted Fascism, the British Ambassador, Sir Michael Palairet, recommended that the island should pass to Greece to cement the alliance. However, despite support from the Middle East department of the Foreign Office, the proposal was blocked by pro-Turkish officials, who had vain hopes of a pro-British policy from Ankara.[28]

At the end of the war the issue was once again raised, this time by the British Ambassador to Athens, Sir Reginald Leeper. However, as SOE veteran and Tory politician C.M. Woodhouse recalled in a letter to journalist Christopher Hitchens, although 'Bevin and the Foreign were favourably disposed . . . the Colonial Office and the Chiefs of Staff strongly objected. . . . Bevin had been in office only for a few weeks, and he did not feel confident enough to force it through cabinet. So that was that.'[29] As Hitchens pointed out, 'From then on, Cyprus was ruled to be a matter in which Greece had no right even to be consulted.'[30] However, this policy did not take account of either Greek nationalists or the Cypriots, who, like inhabitants of British colonies around the world, were becoming increasingly restive and strident in their demands.

Indeed, unknown to the British, Archbishop Makarios III, the recognized political leader of Greek Cypriots, had in 1952 become the head of a revolutionary committee committed to Enosis. The committee, which met in Athens, had recruited as a military organizer Col George Grivas. Grivas, a Cypriot by birth who had served in the Greek Army since 1915, had spent the Second World War eliminating Communists with weapons supplied by the German occupation forces and had a reputation for extreme right-wing politics, chauvinism, ruthlessness and violence. Nevertheless, Makarios was convinced that Grivas was the right man for the job of leading a secret army to apply pressure on the British to leave.

Then what had been a discreet British rejection of Greek and Cypriot aspirations was made public on 28 July 1954. Henry Hopkinson, Minister of State at the Colonial Office, made an announcement regarding the new constitution for Cyprus. Owing to possible revolt by Conservative MPs over the prospective withdrawal of British troops from the Suez Canal, Hopkinson had been instructed to bolster support by making it clear that from Cyprus, the new British Middle Eastern headquarters, there would be no withdrawal. The new constitution was not to be a step on the way to self-determination. In answer to a question on the ultimate aim – dominion status or self-determination – Hopkinson stated that 'It has always been understood and agreed that there are certain territories in the Commonwealth which, owing to their particular circumstances, can never expect to be fully independent. I think the Right Hon. Gentleman will agree that there are some territories which cannot expect to be that.'[31] As Lapping noted, 'The Greek Government had kept trying to settle the issue by talking to Britain, had kept trying to restrain Makarios and Grivas. But 28 July 1954 was the last straw: the British were not only refusing to talk, they were being publicly insulting as well.'[32]

With an unwanted international debate on the Cyprus crisis looming at the UN, the British were faced with the distinct danger that the Americans, and the rest of international opinion, might side with Greece and accept that Cyprus was an issue of self-determination. To prevent that, the British delegation sought to place the Cyprus question within the overall context of the Cold War and thereby ensure American support. The delegation contacted Whitehall for the evidence to back up their assertions. Adam Watson, now in Washington, sent a telegram to IRD on 13 August 1954. His secret message read: 'United Kingdom Delegation New York have asked me for any IRD material showing nature of Communist activity and aims in Cyprus, which might be suitable for quotation in prospective United Nations debate. Many delegations will hesitate to vote for something which can be shown to resemble the Communist party line.'[33] Three days later, on 16 August, Donald Hopson, assistant head of IRD, outlined IRD's response in a note to D. Williams at the Colonial Office. Watson suggested a reply that detailed 'the extent of Communists in the Cypriot political parties with details about their activities, and also one or two annexes dealing with the propaganda put out by Moscow, the Greek Communists and the Communist International organizations.'[34]

The need to divert attention from the fact that Britain was occupying a country in which the majority of inhabitants wanted self-determination was clearly recognized by the British UN delegation, a telegram from which suggested:

> it seems to me that, in putting over our case to American public opinion, more emphasis could be laid on two points: the Communist danger and the Island's strategic value. As seen from here, the argument about Communist danger will carry most weight with the American opinion. I hope therefore, that we may be sent as soon as possible material on the Communist Party in Cyprus, its origin, size, strength in the Trade Unions, programme, links with Communist countries, the action taken against it, extent of cooperation between it and nationalist advocates of Enosis etc. It would be particularly useful if we could insinuate that the issue of Enosis has been gradually exploited and blown up by the Communists, both in Cyprus and Greece, as a Cold War gambit, until the Greek Government felt obliged to come forward themselves as its public champion.[35]

The report, which was compiled by IRD for the delegation, followed this advice and aimed to ensure that the problem was understood within the context of the Cold War and the Communist threat. The IRD briefing stated that 'the real purpose of Communist policy on Cyprus is to exploit the Enosis issue with a view to creating difficulties in the fulfilment of the strategic arrangements of the free world in the Middle East, and breaking the ties of friendship and strategy which bind the United Kingdom with Greece and Turkey. Cypriot Communists have egged on the Church and Nationalists in Cyprus to pursue the Enosis issue, and Greek Communists have similarly egged on the present Greek Government.'[36]

This argument was, according to the UK delegation, extremely successful. Indeed, the Greeks had attempted to play the British at their own game, trying to make the most of American anti-Communism to ensure support for their position. On 26 August the UK delegation informed the Foreign Office that:

> It looks as if the Greek Delegation have been worried by the amount of space given by American journalists to that part of our guidance on the Cyprus question which

dealt with Communism. They, therefore, attempted to turn the tables on us by suggesting that we were the ones who were collaborating with the Communists on the Island. You will see that Mr Palamos alleged that the Administration of Cyprus had been using the Communists to break up the 'national front' for Enosis and to discredit it abroad.

Nevertheless, W.B. Hesmondhalgh of the UK delegation concluded that 'Mr Palamos' arguments did not impress the correspondents and we have had little difficulty in dealing with them. It does, however, seem that this theme of Communist backing for Enosis, with its attendant dangers, is paying dividends and should be exploited.'[37]

However, the adoption of this line was not without opposition within Whitehall, where officials could not but perceive real difficulties with the Communist angle on Cyprus. IRD's input was just one out of a number from departments concerned with the propaganda line to be taken. Historian Susan Carruthers wrote:

> The Colonial Office Information Department (COID) was the principle source and co-ordinator of publicity in Britain on Cyprus. . . . The international dimension of the problem also necessitated the involvement of several Foreign Office departments: the Information Policy Department (IPD), Southern Department and United Nations Department all fed policy and advice to the Colonial Office, while Information Research Department advised on the Communist aspect of the Cyprus Emergency and the propaganda mileage that could be gained from exploiting it.[38]

In response to the UK delegation's argument for concentration on Communism and strategic considerations, an official in the Department of Defence minuted: 'The fact that the American public likes to see Communists behind every trouble in the world does not mean that we must gratify their taste at the expense of truth or wise policy. The Enosis problem existed before Communism and would continue without it. The present appeal to the UN does not, so far as I know, owe more than a part of its origin to Communist meddling.' The official pointed out that the propaganda line opened Britain to two logical comebacks from the American public. Why had Britain not been tougher with the Communists in Cyprus? And why not remove the grievance that the Communists were exploiting?[39] A fellow official minuted in response, 'I have never felt that logic was a vital element in the American attitude to Communism.'[40]

While the British government was able to deal with Enosis on a political level at the UN, in Cyprus, EOKA initiated a guerrilla war against the British. On 1 April 1955, EOKA exploded sixteen bombs around the island. EOKA was soon carrying out raids on police stations and targeting British officials, including the governor, Sir Robert Armitage, and British Army bases, wounding numerous British soldiers. As the campaign developed, it became clear that the majority of Greek Cypriots were backing EOKA. Negotiations to end the fighting between Makarios and the new governor, Field Marshal Sir John Harding, broke down. Suspecting, correctly, Makarios's involvement in EOKA, the British arrested him and deported him to the Seychelles. The decision caused an uproar. As Brian Lapping noted:

The Archbishop of Canterbury said . . . that the action made Christians everywhere feel shocked and uneasy. The Greek Government . . . condemned the deportation as an uncivilised act of violence. . . . The United States Government pointedly announced that it favoured the continuation of negotiations in Cyprus. And in Britain Labour Party Leaders who had played down the Cyprus issue during the Harding-Makarios talks were roused by the deportation to outraged opposition.[41]

This became a constant worry for IRD officials. Doubts and criticisms expressed by Labour MPs about the conduct of British troops, government foreign policy and the Communist threat could seriously undermine the work being done by IRD in presenting a coherent and consistent propaganda line. For example, in 1956, John Peck in the United States, trying to get across the British government's line on Cyprus, complained that 'Our efforts are . . . being largely undermined by what appears from here to be the purely adolescent attitude of Her Majesty's Opposition to this question of self-determination . . . this letter is a plea that a special effort might be made to try to get some rational and realistic views propagated in England on this specific issue of self-determination.'[42]

The response of leading members of the Labour opposition to Hopkinson's speech had been uproar and demands for an emergency debate. Lapping noted:

> This was 1954: India, Pakistan, Burma, Ceylon and Palestine were independent; the Sudan and Gold Coast were close to it; the principle that Britain's purpose in running the Empire was to advance subject peoples to self-rule had been published by the Labour Government in a white paper in 1948 and accepted, though without enthusiasm, by their post-1951 Conservative successors. Many Labour MPs believed that Hopkinson's words revealed that the Conservatives were about to back away from this consensus.[43]

Over the following years, Barbara Castle, in particular, continued to campaign for self-determination for Cyprus, inadvertently making it far harder for the government's propaganda machinery to present a clear line. Indeed, as far as the senior civil servants in charge of propaganda were concerned, 'the attitude of the Opposition constitutes the greatest weakness in the presentation of our Cyprus policy in the USA and abroad generally.'[44]

There is some evidence that Peck's request did not fall on deaf ears and that IRD's media contacts were put to good use. In an article in the *New Statesman* in 1957, Castle complained that 'the Foreign Office has "moved in" on the Greek service of the BBC'. Castle cited the fact that Labour MP Francis Noel-Baker, a noted expert on Cyprus and Greece who had reported Liberal and Labour Party resolutions critical of the government's handling of the crisis, had been dropped by the BBC for being too 'partial'. Preparation of the service's daily and weekly press summaries had been taken out of the hands of the Greek staff and all scripts were being sent to the Foreign Office. The effect of all of this, according to Castle, was beginning to show:

> On 22 March the weekly press in this country commented extensively on Lennox-Boyd's [Secretary of State, Colonial Office] announcement of new proposals, follow-

ing EOKA's truce offer. The *Spectator* commented at the greatest length in an excoriating attack on the government . . . in which Lennox-Boyd's proposals were dismissed as 'obviously quite inadequate'. The *New Statesman* ran a scathing note . . . But pride of place in the Greek service's weekly press review was given to a placid little pro-government note in *The Economist* rendered almost word for word.[45]

In April 1957, the new British Prime Minister, Harold Macmillan, decided to release Makarios, but by 1958 the situation in Cyprus was becoming ever more violent. While Grivas turned EOKA against the Cypriot Communist Party (AKEL), left-wingers and trade unionists, fighting broke out between Greek and Turkish Cypriots, both secretly supported by their mainland governments. In return for Cypriot independence from Britain in 1960, Makarios abandoned Enosis with Greece. However, three years later the British were back, this time not as colonial occupiers but as a force attempting to keep the peace between the warring Greek and Turkish Cypriot communities.

CHAPTER ELEVEN

Spreading the Word: IRD Publishes

George Orwell's reputation as a left-wing icon took a body-blow from which it may never recover when it was revealed in 1996 that he had cooperated closely with IRD's Cold Warriors, even offering his own blacklist of eighty-six Communist 'fellow travellers'.[1] As the *Daily Telegraph* noted, 'To some, it was as if Winston Smith had willingly cooperated with the Thought Police in *1984*.'[2] IRD was then taking the first steps in building a major covert publishing operation that was to last nearly thirty years, and its involvement with Orwell was a reflection of the importance that it placed an the power of the book as a propaganda tool. As a CIA officer was later to remark to a US Congressional committee, a book is always the most influential form of propaganda in the long run, even if apparently no one reads it, like Marx's *Kapital*.

During the Cold War years, Orwell's novels, *Animal Farm* (published in 1944) and *1984* (published in 1950), with their compelling anti-totalitarian messages, were widely read. These short, and very direct books, were to be used as the most prominent warning against the evils of Communism. Terms like 'Big Brother is watching' and 'the Thought Police', or even 'Orwellian' entered popular culture. The simple story lines and chilling morals made them an accessible choice for a wide audience. Both books were widely taken up by anti-Communists as metaphors for the evils of the Communist system. For IRD, part of their attraction was that they did not directly mention Communism, so they could not be dismissed out of hand as propaganda.

Although an old Etonian, Orwell's credentials as a left-winger, including service against Franco in the Spanish Civil War, gave the books even greater credibility. IRD officials looked at a number of international figures with left leanings who might be used in their anti-Communist crusade. Orwell, Arthur Koestler, A.J.P. Taylor and Bertrand Russell were among those discussed. Wherever possible, feelers were put out towards these figures. Foreign Office officials were well placed on the social circuits of the time to make discreet contact. Orwell, for instance, was friendly with Mrs Celia Kirwan an IRD officer. Kirwan, née Paget, and her sister were 'noted beauties' who, in pre-war London society had apparently been the most photographed débutantes of their year. Celia had been at boarding school and then a Swiss *pensionnat de jeunes filles* on the shores of Lake Geneva. She had first met Orwell at Christmas 1945 at the house of her brother-in-law, Arthur Koestler. Kirwan was an assistant editor of *Polemic*, a magazine of contemporary ideas, and Orwell was so entranced that he proposed marriage in 1946. She politely rejected his offer of marriage, or least an affair, but they remained close friends.

By 1949 Mrs Kirwan had been recruited to IRD. She was later to say of the department, 'You had to be above board to be working on the unit. But at the time you weren't supposed to say what it was all about. I think the work we were doing was a good thing because people were misinformed about Communism in those days in a big way. And it was about time they got the record right.'[3] The names of both Orwell and Mrs Kirwan's brother-in-law had come up as possible IRD assets. Koestler, another major writer and former Communist, had also written brilliantly on anti-totalitarian themes, most notably his book *Darkness at Noon*. At the behest of her departmental head, Mrs Kirwan went to visit the now terminally sick Orwell on a number of occasions at a sanatorium in Cranham. She encouraged his cooperation and this he readily provided.

Documents released from 1996 reveal that IRD made great efforts to maximize the international political impact of George Orwell's work.[4] It was anxious to distribute the books wherever they were not readily available. In a memo, the IRD's Ernest Main told Ralph Murray that he had been 'taken with the relevance of Orwell's fairy story' in *Animal Farm*: 'Translation into other languages might be considered if this has not been done already. The idea is particularly good for Arabic in view of the fact that both pigs and dogs are unclean animals to Moslems.' One file discusses copyright clearance for *Animal Farm* for proposed distribution in Egypt. On 4 April 1949, IRD official Adam Watson wrote: 'I think *Animal Farm* has been done in a number of languages – even Polish. Has it ever been done in Arabic? In any case, the more the merrier. Whatever does transpire, Kirwan might keep Mr Orwell in the picture.' Ralph Murray wanted to help to get *Animal Farm* released in Russia.[5] He requested assistance in raising 2,000 marks for the purpose of the publication in the Russian language version. On 24 June 1949, IRD contacted Orwell on behalf of the social and political review *Possev*. IRD informed Orwell of the journal's efforts to publish his 'remarkable satire' in the Russian language. *Possev*'s Mr V. Puachev then approached Orwell to ask for advice on potential investors who might be interested in publishing *Animal Farm* in book form for distribution in the USSR. Puachev concluded: 'We ask you please not to think that this letter has been sent to you with any mercenary motives, but exclusively in the interests of the cause of combating Bolshevism, which cause your book serves so brilliantly.' On 18 July 1949, Kirwan informed Jack Brimmell, 'If *Animal Farm* does get through to the USSR as *Possev* claims it would, I am sure it would be most effective in a very good cause.' In addition to plans to publish *Animal Farm*, IRD had high hopes for the new book, *1984*. On 4 November, Kirwan told Charles Thayer, the director of Voice of America broadcasts in Washington, that IRD was translating *1984* into Italian, French, Swedish, Dutch, Danish, German, Spanish, Norwegian, Polish, Ukrainian, Portuguese, Persian, Telegu, Japanese, Korean, Hebrew, Bengali and Gujerati.[6]

During a visit to Cranham, Mrs Kirwan asked Orwell's advice on another matter. IRD was looking for a publisher to 'front' a series of IRD-sponsored anti-Communist books. It had in mind a publishing house with known left-wing affiliations to help to disguise the motivations for these books. Orwell had told Kirwan that Victor Gollancz, one of the best known left-wing publishers, was too preoccupied with the question of Palestinian dispossession in the wake of the creation of the state of Israel, so 'Orwell suggested that it might be a good plan to allow him to get these Arab refugees out of his system before trying to interest him in our plan. However according to Orwell because his books always sell very well, are well displayed and given the widest publicity, Gollancz was "undoubtedly" the best person to publish a series of books that bore the imprimatur but not the imprint of IRD.' Orwell told Kirwan that, had he been in better health, he would have been 'very willing' to act as an intermediary between IRD and Gollancz. However, he would 'try to think of someone else' to perform this role.[7]

Kirwan also asked Orwell to think of some writers who might produce articles for IRD. According to the files, he expressed his wholehearted and enthusiastic approval of the department's aims and, although too ill to write anything himself, he suggested some other names, including Darcy Gillie, the Paris correspondent for the *Guardian*, Franz Borkenau, who wrote for the *Observer* and the critic Gleb Struve.[8] What Orwell then wrote to Kirwan was, forty-five years later, to provoke a re-evaluation of his role as one of Britain's most eminent left-wing thinkers: 'I could also, if it is of any value, give you a list of journalists and writers who in my opinion are crypto-Communists, fellow-travellers or inclined that way & should not be trusted as propagandists. But for that I shall have to send for a notebook which I have at home, & if I do give you such a list it is strictly confidential, as I imagine it is libellous to describe somebody as a fellow-traveller.'[9]

Orwell did identify those whom he believed were Communist sympathizers. The files show that he had named a naval officer, one Cdr Young, as a member of the Communist Party, in his previous meeting with Kirwan. IRD historian John Savile points out that Edgar Young never made any secret of his pro-Soviet and pro-Communist Party attitudes and was certainly interested in a list of crypto-Communists. Kirwan wrote to Orwell on 30 April 1949: 'Dear George, Thanks so much for helpful suggestion. My department were very interested in seeing them . . . they have asked me to say they would be very grateful if you would let us look at your list of fellow-travelling and crypto-journalists: we would treat it with the utmost discretion. Yours ever, Celia.' The IRD wanted details as well as names. 'I hope the list gives reasons in every case,' stated IRD official Adam Watson. Indeed, the notebook was sent to the department and was copied and returned. It contained the names of 130 writers listing their jobs, and including notes by Orwell. For a long time the only insight into who was on the list had been given by Bernard Crick, Orwell's biographer. Crick had seen the original notebook of suspects and wrote that, 'Many were plausible, a few were far-fetched and unlikely', he said.[10]

But in June 1998 the *Daily Telegraph* ran a story announcing that Orwell's original list of 130 'crypto-Communists' was to be made public, with the exception of some three dozen still living. Those identified by Orwell included Charlie Chaplin, J.B. Priestley and George Bernard Shaw, as well as politicians and Labour MPs such as Tom Driberg and Richard Crossman. Priestley's qualification as an 'FT', or Fellow Traveller, appears to have been that he was 'very anti-American' and 'makes huge sums of money in USSR', while Shaw was 'reliably pro-Russian on all major issues'.[11] It must have been perfectly obvious to Orwell that he was handing the names, in effect, to the Security Service, MI5, with whom IRD obviously had clear links.

Surprising as Orwell's behaviour was, it is clear that, unlike many of his contemporaries, he was cynical towards the Soviet Union. As Australian historian Phillip

Deery has pointed out, 'Orwell's opposition to Soviet totalitarianism predated the Cold War. Its genesis lay in the Spanish Civil War. It was there that he witnessed at first hand how Stalinists and NKVD agents brutally trampled the tender shoots of libertarian socialism and how they deliberately falsified history.' In 1947 Orwell wrote that, in Spain, 'I understood, more clearly than ever, the negative influence of the Soviet myth upon the western Socialist movement. . . . Indeed in my opinion, nothing has contributed so much to the corruption of the original idea of Socialism as the belief that Russia is a Socialist country. . . . And so for the past ten years I have been convinced that the Destruction of the Soviet myth was essential if we want to revive the Socialist movement.'[12]

When the IRD file was revealed in the *Guardian* in 1996, it caused a great furore. A former leader of the Labour Party and a close friend of Orwell, Michael Foot found the offer of the blacklist 'amazing'. Tony Benn was saddened to learn that Orwell 'gave in' to the pressure of the intelligence services. For many years after his death some in the left had often argued that Orwell had never meant *Animal Farm* or *1984* as anti-Soviet parables and claimed that the books had been hijacked by Cold War Warriors of the right. These files show that this was not the case.

Orwell's works were among the many sought by IRD. From its inception, the department had recognized the importance of the book in getting across its anti-Communist message. It discreetly sought ways to get anti-Communist books into print and to ensure their wide distribution. Mayhew's first paper had called for an anti-Communist textbook to be produced, and he later stressed the need to attack 'Communist theory and practice'.[13] In December 1948, the Foreign Office published internally a red-covered paperback, *The Theory and Practice of Communism*, with no attribution, which was handed out to diplomats and selected journalists.[14] In January 1950 the first public edition was printed by an obscure publisher called Geoffrey Bles, but it was later to go into many editions as a Penguin paperback. The book was to prove very influential in setting views towards the Soviet Union. It is on the reading lists and shelves of universities around the world to this day. The author was R.N. Carew Hunt: described as a Foreign Office official, Robert Carew Hunt was actually an officer of MI6. Born in 1890 the eldest son of Canon Carew Hunt of Christ Church, Oxford, he had been educated at Bradfield College and Merton College, Oxford. In the First World War he served as an officer in the Oxfordshire and Buckinghamshire Light Infantry. In 1919 he joined the Foreign Office. He had been part of Section IX (the anti-Soviet Desk), which had been set up with Kim Philby as its chief late in the Second World War.[15]

Carew Hunt had academic aspirations and was considered to be one of the Foreign Office's leading Sovietologists, specializing in the intricacies of Marxist-Leninist doctrine. He was an intelligence officer, publishing while still in post, and his book reveals some of the beliefs held within MI6 at the time. Generally, Sovietologists were divided into two camps regarding the role of doctrine in Communist politics. On one side were those who believed that all Soviet decision making was based on Marxist-Leninist dogma. On the other, there were those who believed that the Soviets played hard and fast with dogma, applying it only when it suited them. Carew Hunt would have none of this attacked those who preferred the latter. In his book this subject forms the core of his analysis, 'Yet there is no doubt that Communists do believe that they are applying to political situations a theory which they fervently accept and which they hold to be scientific.' Even his close friend and fellow IRD writer, the academic Leonard Schapiro, could not swallow this one whole. Writing a foreword for a new edition of the book after Carew Hunt's death in 1959 he said, 'I am inclined to think while this may be true sometimes, it is generally an overstatement.' *The Theory and Practice of Communism* was one of nine books bought in bulk by IRD in the latter half of 1949 and distributed to British posts aboard. Other books included Julian Huxley's *Soviet Genetics and World Science*, and Jan Stransky's *East Wind over Prague*.

Another early venture into publishing came when IRD played a part in arranging the publication of the first book by a Soviet defector to Britain, Lt Col G.A. Tokaev, though this proved 'a less than happy experience'. The idea, a book called *Notes on Bolshevism-Communism*, was designed to provide an unemotional and interesting account of Soviet life, and the Foreign Secretary agreed to Tokaev publishing the book. However, both the text and the author proved difficult to handle, Tokaev causing considerable confusion by revealing himself to the British press before extracts of the book were ready to serialize.[16] However, important lessons were learned about the handling of defectors for propaganda coups. Despite IRD irritation, it was later revealed that Tokaev had been an important military intelligence source shared with the Americans. It was he who had revealed that the Soviets were building a strategic air force based on a copy of the B-29 bomber, a revelation that was a catalyst later for the Pentagon's mythical 'bomber gap'.

On 28 January 1949, Murray informed his boss, Christopher Warner, that 'We are now at a stage of considering plans for attempting to influence, and perhaps to enter into, the book market abroad, particularly in Asia.' Subsidizing cheap book productions was considered 'essential for the proper extension of our work abroad', as publications would 'tackle the themes on which public opinion needs to be enlightened . . . in the national interest.' It could become 'politically quite important [to] intervene unobtrusively to cause them to appear in suitable cheap editions'.[17]

Although Orwell's suggestion to get Gollancz to publish its books was not realized, IRD continued to look for a possible left-wing publisher. It also tried Odhams, which was considered to be the ideal publisher because of its 'association with the Labour Party'. Murray told the company that he wanted discreetly to influence publishers to project 'social democracy as a successful rival to Communism'.

Murray's memos reveal that earlier attempts to use the TUC were stymied by its bureaucracy:

> We have had a dismal experience trying to induce the TUC to take some action. We shall never get any satisfactory results out of the TUC alone: they are too cumbersome, too unpublicity minded and too short staffed to make a significant contribution in practical publicity . . . neither the Labour Party as such, and still less the TUC as such, is capable of producing a flow of literature, either in this country or abroad, which can compete with the Communist propaganda machine. . . . They are incapable of writing down the useful facts by themselves, but if tactfully and discreetly interviewed by someone saying he came from the Labour Party or the Fabian Society (Not H. M. G. which would frighten them) they would talk and produce much valuable information.[18]

None of these approaches appears to have come to fruition. IRD's entry into full-scale publishing only came with the cooperation of the IRD/MI6 'front' team of Sheridan, Maturin and Cannon-Brookes: it was to be another combined operation. In 1946, Leslie Sheridan had registered at Companies House a publishing company called Ampersand as a commercial venture. In 1950 it was to become the first of IRD's covert publishing operations.

The first Ampersand titles were the Bellman Books series, edited by Michael Goodwin, who was to work for Ampersand from 1952 to 1955. He was to become a ubiquitous figure among the professional Cold Warriors. He had joined the BBC in 1935 and stayed with it except for a break for active service with the Royal Artillery (1940–3). From 1947 to 1952 he edited the magazines *19th* and *20th Century*.

Bellman Books were a dozen concise handbooks, each on a different anti-Communist theme. One by Denis Healey, entitled *Neutralism*, implied that neutralism was akin to Communism. The books did not sell well, probably mainly because Ampersand lacked a proper distribution system, a defect that was later corrected by arrangements made with an established publisher, Allen & Unwin. Between the early 1950s and 1977, more than twenty titles were published by Ampersand, including works by Robert Conquest, a former employee of IRD, and the ex-Communist Douglas Hyde, who had once been news editor of the *Daily Worker*. Hyde had left the Communist Party in 1948, and his 1951 bestseller *I Believed*, published by Heinemann, was an exposé of the workings of the Communist Party of Great Britain.

However, by far the largest IRD publishing operation was not under the Ampersand imprimateur but was published by companies that may have been unaware of any relationship with the department. This operation was fronted by Stephen Watts, a pre-war *Sunday Express* film critic, who had worked for MI5 during the war. A series of books was published under the general title of Background Books, with Watts as editor. The first titles in the series were published by Batchworth Press in 1951, with a large white question mark on a bright red cover. Through the question mark was printed the title and the author's name. The first books were *Why Communism Must Fail*, by Bertrand Russell, and *Trade Unions: True or False*, by Vic Feather, then Assistant General Secretary of the TUC. An introductory note explained that Background Books were

> designed to provide ordinary people, interested in the world today, with some background information about events, institutions and ideas. They will not interpret current history for you but they will help you to interpret it for yourself. Background Books will range widely in subject, dealing with what lies at the roots of the questions thinking people are asking, filling in the background without which world affairs today cannot be properly seen or judged.

From 1951 Batchworth Press handled the Background Books series, printing 20,000 copies of each title with a cover price of 1*s* 6*d*. Batchworth was an odd choice of publisher. It was a small company run from a 'sleazy' first-floor office in Bloomsbury by William Sydney Shears, who liked to use his wartime rank of major. He had a been a POW for most of the war. The company counted a number of aristocrats on the board, including the then Duke of Buccleuch and the Earl of Ellesmere. Maj Shears seems to have had connections with the Special Operations community, as his most successful coup was publishing Col Maurice Buckmaster's account of SOE operations in Europe, *Specially Employed*, in 1952. One of the directors of a subsidiary company had worked for the SOE. But all was not well. Fresh out of university, Jackie Latham was one of the two staff and had a small batch of shares. Latham became concerned with the accounts that he discreetly warned shareholders. Even IRD could not keep Batchworth a viable concern. In 1954 the accountants qualified the accounts, and in 1956 the company collapsed with debts of more than £26,000 and was bought out.[19]

The Background Book series was to be transferred to Phoenix House (1955–9) and finally Bodley Head (1960–71).[20] Nearly 100 titles were published in the series over two decades. Through Stephen Watts, IRD not only selected writers but also subsidized production through bulk orders amounting to tens of thousands of pounds.

Many of the Background Books are rather simple anti-Communist propaganda. Authors were well-known as writers, public figures in the trade unions, politics or universities, or Cold War protagonists, some – like Leonard Schapiro, Sir Robert Bruce Lockhart, Christopher Mayhew, Francis Noel Baker, Bickham Sweet-Escott and Monty Woodhouse – with intelligence backgrounds. Other titles included in the series, all on anti-Communist themes, were *The Fanatic and the Sane*, by Oxford academic G.F. Hudson, and *Economic Imperialism: the Lesson of Eastern Europe*, by Alfred Zauberman. Nearly all of these books were widely distributed by IRD through Foreign Office information officers in the Third World. Half a dozen of the authors, who together wrote eleven titles in the series, had extremely close links with IRD. These included the Czechoslovakian émigré Walter Kolarz, recommended to IRD by Denis Healey. His book, *How is Russia Ruled?*, was published in 1953 by Batchworth. Mayhew contributed two books to the series, the first in collaboration with his wife Cicely: *What is Titoism?* (1951) and *Coexistence Plus* (1962). Another author with close links to IRD, and who contributed four titles to the series, was Guy Wint, a journalist and, for ten years, a leader writer for the *Manchester Guardian*. Wint was an authorized client of IRD with access to IRD's research desks, as was academic Hugh Seton-Watson, who wrote the Background Special, *The New Imperialism*, in 1961. IRD writers, like Tosco Fyvel who wrote *What is Culture?* (1953), merely reformulated existing IRD research papers to be published as Background Books – presenting government propaganda material as independent research. Brian Crozier, at one time a consultant to IRD wrote two titles for the series: *Neo-Colonialism* (1964) and *The Struggle for the Third World* (1966). He revealed in his autobiography that 'Before leaving *The Economist*, I had on contract, transformed a thick folder of IRD documents into a short book called *Neo-Colonialism* to demolish the Communist claim that "imperialist" companies continued to exploit colonies after independence had been granted.' Similarly, *The Struggle for the Third World*, which dealt with the 'competitive subversion' between China and the USSR in the Third World, was based on a 'sanitized' report the Crozier had earlier produced for IRD and a Chatham House article of the same name.[21] According to one IRD insider, 'Lord Bottomley wrote a book . . . and I should think that 80 per cent of that was material researched by IRD and made available to him.' *The Use and Abuse of Trade Unions* was published in 1963. Primarily an attack on Communist involvement in the trade union movement globally, it attacked the World Federation of Trade Unions

(WFTU), one of IRD's targeted Communist front organizations: 'the WFTU and its affiliates urge workers to press for higher wages, shorter hours, more social benefits and protection from automation. These are the legitimate objects of all trade union activity. But the Communist inspired bodies exploit them to an unreasonable extent with the aim of damaging the economies of non-Communist countries.'[22]

Many of the authors seem to have had no links with IRD or even knew that it existed. It was not necessary for them to do so because they could be chosen with their known views in mind. And while Bertrand Russell, another left-wing intellectual in contact with IRD, would not be asked to write a book on the question of nuclear deterrence, he would be approached, as an anti-Communist since visiting the USSR in the 1920s, to write *What is Freedom?* (1952) and *What is Democracy?* (1953). As historian Lyn Smith concluded: 'There is no evidence that writer's views were trimmed to particular lines; for Background Books or Background Specials rather it was the case that if their independent opinions fitted in with IRD's requirements then their output would be used.'[23]

According to Bryan Magee, Stephen Watts approached him having recently read Magee's book *The New Radicalism* (Secker & Warburg, 1962). Magee, at the time an active member of the Labour Party, who had recently stood twice for parliament, had argued that to win the next election, survive as a party of government and be truly radical, the Labour Party should cut itself free from what he saw as an attachment to Marxism and support for the Soviet Union. Watts had asked Magee whether he would write a book with a corresponding message for people overseas. Magee agreed and wrote *The Democratic Revolution* (1964). According to Magee:

> The thesis was that Communism was already a failed system and was already being abandoned from the top, and that its many attractions for Third World countries were entirely illusory. Far and away their best prospect of achieving societies that embodied social justice, I argued, was to opt for democracy, which would revolutionise their societies radically and in desirable ways. No one had attempted to influence what I wrote, and my book was published just as I wrote it, down to the last comma.

Magee had been unaware that Background Books had links with any organization and was outraged when he found out about the link with IRD.[24] Michael Kaser, who had worked in the Foreign Office's Economic Intelligence Department between 1947 and 1951, knew that IRD existed but said that he was unaware of its relationship with Background Books. Interestingly, Kaser was not approached by Watts but by the Warden of St Anthony's College Oxford, Sir William Deakin, who had been seconded to the SOE during the war and led the first British mission to Tito.[25] Deakin was a close friend of Adam Watson, who visited him frequently in Oxford, discussing, among other things, IRD.[26]

It seems that the main IRD target audience for the series was the educated middle-class, particularly in the Third World. Information officers overseas would distribute editions of the series in colleges and libraries free of charge, as well as passing them on to selected contacts.[27] According to Bryan Magee, commissioned by Stephen Watts to write *The Democratic Revolution* (published in 1964), Watts had explained to him that 'These books . . . were aimed mostly at readers in the Third World who were getting a higher education in English even if that wasn't necessarily their first language, e.g. university students in India and Africa.'[28] Background Books were available in Britain, distributed through the normal channels, and can still be found in significant numbers in university libraries to this day.

The investigation by the *Observer* in 1978 first revealed IRD covert publishing operation and the fact that IRD/MI6 had reimbursed all Ampersand's expenses – both publishing and overheads – at the end of each year, using funds allocated to the Secret Service.[29] In this way, Watts explained, the operation was safe from scrutiny by Parliament. (The Secret Vote, by convention, is never debated.) Ampersand was, in effect, acting as a 'cut out'.[30] However, it was this peculiar subsidy that confirmed to Richard Fletcher that these publishing companies were fronts for MI6 and IRD. Watts was required to deliver detailed annual accounts to MI6, but rather than have the bother of sanitizing them to the minimum information required under Companies Law, he simply sent the same accounts to Companies House as part of the annual return.

Ampersand also bought books for IRD from other publishers. Its accounts[31] show that for the ten years up to 1977 £55,991 was paid to Bodley Head alone, where the deal was arranged through Max Reinhardt, Managing Director of Bodley Head. Leslie Sheridan for Ampersand had negotiated a different arrangement with Allen & Unwin Ltd – through Rayner Unwin, the chairman – in which Ampersand paid all publishing costs. The books were sold by Allen & Unwin which returned a proportion of the proceeds to Ampersand. Allen & Unwin thus received a return on all Ampersand sales at no risk and with no financial outlay.

Ampersand was still operating in this way in 1978. Using Secret Service funds it seems to have been remarkably successful at providing the cheap, short publications of a popular nature and free from government labels which the Foreign Office had called for thirty years earlier. Background Books represents one of the means by which IRD managed to link its propaganda with the 'voice' of the independent media. As a means of influencing opinion, this method was highly effective.

CHAPTER TWELVE

Internal Affairs: IRD's Domestic Campaigns

In November 1956 the *Daily Mail* ran a front page splash accusing Communist union officials in the Fire Brigades Union of squandering 'more than £20,000 of union funds'. The article said that union members alleged that the money had been spent on 'Communist directed political activity in Britain which brought no benefit to members', and that 'the rest of the money . . . has been squandered by three officials on personal luxuries including expensive living and entertainment of women friends.'[1]

Although the vast majority of the rank and file of the Fire Brigades Union (FBU) were not Communist, they were content to elect Communists or Communist-inclined officials at a district and national level. The union's two leading figures in the 1950s, the General Secretary, John Horner, and the Assistant General Secretary, Jack Grahl, were both in the British Communist Party. These officials were the subject of government and sometimes rank-and-file suspicion, exacerbated by the left-wing policies and issues that the FBU both followed and pursued. These included affiliation to the Campaign for Nuclear Disarmament (CND), the National Council for Civil Liberties and the Movement for Colonial Freedom. Such associations proved enough to provoke active state intervention by IRD.

Earlier that year the Conservative MP Douglas Dodds-Parker, then Under-Secretary of State at the Foreign Office, had been approached by Norman Reddaway. The year before, on his return from a posting to Canada, Reddaway had, to his disappointment, found himself in IRD, appointed assistant to the then head, J.O. Rennie. However, he set about his task with energy. Dodds-Parker had been elected a Conservative MP in 1945 and was appointed to the Foreign Office in 1953. During the Attlee government, Dodds-Parker had collaborated behind the scenes with Bevin on anti-Communist issues, and on request he would write letters drawn up beforehand in the Foreign Office for publication in *The Times*. Dodds-Parker, like Reddaway, believed in getting things done:

> There is not very much you can do in the diplomatic world . . . but if you could discredit a dictator in his own country by getting information through the press in his country on what his private life was like, whether he stashed away money abroad, things like that. If those were known, it could work . . . and this is one of the ways you can weaken a dictatorship, or incompetent organization . . . by getting the truth told. And that seemed to me to be one of the few useful ways one could do something and not just sit at the back of the smoking room, saying, 'Tut-tut. Isn't it awful.'[2]

Reddaway wrote a short minute, alerting Dodds-Parker to a potential gold mine of information to undermine British Communists. Whitehall's Home Region Committee, set up in the 1950s to gather information on the activities of Communists in British Industry, comprised members from the Department of Trade and Industry, the Ministry of Labour, the Home Office, the Police, Foreign Office (IRD) and MI5. The committee had been discreetly gathering information on the damage that Communist-led industrial action was doing to British industry. As ex-MI5 officer Peter Wright recalled, 'In the late 1940s, MI5 began to devote resources in an effort to monitor and neutralise CPGB activity in trade union movement. By 1955 . . . the CPGB was thoroughly penetrated at almost every level by technical surveillance or informants.'[3] The committee did not, however, see it as part of its job to exploit the information that they had gathered, despite its obvious attraction for sections of the press.

Dodds-Parker, like Reddaway, of whom he thought highly, saw the opportunity to undermine Communist influence and power in the trade unions – continuing Bevin's good work – and immediately convened a meeting under Cabinet Secretary Norman Brook to see what could be done. The other members at the meeting were Norman Reddaway for IRD, the late Patrick Dean for the Foreign Office, and Roger Hollis, director of MI5. Hollis, who in the late 1940s had been responsible for Communist Affairs in MI5 and would later become alarmed enough to place CND on the MI5 list of subversive organizations, was, after a short discussion, ordered by Norman Brook to ensure that MI5 intelligence on Communists in the trade unions would be provided to IRD for exploitation.[4]

Liaison between MI5 and IRD was maintained through an experienced IRD hand and an MI5 man assigned to liaise with him. Whenever the MI5 liaison officer identified material that had news value, he would get in touch with his IRD contact to discuss its possible use. They would then talk about how the information should be handled to get it out in the right format, at the right speed and into the right hands. One pair of right hands was Woodrow Wyatt, a good friend of Reddaway's, who became a prime journalistic outlet for the MI5/IRD material.

Officially the line has been maintained that IRD never became involved in domestic politics or smear campaigns. Yet we can reveal that the Horner story was just one result of the MI5/IRD liaison agreed at that meeting in 1956. IRD planted the Horner story. It was one of a number of smear operations against Communists in which IRD had a hidden hand and was often based on information gathered by MI5, reflecting the close cooperation between the two agencies. In the FBU case, a trusted contact of Reddaway's, *Daily Mail* diplomatic correspondent Walter 'Jack' Farr, had agreed to oblige IRD as he had previously been given defector stories. Along the way a sentence had been added at the end saying that the Horner brothers kept a luxury flat in which they entertained ladies of easy virtue. This produced a writ from the FBU.[5] The problem for the *Daily Mail* was that the allegation about ladies of easy virtue was not provable. However, in classic *Daily Mail* style – attack being the best means of defence – it put half a dozen hard-nosed reporters on the case to dredge up anything else they could about Horner and his comrades to blacken the Horner name. Grahl had, by now, quarrelled with Horner and began to feed inside dirt on what was going on in the FBU to journalists. The writ meant that the *Daily Mail* felt it could not publish new material, so it went to ex-Trotskyite called Hugh Chevins, who was the industrial correspondent of the *Daily Telegraph*. Through Chevins, the pressure was maintained on Horner and the left-wing leadership of the FBU.

The FBU had been attacked by the *Daily Mail* before in the press, in general with accusations of Communist domination and malpractice. In November 1951, in a two-day dispute that marked a watershed in the history in the union, the FBU took the first national industrial action in its history. The 'spit and polish' demonstrations, as they became known, were aimed at regaining pay parity with the police and involved union members refusing to do all domestic and 'brass-bashing' chores, while continuing to answer all fire calls. Nevertheless, on the last day of the demonstration, Henry Brooke, Conservative leader of the London County Council, referred to it as a 'Communist inspired mutiny', and the *Daily Mail* picked up the story and condemned Communist influence in the union. However, as Victor Bailey, in a contribution to the FBU's official history, commented:

> Dragging in the red bogey came as no great surprise to the union; it was not the first time it had suffered a smear campaign in the press. . . . In the 'red scare' climate of 1949–51, moreover, it was *de rigueur* to ascribe any organization demanding a wage increase, or taking industrial action to secure one, as the tool of Communist agitators. Critics of Labour's policy of wage restraint, of which the FBU was one, had invariably aroused government accusations of Communist infiltration. Unofficial strikes were always described as Communist-fomented, part of a master plan to intensify Labour's economic difficulties.[6]

The Horner story came immediately after both British intervention in Suez and Soviet intervention in Hungary. On 31 October 1956, Royal Air Force bombers had attacked Egyptian targets and Britain's military action against Nasser began. As we have seen, the British intervention was fiercely criticized across the political spectrum. In response to the events of 31 October John Horner had called on the TUC to go on a general strike in protest. Although Horner's call was ultimately unsuccessful, it was probably this inflammatory act that provoked the attack from IRD.

In the ensuing days the *Daily Mail* continued to pursue Horner and his colleagues, portraying them as die-hard Moscow-controlled Communists. The facts were not always so convenient. Horner, who was forty-five years old, had left the Labour Party to join the Communist Party after the Second World War. However, on 14 November 1956 he had announced his resignation from the party in protest over Soviet suppression in Hungary. In a letter to the Communist Party's general secretary, John Gollan, Horner stated, 'I feel I have been responsible for propagating and advancing policies which have produced this latest tragedy. . . . I am no longer convinced that a party of our type is a necessary condition to achieve socialism here.'[7]

The opportunity to go on the offensive against British Communists, which the Soviet invasion presented, was not to be wasted. The party was in turmoil. The hardliners followed the Soviet line, that the uprising was of 'Fascist and counter-revolutionary elements'. Many other members left in disgust. This included a third of the journalists working for the party organ, the *Daily Worker*. Despite the fact that Horner had already resigned, the *Daily Mail* reported that delegates representing 250 Manchester firemen had demanded the immediate resignation of Horner and other Communist and ex-Communist officials.[8]

★★★★

This story reveals that the IRD not only directed its operations abroad but also intervened directly in domestic politics. Although membership of the Communist Party was legal in Britain, IRD waged a covert war against it. IRD assumed that a Communist trade unionist acted as a tool of the Soviet Union and not to eradicate legitimate grievance. As we can see, IRD carried out campaigns against individual trade unionists of whom it disapproved.

IRD had tried to change the political face of Britain early on. Official government policy banned overt propaganda against the Communist Party of Great Britain. A report to a cabinet meeting of 19 December 1949 had recommended that 'the Government should take in the United Kingdom any such action as might be necessary to discredit the Communist Party in the eyes of the people and should, in particular, undertake for this purpose a campaign of educative publicity involving the use of public funds and the employment of Government agencies.' The cabinet decided 'from the constitutional point of view it would be very difficult for a Government to take official action of this kind against a political party which has not been declared an illegal organization and in fact represented in the House of Commons'.[9] However, the cabinet discussed informal methods of countering 'Communist infiltration in this country', including an approach to Mr Surrey Dane of Odhams Press to secure anti-Communist material in papers that he controlled.

Domestic anti-Communist propaganda was to be covert. IRD briefings were distributed to ministers on a regular basis for their use whenever appropriate. Mayhew suggested that they should be given anti-Communist talking points and that the texts of any useful speeches that they made should be passed on for wider distribution. Bevin, Mayhew thought, should consult IRD before all speeches for the possible inclusion of IRD material. Similar arrangements were made for selected 'friendly' MPs, in particular to aid anti-Communist MPs in the Labour Party. IRD files show that Col Sheridan was meeting with the Deputy General Secretary of the TUC, Victor Feather as early as 1950. This was to discuss 'placing articles'. The two men discussed their concern about the ineffectiveness of the anti-Communist propaganda of the international Trade Union body, the ICFTU, which had been set up primarily to split the Soviet international Trade Union 'front', the WFTU.[10]

Another IRD domestic target was organizations perceived to be Soviet 'fronts'. This was part of a wider campaign. Col Douglas Dodds-Parker, when Parliamentary Under-Secretary at the Foreign Office, was responsible for liaison with MI6. According to Kim Philby, he was also chair of the Psychological Warfare Consultations Committee, know as the Dodds-Parker Committee. This carried out 'psychological operations against any peace movements . . . and planned Intelligence Service operations against progressive organizations in England'.[11]

IRD worked closely with MI5 on the domestic side, and it was clearly receiving intelligence from MI5 on suspected Communist fronts. One file in the Public Record

Office is entitled 'Association with the National Council of Civil Liberties of Certain TUC Affiliated Trade Unions'. In one letter, Ralph Murray wrote to H.G. Gee of the TUC on 3 February 1949, expressing concern that 'a number of Trade Unions' who were 'in some way affiliated to, or who lend support to, the National Council of Civil Liberties' were helping the Soviet propaganda cause: 'The National Council of Civil Liberties is heavily Communist-penetrated and is in fact being used for little if nothing more than attacking our Colonial administrations and politics at every opportunity. You will remember that E.M. Forster, who was a prominent member of the Council in its heyday in the '30s, resigned last May precisely because the Council was being used for political matters of which he did not approve'. Murray intended to sever the 'connection of the Council with Trade Unions' by persuading those concerned to 'withdraw their support, affiliation or connection with the Council'. On 18 February, Gee responded that the TUC was 'under no illusions about the present complexion of the National Council of Civil Liberties . . . it is obvious that all those with a powerful Communist element will have joined, especially the AEU, ETU, Construction Workers, Tobacco Workers, Fire Brigade Unions and CSCA etc.' Although the TUC was aware of the link between individual unions and the National Council, Gee informed the IRD that the TUC could not force individual unions to cut their ties. However, the TUC was able to educate its members into taking action themselves as part of its 'general anti-Communist drive'. In a handwritten note on 25 April 1949, Murray wrote, 'this is now going quite well, as regards the TUC'.

In 1953, the Labour Party suddenly increased the number of organizations on its proscription list – organizations to which Labour Party members could not belong – by eighteen. The information on which this decision was based had come through the International Department from 'the Foreign Office and Special Branch'.[12] The main conduit for propaganda from IRD into the Labour Movement was the Labour Party's own International Department. In the late 1940s, material was sent directly by IRD to Mayhew's friend and the secretary of the International Department, Denis Healey. The type of material sent to the International Department varied. Briefings in the archive include titles such as 'Soviet Suppression of Liberty in Germany's Eastern Zone' and 'Russian Trades Unions and How They Operate'.

IRD would also provide the International Department with the means to rebut Communist allegations against Western powers. For example, a 'Memorandum On The *Daily Worker* editorial of 12 July 1951', sent to the International Department 'With the Compliments of J.H. Peck', head of IRD between 1951 and 1954, presented an analysis and rejection of the editorial's estimate of comparative Western and Soviet military strength and rearmament. Material like this could then be used by the International Department or sent on to reliable anti-Communists and other parties to use themselves, probably unaware of the material's origin. The instant rebuttal was a technique developed by IRD to a high state of perfection, long before the Labour Party's much vaunted rebuttal unit was formed in the run up to the 1997 election. When officials spotted an article or letter in a newspaper that they felt assisted the Communist cause, they would look for errors and immediately have a response sent off to the paper. These rebuttals were usually fronted by an apparently neutral and well-known figure – MPs were preferred and many were happy to see their names in print for no effort.

Another route of IRD influence into the Labour Movement was through the Trades Union Congress. An early link was established with Herbert Tracey, the influential TUC publicity officer who also ran an anti-Communist organization called *Freedom First*. Through Tracey, IRD was able to insert its material into his organization's newsletter, which was read by several hundred influential trade union organizers. An international edition of the newsletter was proposed and covertly funded by IRD. It would purchase a sufficient number of copies for distribution through its own channels to ensure the newsletter's continued financial viability and thus the propagation of its views through an apparently independent medium. Through Tracey, 'mutual assistance between the Foreign Office and TUC on publicity overseas' was established.[13] In this he was helped by leading members of the TUC general council, Percy Cudlipp, then editor of the *Daily Herald*, and Denis Healey.

A self-proclaimed Cold Warrior, Healey was to be one of IRD's key contacts. Born of middle-class parents in Kent at the height of the First World War, Healey went to Balliol in 1936 where he joined the Communist Party for two years. During the Second World War he had joined the Royal Engineers and seen action in the Army, rising to the rank of major. In 1945, after failing to win a seat, he had been given the job of International Secretary of the Labour Party. 'As International Secretary it was my job to explain the Government's foreign policy to the Party and the world,' he wrote in his autobiography. 'Bevin gave me a pretty free run of the Foreign Office, and I made many friends among its officials – notably Gladwyn Jebb, a lordly radical who had been Dalton's diplomatic adviser at the Special Operation's Executive . . . and the intellectual Evelyn Shuckburgh; he once startled me, in a discussion of Tito's break with Stalin, by suggesting that it might have been a trick to deceive the West.'[14]

It is hard to underestimate Healey's influence over early perceptions of the Cold War. The *Keep Left* pamphlet was published in mid-1947. In part written by Michael Foot, it derided Ernest Bevin for his pro-Americanism and anti-Soviet inclination. Although Foot was a *Daily Herald* commentator, the paper offered its full support to Bevin's counterattack, the pro-Atlanticist anti-Soviet *Cards on the Table* written by Healey.

The Labour Party's International Department became a major conduit for disguised IRD propaganda to penetrate into the Labour Movement. It is worth noting that the flow of information was two-way. In a letter written in November 1948, Denis Healey wrote to IRD, recommending possible contacts for them. One of the three on his list was a Czechoslovakian Social Democrat who had recently emigrated to Britain called Walter Kolarz. Healey enquired whether IRD 'could make use of his abilities?'[15] It did. Healey also developed a sideline that made him an even more important asset for IRD. According to Healey, he and his wife Edna and newborn daughter found it hard to live on their Labour Party salary, so he took up journalism and broadcasting. 'Bush House, the Headquarters of British broadcasting overseas, became my second home. I did a weekly commentary in French on whatever caught my fancy in the news; I broadcast occasionally in German and Italian, and before long I was doing a great deal in English, for audiences abroad,' he recalled.[16]

IRD material was supplied to Healey and his successors in publications such as *Digest*, and in 1949 the department began to produce two specialized publications. *Speaker's Notes* developed from material provided to ministers for use in speeches to counter the allegation that the Western powers were failing to cooperate with a willing Russia. And *Points at Issue*, a small booklet, was intended to supplement *Speaker's Notes*. Mayhew wanted it sponsored by an organization like the TUC for wider publication. However *Newsweek* (9 May 1949) spiked this gun by reporting that 'the British Foreign Office distributed last week a guide for official speakers on Soviet-Western relations . . . [which] reflected British distrust of current Berlin blockade peace talks.' It was heavily circulated but never published. The unattributable nature of the publication frustrated one potential customer. The Foreign Office ruled that the War Office, which had suggested supplying every single officer with a copy, would have to take political responsibility if mass distribution of an imprintless publication gave rise to any questions, possibly in Parliament. The service ministers failed to agree this condition.[17]

Mayhew also arranged that answers to 'unhelpful' resolutions sent to the Labour government from constituency Labour Parties on 'familiar Communist themes' (including Greece, Eastern Europe and the colonies) would be drafted by IRD on behalf of the departments to which they had been addressed.[18] The 'Communist theme' in Greece was the arbitrary execution and imprisonment of trade union leaders by the Greek government.[19]

International Department archives show a steady stream of material from IRD and intimacy between the two departments' senior officials. In 1955 the department began receiving IRD's new bimonthly publication *Quotations*. The new head of IRD, John Ogilvy Rennie, wrote to Healey's successor, Saul Rose, inquiring whether he would be interested in receiving it under the usual unattributable conditions: 'It consists of a selection of quotations from the Soviet Press and radio, the *Large Soviet Encyclopaedia* and the Marxist classics, reflecting trends, shortcomings and anomalies in Soviet internal and external propaganda.'[20] A letter dated 18 March 1955 from Rose to Rennie expressed the wish to receive the new publication 'under the usual conditions'.

One of the most effective methods used by IRD was the placement of propaganda by contacts in the Labour Party and the TUC, to bolster anti-Communists against Communists and those less enthusiastic about the Cold War, the Atlantic alliance and nuclear deterrence. This was done with the help of both 'witting' and 'unwitting' journalists and academics. Woodrow Wyatt, for example, was at the forefront of those to claim that the influence of the Russian front organizations on trade unions was causing disastrous damage to the country. In about 1956 he wrote a book called *The Peril in Our Midst*,[21] which claimed that, under the influence of the WFTU, people like Horner in the FBU, and, more seriously, Foulkes and Haxell[22] in the Electrical Trades Union, were working in the interests of Moscow. This was a continuation of the operation of which the Horner story was but a part. Wyatt had close links with British intelligence. He had been a shareholder of an MI6 news agency since 1952. Wyatt's information came from MI5 via IRD and Wyatt's inability to find a publisher for *The Peril in Our Midst* was solved when IRD's Leslie Sheridan stepped in and had it published by one of the department's front operations.

Wyatt also campaigned against Communist ballot rigging in the trade unions especially the leadership of the Electrical Trades Union (ETU).[23] In a spectacular court case, the judge, Mr Justice Winn, found that a group of Communist leaders of the union, including Foulkes and Haxell, had 'conspired together to prevent by fraudulent and unlawful devices the election of the plaintiff Byrne in place of the defendant Haxell as general secretary of the defendants union'.[24] Justice Winn found that 'not only was the ETU managed and controlled by Communists and pliant sympathizers, but it was so managed in the service of the Communist Party of the United Kingdom and the ideas of that party.'[25] Haxell was immediately replaced by Jock Byrne as General Secretary and Foulkes was replaced in 1963 by Les Cannon. As one insider commented, the combination of Wyatt, IRD and MI5 material proved highly effective as part of 'an extraordinarily successful operation.'[26] As a result the union was taken over by a moderate leadership under John Byrne, Les Cannon and Frank Chapple, who led the ETU as General Secretary until 1984.[27] Under their leadership, in 1965, Communists were banned from holding union office.[28] Alec Douglas Home was so impressed that he sent a personal note of congratulation to Reddaway, who was by that time in Beirut.

The historical version of these events has largely remained that recorded by the New Statesman. In an article in July 1961, following the court's decision in favour of Byrne's replacement of Haxell, the anti-Communist campaign was described as having been waged by 'a handful of "revisionists" and Labour Party members who have neither the resources nor the opportunity to compete with a machine of 2,500 CP members'.[29] Indeed, Arthur Bottomley, in his book The Use and Abuse of Trade Unions, published by IRD front Ampersand in 1963, wrote that 'the ETU was cleaned up, not as a result of outside protest and agitation (though this undoubtedly played a part) but by the slogging, painstaking and dedicated efforts of a group of socialist trade unionists.' Bottomley commented that the case was, 'One of the best documented exposures of the ruthless Communist minority domination of a trade union . . . and has already been hailed as a landmark in the history of labour struggles'.[30] Not for the last time, IRD and the discreet machinery of the British State would miss out on the credit that it was due. Those in IRD and MI5 who had been involved had to remain silent about their role in, what the historian of the ETU, John Lloyd, described as 'the single most important political change in the union since the war'.[31]

The relationship between intelligence agencies and the right-wing press was close, and none more so than with the Daily Mail. One example from the mid-1950s was provided by a former IRD official. ETU leaders had denied that they had a caucus to decide on tactics during the TUC conference. MI5 intelligence, passed through IRD to the Daily Mail, revealed that the ETU leaders would be at the headquarters of the British Communist Party in King Street shortly before conference. The group was photographed from a window opposite in King Street. The Daily Mail published this and said that this was evidence of a caucus meeting.

In 1962 the Radcliffe Committee, set up by the Macmillan government in the wake of the Vassall spy case, alleged extensive Communist Party control over the civil service unions. In the same year the former Labour, later Conservative, MP and journalist, Aidan Crawley, claimed that the CPGB was strongest in the NUM, building workers unions and the AEU, warned that they were making inroads into the clerical unions, and cited sections of the woodworkers, the plumbers and the painters unions as being under CPGB control.[32] Aidan Crawley, like Mayhew, was one of the first postwar generation of BBC TV presenters and also close to IRD. The media, especially right-

Christopher Mayhew proposed the formation of IRD while a junior Foreign Office Minister in Attlee's government. (Universal Pictorial Press)

John Cloake, an early recruit to IRD. (John Cloake)

Norman Reddaway, one of IRD's most influential figures. (Norman Reddaway)

Lenin and Stalin, the architects of Soviet Communism that IRD strove hard to undermine. (Russian Archives)

Winston Churchill 'set Europe
ablaze'. SOE and IRD blossomed
in the Churchill years of the 1950s.
(Press Association)

SOE veteran Sir Douglas
Dodds-Parker provided the
necessary political backing for IRD's
domestic campaign in the mid-
1950s. (Sir Douglas Dodds-Parker)

North Korean Communist Prime Minister Kim Il Sung with Soviet advisers during the Korean War, 1951. (Paul Lashmar Collection)

Michael Ivens, head of right-wing lobby group Aims of Industry and leading advocate for Britain joining the EEC. (Michael Ivens)

John Horner, Communist leader of the Fire Brigades Union who was targeted by IRD. (Fire Brigades Union)

Nikita Khrushchev. IRD did not believe he would liberalize Soviet Communism and foreign policy. (Russian Archives)

President Sukarno of Indonesia with his wife Dewi. Sukarno's leadership was perceived as a threat to the West which assisted in his overthrow. (Hulton Getty Picture Library)

Gen Soeharto, who came to power in 1966 aided by Western efforts to topple his predecessor President Sukarno. (Associated Press)

Harold Macmillan's government ordered IRD to help destabilize Sukarno's Indonesia. (*Daily Telegraph*)

Foreign Secretary David Owen, seen here with Leonid Brezhnev, found IRD's Cold Warriors an embarrassment and closed the department down in 1977. (Lord Owen)

Hilary W. King, former Ambassador to Guinea, a critic of IRD's Cold War black propaganda. (Hilary W. King)

Roland Challis, BBC correspondent in South-East Asia during the rise of Gen Soeharto in Indonesia. (Roland Challis)

wing newspapers like the *Daily Express* and the *Daily Mail*, frequently carried lurid 'red-under-the-bed' stories.

IRD's activities had clearly gone beyond the 'informal' distribution of propaganda referred to in IRD's original brief. All of these examples of IRD's intervention in domestic politics were part of the attempt to achieve what was, according to Mayhew, IRD's principle aim on the domestic front: to support anti-Communists in government, the Labour Party and the trade unions. To what extent this intervention was successful is difficult to determine, but according to Mayhew, 'It is amazing how those to whom one sent it [IRD material] were, even if they didn't use it, influenced themselves to see that Stalinism was an evil thing, and certainly IRD's propaganda coincided with a considerable political defeat of the extreme left in the Labour Party.'[33]

It was not only the Labour Party. As IRD grew and became more confident, it became more interventionist. Early IRD documents show that it was prohibited by government from domestic operations – the rules of etiquette were explicit: carrying out domestic propaganda was Home Office territory. However, this hurdle seems to have been overcome. From 1951 a more aggressive approach was taken under the new head, John Peck, an Oxford classicist and writer of light verse. Peck had been a private secretary to Churchill during the war. His former Foreign Office colleague Michael Cullis later wrote of the effectiveness of Peck at IRD, 'Having myself in part worked for it in the field, I was well placed to admire what he did (perhaps occasionally overdid) by way of getting this whole, very necessary, operation off the ground at an important juncture in world affairs.'[34]

Peck's Cold Warriors became particularly concerned when support was given to the peace movement by opponents of nuclear weapons who were respectable establishment figures. Early on, IRD had built up a relationship with the Church of England and had spent a great deal of time enlisting leading Church figures to the pro-nuclear and anti-Communist cause. The main point of contact was the Church's Council for Foreign Relations (CFR), which had enormous influence over the political line dictated to its congregation, not only throughout the country but also abroad. Through Canon Herbert Waddams, General Secretary of the CFR, IRD was able to disseminate a great deal of covert propaganda. Waddams had been in the Ministry of Information during the Second World War and well understood the use of propaganda. The archive reveals the council in constant contact with IRD. Waddams had initially been a hesitant entrant into the Cold War, but by 1948 he took up the role with some vigour. IRD was prepared to provide sensitive material to the CFR providing that it was all returned including the original cover letter. On one occasion Canon Waddams failed to return the covering letter, so it is now in the CFR archive. IRD was offering personal information on the 'Red' Dean of Canterbury, Hewlett Johnson, clearly wanting to rid themselves of this turbulent priest. Peck wrote to Waddams:

I wonder if you would mind looking at the attached? These notes came to us by a roundabout route in case we could make any use of them. It is quite a formidable collection, and I see no reason why we should be very tender in our treatment of the Dean. In general we do not like to publicise overseas British nationals who have gone off the rails in any manner, but he has become such an international figure that I think anyone wishing to refute him should have some material at his disposal.

I think however that you should know what is going on, and if you wish to use any of this material yourself there would be no objection. If on the other hand you would prefer to know nothing of this, please return the letter and the enclosure which will then have never been sent.[35]

This was clearly MI5-generated material on Hewlett Johnson. To his credit, Waddams did not use it and returned it to Peck, saying, 'I agree that there is no reason why he should be tenderly treated and I should be very glad to see him debunked. But I am pretty sure that the kind of notes you enclosed are not the right way of doing it. . . . I think you would be making a mistake to use this material.' Hewlett Johnson had a long history of tolerance towards Communists and Peck's correspondence took place shortly after Johnson had returned from China. He carried a number of appeals from Chinese Christians who were well known and respected in the West, complaining about the American use of germ warfare in China and North Korea. This resulted in an onslaught against Johnson by the media and politicians.[36]

This is not the only example of Foreign Office intervention. Church of England archives also show that, in May 1953, a Mr John Egg of IRD called in person on Col Barron of the CFR. Egg, for reasons we think are obvious, later, changed his name and was IRD's liaison officer to MI5. He drew Col Barron's attention to a letter in the *Manchester Guardian* of 8 May, in which the Dean of Manchester stated that he welcomed the holding of a peace congress in Manchester on 17 May, and that every Christian should do likewise. As Bishop of Singapore, the dean had been a prisoner of the Japanese and was a respected figure. He openly acknowledged that he knew nothing of the organization behind the peace congress, but he nevertheless authorized the Revd W. Watts, who was associated with it, to make use of his letter in anyway he chose in the interests of peace. Egg informed Barron that the Foreign Office saw this as a typical example of an intellectual who was being hoodwinked by Communist peace propaganda and lending it support without any knowledge of the facts. Egg gave Barron a unattributed IRD paper, 'British Peace Congress 1953', and asked him to send a copy of it to the Dean of Manchester. According to historian Dianne Kirby, he also asked whether the CFR could help in getting over this type of document to members of the clergy, and if it would submit for their guidance a list of Church newspapers, societies, women's guilds, etc, 'which we think would benefit by an unofficial circulation if necessary by the Foreign Office, of this kind of pamphlet'. Kirby said, 'The correspondence between the CFR and the Foreign Office demonstrated that the latter wished the former to disseminate what was effectively grey propaganda without attributing its real source.'

In August 1953, John Peck sent Herbert Waddams a paper 'on propaganda moves which the Soviet Government might take to further its campaign to secure world-wide favour as the champion of "peace and friendship" between nations,' and told him that, 'should you wish to use any of the information contained in this paper, please do so, but I must ask you to ensure that neither the paper itself, nor the speculation it puts forward, is attributed to the Foreign Office.' The CFR was certainly interested in what the Foreign Office had to say. On 22 October 1954, Waddams asked for a list of front organizations that might tempt clergymen. J.O. Rennie at IRD replied that the

'Communist-tainted' bodies that clergymen might be induced to support were divided into three categories: those aimed specifically at practising Christians; secular organizations whose aims might attract clerical support; and organizations that, while not proscribed by the Labour Party, could fairly be described as Communist in aim and character. The organizations existing to mobilize Christian opinion were the Society of Socialist Clergy and Ministers (SSCM), whose origins lay in the 1942 Malvern Conference organized by William Temple, the Christians and Crisis Group and the Christian Peace Group – (the latter two, thought to have merged, were seen as less 'dangerous' than the SSCM).[37]

IRD had therefore defined and covertly harried its enemies by the mid-1950s, but it had also defined and covertly nurtured its friends.

CHAPTER THIRTEEN

IRD's Fellow Travellers

In the strange 'wilderness of mirrors' world inhabited by IRD, it was often hard to tell who were government propagandists and who were journalists. In many cases, individuals were both at the same time or changing hats effortlessly between the two. One year they would be working for the MI6 'friends', the next for a Fleet Street newspaper. MI6 and IRD both had a close relationship with *The Economist*. Brian Crozier, who freelanced for IRD as well as working at *The Economist*, illustrated the extent of the relationship in his autobiography, *Free Agent*. While he was a writer of *The Economist's Foreign Report*, Crozier was taken to MI6's headquarters, Century House, by his SIS contact: 'I met a number of people whom I had talked to . . . in the belief that they were "Foreign Office". One of them I had known as a colleague when he had worked for the Economist Intelligence Unit.'[1]

One ex-Foreign Office source said that, in the 1950s, *The Economist's Foreign Report*, a by-invitation-only subscription newsletter started in the late 1940s, was a major conduit for IRD material. Ruth Dudley Edwards wrote in her study of *The Economist*, 'Since it was first launched people have tried to define the difference in content between this blue, eight-page, expensive newsletter and *The Economist*.' She quoted a vague Geoffrey Crowther, editor and later chairman of *The Economist*, as saying that 'There are things that one doesn't want to put into print and have quoted on the Moscow radio next day; or things that we think are correct but aren't sure; or which, for one reason or another, get displaced from a paper that is pretty rigid in size and form.' Brian Beedham, the foreign editor of *The Economist* between 1964 and 1989, was equally obscure: 'It has always seemed to me that the good Foreign Report piece fell into one of two categories – either the under-the-bed piece, reporting on something not yet known to the public press, or not properly, or the novel item of analysis and interpretation looking farther into the future than other eyes can see.'[2]

The Economist's Foreign Report was started by two of Crowther's protégés, Jean Bird and Alison Outhwaite. During the war, Outhwaite had been a European expert in the Foreign Office's Political Intelligence Department and Jean Bird, 'an American who had served in the American embassy in London on similar work', had written a Background Book for Batchworth Press in 1954 entitled *East-West Trade*. According to Edwards, 'From the very beginnings of *Foreign Report* . . . there were tensions with the foreign department, whose editor was nominally responsible for *Foreign Report*'s contents. . . . Outhwaite in particular was too much of a cold warrior for John Midgeley's liking and her critics thought her sources were too 'Establishment'.'[3]

In fact, IRD appears to have established an effective outlet with the *Foreign Report*. Staff working on this eight-page confidential letter included Brian Crozier and Andrew

Boyd, who introduced Crozier to his IRD contact, H.H. 'Tommy' Tucker. Crozier said that much of the material presented in the *Foreign Report* came direct from IRD: 'If I were to try and put a percentage to it, it would be round about maybe 20 or 30 per cent. But it varied, I mean every now and then they'd have something really sensational and so one used it, but there were a lot of other sources.' Crozier was introduced to IRD over lunch at the Travellers Club early in 1955. 'I already knew of their existence but I hadn't contact, so one of my colleagues took me for lunch and after that I was involved with them, not on a paying basis until I actually left *The Economist*, but exchanges of information, that kind of thing.'[4]

Many of *The Economist*'s staff were very close to the intelligence establishment. Deputy Editor Donald McLachlan had been part of Sefton Delmer's black propaganda team. John Midgeley, Foreign Editor in the late 1950s, had worked for the *Guardian* before and after the war during which he had served in military intelligence. Another member of the foreign department was the historian and ex-director of the Middle East division of the Ministry of Information, Elizabeth Monroe. The journalist and foreign editor Patrick Honey, for a period the Foreign Editor at *The Economist*, became a friend of Crozier's and wrote articles and books for IRD.

From the mid-1950s, IRD developed a hard core of trusted and like-minded journalists and academics who were to remain remarkably consistent throughout its existence. This inner caucus was refined from a wider, more politically diverse circle of contacts. IRD strove to make links with the media through relationships with individual journalists, both directly and through the contacts of the Foreign Office's information officers in diplomatic missions abroad. They would be approached with the offer of material produced for the diplomatic service but available to a few people outside the service who might find it useful. The journalist was free to use the material however he or she wished on condition that it was not passed on to anyone else and that it was not attributed to Her Majesty's government. Many agreed.

IRD had its own in-house team of writers: some career Foreign Office people, others professional journalists. Of the ninety-one articles sent out during 1948, some forty-one had been written by IRD staff writers using pseudonym's like 'John Cardwell' and 'David Laidlaw'. In the initial wave of recruitment, IRD wisely hired a number of contract staff with leftist credentials, like Celia Kirwan, in much the same way that it sought to use left-wing publishers and figures. It suited the mood of the times and gave articles an anti-Communist credibility that a right-wing writer might have lacked.

The rest of IRD's journalistic output came from outside contributors. In November 1950 the new member for Bristol south-east, Tony Benn, was confidentially approached by IRD's Col Leslie Sheridan using his public relations consultant cover. (Sheridan wrote to his boss, Ralph Murray, that Anthony Wedgwood Benn 'is a really brilliant young man'.) Benn recalled that he was offered a substantial annual salary to write anti-Communist articles for IRD. He declined the offer. In a letter to Sheridan he wrote, 'I have been thinking over the matter we discussed yesterday + have come to the conclusion that I cannot take on the work. I feel that it would be incompatible with my independence as an MP + in any case it's not really up my street at all. I wouldn't be any good at it.'[5] Tony's brother, the historian David Benn, pointed out that it is technically illegal for an MP to be paid in such a way by the Crown.

Tony Benn may have rejected IRD overtures, but how many other MPs were recruited by IRD and what were they paid?

Other left-wingers, like the writer Tosco R. Fyvel, were also approached and recruited. Fyvel had been *Tribune*'s literary critic from 1946 to 1950 and became a regular writer for IRD. A well known figure in pre-war left-wing circles, Fyvel was a friend of both Orwell and Koestler. He went to Cambridge after attending various Swiss and English schools, and during the war he too became involved in psychological warfare. In 1939–40 he had co-edited with George Orwell, a series of pamphlets on war aims for the British Army called the Searchlight Books. He then worked on psychological warfare in North Africa with both the British and the American armies. From 1951 Fyvel became involved in IRD's continued efforts to exploit the propaganda potential of Soviet military defectors, the technique that had started off very unsurely with Lt Col G.A. Tokaev in 1948.[6] They quickly became more skilled in defector handling. In March 1952 IRD published the tale of a young Russian rifle regiment non-commissioned officer, entitled 'Sergeant Shutov reads the road signs'. It was by-lined T.R. Fyvel, who was described as a 'leading left wing critic of Stalin'. Fyvel and his colleagues industriously produced articles that, in keeping with IRD practice, if not with journalistic ethics, did not say that they were paid by the Foreign Office.[7] Other journalists came from Fleet Street, like the diplomatic correspondent of the *Daily Telegraph*, R.H.C. Steed. Hugh Chevins, the *Daily Telegraph* journalist who played a pivotal role in the Horner Affair, was paid to write articles for IRD. In the summer of 1949 he wrote *Progress Towards a Free T.U. International*, which was distributed to all Foreign Office posts. Woodrow Wyatt MP wrote on *The Two Imperialisms*. Other well-known names included Freda Utley, Oscar Hobson, Rhys Davies MP, Harold Laski, J.A. Hough and Paul Anderson of the *Picture Post*. Additionally, IRD bought second rights for thirty-seven published articles in that year from such authors as Prof Gilbert Murray and Julian Huxley.[8] These articles were sold very cheaply and appeared in newspapers all over the world.

As well as contact with individual journalists, IRD made arrangements with several newspapers, including the *Observer*, *The Times* and the *Sunday Times*, by which IRD bought the right to republish selected articles abroad without alteration and with acknowledgement for the author and original publisher only. By these means IRD could ensure the distribution of favourable and independent articles throughout the world.[9]

IRD assiduously built up a network of journalist contacts: a circulation list for 1976 lists ninety-two British journalists working for publications including the *Observer*, the *Guardian*, the *Financial Times*, *The Times*, the *Daily Mirror*, the *Daily Mail*, the *Telegraph*, and the *Sunday Express*, as well as freelance journalists and journalists working for ITN and Reuters. Many of these had only loose contacts with IRD and some treated IRD material with caution. Perhaps the most interesting and questionable relationship was that between IRD and a carefully selected, small group of influential journalists. In the 1976 list there were a number of people who, in some cases, had been key IRD contacts for more than twenty years. As each showed that they could play the game according to IRD's rules, he or she found that they were rewarded with 'exclusives' that in turn would get them the appreciation of their editor. We have already seen how this could work in the case of Walter Farr and Hugh Chevins. The attraction of free research on topics of interest to the selected journalist is obvious as it relieves him or her of a great deal of work. Effectively, those journalists were able to pass off the enormous intelligence collection ability of the Foreign Office as their own work, the source never being attributed. For IRD it was a means of getting material into circulation and encouraging a news focus on the failures and evils of Communism and the USSR. Journalists were influenced both through the material and through the potential threat of withdrawing the information should the journalist behave in a way that IRD disliked. As late as the 1970s there was a whole bevy of journalists on the more right-wing tabloid newspapers who made their living out of such stories, some just plain ludicrous and many supplied by IRD.

The department was able to help to build the reputations of journalists of whom it approved. Victor Zorza of the *Guardian* was very close to IRD. 'The word Kremlinology was not invented for Victor Zorza . . . but for more than twenty-five years he was its leading exponent,' observed one close friend.[10] He is attributed with journalistic coups that included the discovery of the ideological split between Moscow and Mao Zhedong's China and the prediction of the Soviet invasion of Czechoslovakia in 1968. Zorza, a Polish Jew, had been part of vast deportations to Siberia by the Soviets just before the Second World War. He had escaped and gradually made his way across Europe, ending up in England and joining the RAF. From 1948 he had joined the BBC monitoring service at Caversham. He began writing for the *Guardian* in the early 1950s, finally joining the staff in May 1956. Zorza covered the Soviet Union, not from Moscow but from his London home. He did not go back to the Soviet Union until 1977. He even moved to Slough, it was said, to have fast access to *Pravda* and *Izvestia* arriving at Heathrow. Zorza specialized in analysing the subtle nuances of Soviet politics. 'For the *Guardian* he also analysed the trends behind the secrecies of Soviet society through a method which though infinitely painstaking in practice, was simple in theory. It depended on considering not only what was said and written but on comparing it with what might have been said and was not.'[11] Many of Zorza's articles were based on Soviet publications and credited them. Other stories are unsourced and presented as bald statements of fact. Zorza's style lent itself ideally to absorbing IRD output. According to a number of former IRD staff, he was a key 'client'. One IRD researcher said 'I recall an article we produced on the Soviet motor industry in the mid 1970s. A week later it turned up word for word in a national newspaper under Zorza's by-line.'[12] Reddaway said that, as an authorized client of the Soviet Desk of IRD, he could easily switch to using information from other desks.[13] This helps to explain how Zorza, working from London, suddenly became an expert in the complexities of the Indonesia Untung coup, producing a series of detailed articles for the *Guardian*. One revealing example began, 'Jakarta Radio, which has not even mentioned the word "Communist" since the beginning of the current troubles yesterday turned on the Communist Party with a demand that it should be disbanded.' Zorza, while clearly getting material from Foreign Office sources, was the one journalist to discern that the Communist probably played no major part in the Untung coup attempt.

It would be naive to suggest that correspondents like Zorza were just mouthpieces of IRD. These individuals were usually highly capable and had their own sources. The relationship between Zorza and IRD can best be described as thriving on creative tension. Zorza, for instance, increasingly came to believe that the Soviet Union was undergoing reform and could coexist with the West – not a popular line with FO hardliners. He also encountered the wrath of the hardliners when he questioned the veracity of the book *The Penkovsky Papers*, originally published in the United States in the early 1960s. This very anti-Soviet text was allegedly written by a high-level CIA spy in Moscow before he was caught and executed just before the Cuban Missile Crisis.[14] It was serialized by numerous major newspapers including the *Washington Post*. Zorza indicated that he thought that it was a piece of ghost-written propaganda, an opinion that earned him vilification by the CIA. He suggested at the time that intelligence agencies in democracies 'suffer from the grave disadvantage that in attempting to damage the adversary they must also deceive their own public'. He also denounced, wrongly as it turned out, Krushchev's memoirs as a CIA fake.

According to IRD sources, Zorza fell out with the department from time to time. In 1964 he implicitly criticized it in a *Guardian* article for failing to see the downfall of Krushchev. 'By far the greater number of Western experts, mostly employed in Government agencies and therefore anonymous, and those in the academic world, tended to pour scorn on analyses showing the progressive weakening of Mr Krushchev's position.' And Zorza was not beyond making some strange pronouncements. The *Guardian* article entitled 'New Soviet attempt to turn Europeans against America' was based on rather thin evidence: 'The Soviet initiative was in the form of a *Pravda* article which welcomed the success of the new dialogue with France, and declared that the time had come to take the next, more specific steps in the search for European security.'

The *Guardian* leader writer Guy Wint also had a close relationship with IRD, as did David Floyd of the *Daily Telegraph*. Floyd said that, on one occasion he had written a booklet about China at IRD's request. It told him that it was to be distributed to diplomats.[15] These correspondents might have asserted their independence from IRD, but there were also lazy journalists who were prepared to be fed by IRD and made a career out of it. Read the tabloids, especially the Sunday tabloids during IRD's lifetime, and you can read wild claims about Soviet activities that were risible nonsense and generally unsourced, but many were supplied by IRD's 'subterranean channels'.

But IRD was selective about who it gave information to. Some journals and journalists were considered unlikely to play the game by gentleman's rules. Norman Reddaway explained:

For example, *Time* magazine would not be suitable, because you could not say to a *Time* magazine man – who is a sort of licensed ferret – look, you must not attribute this and you must not reveal the source and so on, because *Time* magazine doesn't work that way. It has its licensed ferrets, ferreting out all over the place, they bung in whatever they can dig out of the holes and bung it into New York. And there is no control over what to put in, say in London, and what comes out in New York, and goes worldwide.

So I am not aware that any *Time* magazine person had access to IRD, I wouldn't have authorised it. And of course the *Daily Worker* wasn't suitable – why would you have the *Daily Worker*? On the other hand a lot of other people were. I mean the

Daily Herald man was a very regular user. Seton-Watson, very regular. I mean, these are the respectable ones. Nicholas Carol, later Victor Zorza, Guy Wint, all these people were judged to be safe to deal with and wouldn't attribute it.

Occasionally they slipped up by making the source of information a little too clear. This incurred IRD's irritation, as the *Sunday Telegraph* was to discover. 'Nicholas Carol, for example, once virtually said that this had come from either the Foreign Office or the researchers or whatever and I had him in and said – "Look, this is the last time you can do this." I remember he wrote a very apologetic letter, *mea culpa* etc, etc. And from then on he was very good. They realized they'd got an absolute gold mine of serious research in there and they valued it enormously of course,' said Norman Reddaway.[16]

Also on the 1976 list were a number of academics who specialized in areas of Cold War and were nurtured by IRD, which provided them with all of the department's latest research. As with the favoured journalist, IRD paid many of these academics to write articles and books as long as they took the correct anti-Communist line. These chosen few were able to build reputations assisted by material fed to them on a plate. Crozier's memoirs explain how this worked. He was asked to write a report on Sino-Soviet subversion in the Third World for IRD and was provided with material from both GCHQ and MI6: 'After the document had been "sanitised" by the excision of secret material, I was allowed to take the scissored typescript home,' he said. The report formed the core of a further Background Book, *Struggle for the Third World* (1966). His next book, *The Future of Communist Power*, was written at IRD offices 'on the basis of a vast supply of classified documents'.[17]

The standard postwar text-book, *The Theory and Practice of Communism* by R.N. Carew Hunt, was prompted by Mayhew. It provided the MI6/IRD officer Carew Hunt with academic respectability. An even more glaring example was that of Robert Conquest. Now based at Stanford University in California, Conquest has the reputation as a leading Sovietologist and is the author of *The Great Terror*, a renowned critique of Stalin. Conquest was employed by the Foreign Office and was on the staff of IRD from 1946 to 1956, before pursuing his successful academic career. According to an ex-IRD official, Conquest produced a huge amount of IRD's early briefing papers and was 'one of our success stories'. After leaving IRD he was able to offer publishers Bodley Head a series of eight books on 'Soviet studies'. These established his reputation. In a later interview he was to admit that much of the material had come from IRD: 'There was very little writing to be done. Only bridging passages really.'[18]

The effect of the Cold War on British academia is a relatively unexplored subject and, despite ideals of academic freedom, there is no doubt that some academics waged the Cold War with fervour. Leonard Schapiro, who was at the London School of Economics (LSE), wrote or contributed to four Background Books as well as number nine in Ampersand's Bellman Books series. Schapiro, 'Professor of Political Science, with Special Reference to Russian Studies', was to become one of the most prominent Cold War Warriors. Born in Glasgow in 1908, he had been called to the bar in the 1930s. From 1940 to 1942 he worked at the BBC monitoring service at Caversham. He then joined the War Office and was in the intelligence division of the German Control Commission from 1945 to 1946 with the substantive rank of major. He returned to practise at the bar, writing extensively for IRD, before joining the LSE in 1955. According to Stephen Watts, Schapiro also suggested several possible authors to him.

Maurice Cranston, professor of political science at the LSE (1969–85), contributed three titles to the series and edited one other. This was *A Glossary of Political Terms* (1966), which included contributions by H.B. Acton and Schapiro. The LSE and especially Schapiro formed a centre for anti-Communist academics. Robert Conquest had a research fellowship at the LSE in the 1950s and the LSE became a centre of 'Sovietology'. Another leading academic, Max Beloff of Oxford University, later the Principal of the University of Buckingham, also wrote a Background Book. However, when contacted in 1995, Lord Beloff replied, 'After forty years one's memory tends to fade. I do not think I wrote any other book for the series and do not know whether or not I knew the series was sponsored by the IRD about whose role I also know nothing.'[19] He was made a life peer by Mrs Thatcher in 1981.

At St Antony's College, Oxford, which had extremely good contacts with the intelligence community, the Soviet Studies Department was headed by an ex-SOE man called David Footman. Places were found for anti-Communist émigrés such as John Erikson, who wrote a book on the Red Army. However, Foreign Office interventions were not confined to the promotion of the work of 'suitable' academics. Direct action was taken to ensure ideological conformity. For example, according to Professor Donald Cameron-Watt, in the early 1950s, at the height of the Cold War, a number of 'fellow travellers' were purged from the School of Slavonic Studies, while a new director was brought in from outside.

If the British can be commended for not entering a McCarthyite witch hunt against Communists in public institutions – Churchill resisted any such suggestions – this must be tempered by consideration of the efficacy of the informal British system in finding out if an individual, in Mrs Thatcher's words, is 'one of us'. This system used (and uses) a system of subtle checks, like an individual's school, college, as well as informal guarantors to ensure someone with the 'wrong' views does not get the job. Besides keeping generations of talent from the 'wrong' social classes out of positions of power, this system could and did go spectacularly wrong, as in the case of the Cambridge Spy Ring. The IRD system was equally informal and beneficial for those who were deemed suitable to partake. Academics would not only benefit from publishing deals but more importantly would also gain access to otherwise unavailable information and research on which they could build. As any modern academic will tell you, the number of papers and books you publish is crucial to your chances of furthering your career.

During the 1950s IRD took a move to the right and the tone of its output gradually changed. A Conservative government was elected in 1951 and was to remain in power for thirteen years. Even the Suez disaster only resulted in a change of prime minister rather than of administration. The number of IRD writers with left-of-centre credentials dropped off as there was no longer a need to pay lip service to social democracy. They were replaced by a more right-wing tendency of Cold War Warriors who saw all Soviet politicians as Stalinists.

By 1960 the IRD inner circle had settled down to a small dedicated band of professional Cold Warriors. They included Brian Crozier, Leonard Schapiro, Hugh Seton-Watson, Maurice Cranston, Leo Labedz and Michael Goodwin, and they were sceptical of any softening of tone from Moscow or Beijing, or indications of a desire to loosen Cold War tensions. They were in a strong position to influence British responses to Moscow. Their position on, for example, Krushchev's 'peaceful coexistence', like Mayhew's, was sceptical.

The effect of all of these operations was staggering. If it was the American free marketers who first realized that think tanks were an effective way of hothousing intellectual traditions, it was the British state that first realized that, by backing potential opinion formers, you could alter the political spectrum. According to historian Christopher Lasch, 'The modern state is . . . an engine of propaganda, alternatively manufacturing crises and claiming to be the only instrument which can effectively deal with them. This propaganda, in order to be successful, demands the co-operation of writers, teachers, and artists not as paid propagandists . . . but as "free" intellectuals capable of policing there own jurisdictions and of enforcing acceptable standards of responsibility within various intellectual professions.'

The IRD had it both ways. Selected journalists and academics who had the resources of the British intelligence service and the Foreign Office at their disposal artificially enhanced their reputations. But IRD was also able to promote the reputation of its own people by slipping them in among the more respectable academics that graced its article and book lists. In addition, IRD's coterie of writers and academics were brought to the attention of American Cold War circles, which in turn could enhance their academic and media reputations even further.

However, throughout it all there were always hidden hands pulling the financial and ideological strings, and they stretched across the Atlantic from Langley, Virginia.

CHAPTER FOURTEEN

A Mirror Image:
the CIA

Four days after North Korea had invaded South Korea and the Cold War had suddenly become hot, 15,000 people gathered in the Frankturm Gardens in the British sector of Berlin. The crowd was addressed by Arthur Koestler, ex-Communist and author of the seminal anti-Communist novel *Darkness at Noon*, who ended his speech with the declaration, in German, 'Friends, freedom has seized the offensive!'[1] Koestler told his Berlin audience, poignantly a small piece of the West just behind the Iron Curtain, that 'the theory and practice of the totalitarian state are the greatest challenge which man has been called upon to meet in the course of civilised history . . . indifference or neutrality in the face of such a challenge amounts to a betrayal of mankind and to the abdication of the free mind'.[2] As historian Paul Kennedy noted, 'There was to be no middle way in an age of Stalin and Joe McCarthy.'[3]

The rally and Koestler's speech, which launched an anti-Communist, anti-neutralist 'Freedom Manifesto', was the culmination of the first international assembly of anti-Communist intellectuals, called the Congress for Cultural Freedom (CCF). The Congress had been sponsored by *Der Monat*, a cultural magazine published by the US occupation government and edited by Melvin Lasky, a short, stocky 29-year-old American with a Lenin-type beard who had worked on the staff of the American anti-Communist fortnightly *New Leader*. In August 1949, Lasky had met in Frankfurt with ex-Communists Franz Borkenau and Ruth Fischer, the former leader of the German Communist Party. There they had come up with the idea of the conference. Fischer outlined the plan to a friend:

> It should be a gathering of all ex-Communists, plus a good representative group of anti-Stalinist American, English, and European intellectuals, declaring its sympathy for Tito and Yugoslavia and the silent opposition in Russia and the satellite states, and giving the Politburo hell right at the gate of their own hell. . . . It would create great possibilities for co-operation afterwards and would also lift the spirits of Berlin anti-Stalinists, which are somewhat fallen at present.[4]

The small organizing group was soon joined by an Estonian American called Michael Josselson who, after working as an interrogator in a psychological warfare section of the US Army in Europe during the war, had stayed on in Berlin to work for the US occupation government. Josselson, a brilliant administrator and organizer, set about helping the conference to become reality. Under his influence it took on a less explicitly political, broader cultural complexion. Invitations were sent out for 26 June 1950 and a distinguished group of philosophers, including Bertrand Russell; the Italian Benedetto Croce and the American John Dewey were approached.[5]

When the congress convened in Berlin, there was an impressive array of Western intellectual, political, scientific and literary individuals. Delegates from the United States included historian Arthur Schlesinger Jr, philosopher Sidney Hook, playwright Tennessee Williams, actor Robert Montgomery and ex-Communist James Burnham. British delegates included philosopher A.J. Ayer, historian Hugh Trevor-Roper and politician Julian Amery. Many delegates were active in the movement for a European Union, such as Denis de Rougemont, Francois Bondy and Altiero Spinelli. Eastern European émigrés included Nicholas Nabokov and the editor of an obscure US fortnightly magazine called the *New Leader*, Sol Levitas. Messages of support were received from André Gide, John Dos Passos, Upton Sinclair, George Grosz and English politician Richard Crossman.

As soon as the congress started, it polarized into factions representing different views on confronting the totalitarian threat. The first was led by Arthur Koestler; the other by the Italian socialist Ignazio Silone. Koestler had already led a varied and active political career, which had led him in turn though Zionism and Communism before his renunciation of Communism in the late 1930s. While in the Communist Party, Koestler had worked underground in Germany, in Spain during the Civil War and in Paris at the office of the World Committee for the Relief of the Victims of German Fascism. This was run by the infamous Willy Muenzenberg, Comintern propaganda chief in Western Europe, and the organization had been the first major Soviet front organization in Western Europe.[6] Koestler's rejection of Communism, expressed most dramatically and influentially in *Darkness at Noon*, was to be as deep and as militant as his previous involvement in it. Koestler was an extremist in an age of extremes.

Ignazio Silone was also an ex-Communist who had joined, together with Antonio Gramsci, when the Italian party was formed in 1921. Silone had become not only a member of the party's Central Committee, but also a member of the Executive of the Communist International. His break with Communism arose from his refusal to condemn Trotsky, which led to his expulsion in 1931. Silone, unlike Koestler, remained a Socialist and served two years as a Socialist deputy in the Italian Constituent Assembly following liberation. In 1942 Silone had written that 'The most important of our moral tasks today consists in liberating our spirits from the racket of gunfire, the trajectory of propaganda warfare and journalistic nonsense in general'.[7] In 1950 he was reluctant to go to Berlin, suspecting that it was a US State Department operation.[8]

Both Koestler and Silone gave opening speeches. While Silone saw the congress as offering the opportunity to reach across national frontiers and urged that the best way to oppose Communism was to promote social and political reform to undermine Communism's moral advantage, Koestler advocated a more aggressive strategy. It was Koestler's sentiments that carried the congress.[9] Koestler castigated the imbeciles who advocated neutrality and more or less called for Communist Parties in the West to be banned. Actor Robert Montgomery argued in a blunt Hollywood sound bite that 'There is no neutral corner in Freedom's room.'[10] The Russian émigré composer and writer Nicholas Nabokov declared that 'Out of this Congress we must build an organization for war. We must have a standing committee. We must see to it that it calls on all figures, all fighting organizations and all methods of fighting, with a view to action. If we do not, we will sooner or later all be hanged. The hour has struck twelve.'[11] Picking up on Koestler's anti-neutralist theme on 28 June, British economist and journalist Richard Lowenthal described the idea of Europe as a 'Third Force', 'as dangerous an illusion as an unarmed neutrality which is simply another name for submission.'[12]

Reactions to the CCF were varied and in some cases, even in Western Europe, hostile. In the *Manchester Guardian*, Hugh Trevor-Roper, who had attended the conference and had subscribed to the resulting manifesto, wrote with some concern of 'Hysterical German applause . . . echoes from Hitler's Nuremberg . . . anti-Russian, perhaps ex-Nazi, and hysterical with a frontier hysteria.'[13] Following Trevor-Roper's article, Bertrand Russell announced that he would be withdrawing from the position he had accepted as one of the honorary chairmen of the Congress's International Committee. Koestler and Arthur J. Schlesinger Jr visited Russell and managed to persuade him otherwise. In a letter to Russell, written the following day, Koestler thanked Russell profusely and outlined his analysis of the situation:

> Both Arthur Schlesinger and I were very happy about the result of our pilgrimage to you. Your withdrawal from the Congress would have caused other members of the Committee to wonder why, and would probably have brought the roof down over our heads. The whole thing is still a very tender plant; we have little money, only a scant paid personnel and no Cominform behind us. But if we can produce results during the next six months, support will grow rapidly, for there is a vacuum in Europe and a reasonable chance that we can fill it.[14]

Nabokov's call for a permanent organization was answered. Despite the lack of money referred to by Koestler, the CCF was placed on a permanent footing with an executive committee, a secretariat based in Paris and national affiliates in countries around the world. Swiss philosopher Denis de Rougemont was made president, Nabokov became secretary-general and Josselson executive director, while Koestler, Silone and American labour leader Irving Brown all became members of the executive committee. A programme of activities, including conferences, festivals of art and the establishment of a range of literary magazines to act as forums for anti-Communist, liberal intellectuals, were soon under way. At its height, the CCF would employ 280 members of staff, have representatives in thirty-five countries organizing conferences and seminars, as well a network of sponsored journals.[15]

These journals were presented as independent entities, although they were financed by the CCF. Josselson later claimed, 'The journals were not organs of any movement. We wanted to provide people with a platform. Of course, we decided who to cultivate; we wanted to put over exciting ideas over a wide spectrum. We didn't expect these people to be our spokesmen. We excluded only the extreme right and the extreme left. We all had a common interest in freedom of expression.'[16] Journals set up by the CCF included *Preuves* in France and *Quest* in India, but the most influential of the CCF journals was set up in the UK in 1953. *Encounter*, the CCF secretariat decided, was to be as much literary as political, and Irving Kristol and the poet Stephen Spender were chosen as its first editors. Kristol arrived in the UK from New York, where he had been assistant editor of *Commentary* and developed something of a reputation as an anti-Communist polemicist. In a *Commentary* article in 1952 entitled 'Civil Liberties, 1952 – a Study in Confusion', Kristol had made the controversial statement that 'there is one thing that the American people know about Senator McCarthy: he like them, is unequivocally anti-Communist. About the spokesmen for American liberalism; they feel they know no such thing. And with some justification.'[17]

Following discussions with Josselson and representations by a number of British associates of the CCF, including Tosco Fyvel and Malcolm Muggeridge, it had been agreed that *Encounter* would be published by Secker & Warburg as an independent journal sponsored by the CCF. Most important, it was agreed that there would no official editorial board to guide the editors. The CCF originally wanted closer control over the journal and had wanted it to concentrate on reaching areas such as Scandinavia and the Far East where, Nabokov told Kristol, 'neutralism is the strongest force'.[18] The objections of the editors and the CCF's British associates won through. As Spender told the CCF's executive committee, 'There was amongst the English intellectuals a suspicion of, and instinctive aversion against, all official or semi-official publications of organizations.'[19] Independence was crucial to the journal's success.

Despite the lack of any overt direction from Paris, some of the themes and issues taken up by the new magazine, when the first issue came out in October 1953, were strikingly similar to those of the CCF. The first 10,000 issues sold out and *Encounter* swiftly became 'the first, the best monthly review in English'.[20] Historian of the CCF, Peter Coleman wrote that, by 1958, even Graham Hough and A.J.P. Taylor – another early critic – were contributing, and Kristol and Spender were able to inform Paris that 'circulation had almost reached sixteen thousand . . . a larger circulation than any comparable monthly review in the English language.'[21]

The reason for this success was partially a result of a toning down of the political and consequential increase in the journal's literary content. However, also, unlike other journals, *Encounter* was able to pay substantial fees to its writers. Journalist Andrew Roth recalled that, at a time when academics and other writers were 'writing articles for £30, *Encounter* was paying up to £200'. Appearing in *Encounter* could also lead to invitations to speak on the American lecture circuit for substantial fees.[22]

By 1963 the magazine's circulation had reached more than 34,000 per issue, which was without doubt substantial for a publication of its type.[23] Despite its literary feel, where politics were concerned *Encounter* maintained and developed some permanent anti-Communist themes. For example, in the June 1955 issue, the ex-ambassador of Britain to Moscow, Sir David Kelly, made the direct connection between the Communist and the Nazi threat: 'The lamentable slowness of the Western peoples and governments in realizing the true nature of the Soviet threat, and in laying the foundations of the Atlantic Union, is not dissimilar to the slowness of the same people in realising the nature of the Nazi menace between 1932 and 1939.'[24] Communism, personified by the Soviet Union, was consistently presented as expansionary and offensive in contrast with the West, which was presented as essentially defensive. In

1958 Peregrine Worsthorne argued that, 'When they write of "victory", they do not mean, as does the West, a mere avoidance of defeat. They have in mind a victory that would result in the spread of Communist control over the conquered area.'[25]

More generally, however, anti-Communism took the form of a marked concentration on the problems of the USSR and Eastern Europe – the oppression of intellectuals in particular – often within articles that were primarily concerned with poetry, literature and music. For example, Nabokov's exposé of the effects of totalitarianism on music in the USSR, 'No Cantatas for Stalin',[26] and the regular series of articles edited by Leopold Labedz, 'From the Other Shore', which first appeared in 1957.[27] According to Coleman, this regular column was highly successful and was distributed separately around the world.[28]

The reaction to unilateralism, as propagated by CND and many on the Labour Party's left wing, was predominantly, if not uniformly, hostile in the pages of *Encounter*. In his article 'Bombs and scapegoats', David Marquand argued that unilateralism was an emotional rather than a rational position to take. It was, 'Useless to argue that nuclear weapons are not the chief cause of world tensions; that although the British people . . . might prefer Communism to war, millions of people in far less fortunate countries do not; that if no nuclear weapons existed, bacteriological weapons might be used instead. . . . Useless to argue so – useless, in fact, to argue at all. One cannot argue with an emotion.'[29]

Under Lasky's editorship from 1957 onwards, *Encounter* became increasingly interested in Africa. Following a tour of Africa suggested by Josselson, Lasky edited a series of articles on Africa for *Encounter* and the journal began regularly to publish articles on the subject by Elspeth Huxley, Colin Legum, Dan Jacobson and Rita Hinden.[30] Under Lasky, *Encounter* also moved closer to the Gaitskellite wing of the Labour Party and by the early 1960s had become one of its main forums for discussion.[31] In 1960, Lasky was able to write to John Hunt that 'Gaitskell has been very glad of our support and has written to me personally to express that gratitude.'[32] Richard Fletcher, who was active in the Labour Party at the time, argued that *Encounter*, through acting as a platform for Labour politicians such as Anthony Crosland, Denis Healey and Hugh Gaitskell in their campaigns to move the Labour Party towards the right and away from nationalization and unilateralism, played an important part in undermining the British Left.[33]

Anthony Crosland was one of the most influential Labour leaders to write for *Encounter* and become involved in the CCF, many of the conferences and seminars of which he attended. Between 1950 and 1960 the CCF sponsored forty-three international conferences in locations that included Beyrouth in West Germany, Tunis, Rangoon and Mexico. Topics included Science and Freedom (Hamburg, 1953), Islam in the Modern World (Karachi, 1959) and Changes in Soviet Society (St Antony's College, Oxford, 1957).[34] It was at a CCF conference that Crosland met the American Daniel Bell, formerly managing director of the *New Leader*. Bell was in the process of developing the ideas that he would publish under the title *The End of Ideology*. His thesis was that growing economic affluence had in effect made the traditional working class indistinguishable from the middle class. Consequently, Marxist theories of class struggle were redundant and the Socialist project would now be limited to the gradual reform of capitalism in the direction of further welfare and equality on the back of economic growth.[35] Crosland was undoubtedly influenced by Bell's ideas, which were evident in his seminal work *The Future of Socialism* (1956).

In an article in the French *L'Observateur* in 1950, commenting on the CCF's first congress in Berlin, Michéle Barat described the gathering as 'A political manifestation, an enormous demonstration of America's will to fight the Soviet power on every level: that was what the Congress was about, notwithstanding the presence of many a man of good will who had come in all good faith to talk about spiritual matters and the defence of cultural freedom.' Barat was scathing about Koestler's speech, which he described as 'an impassioned attack against the fundamental principles of intellectual freedom, i.e. tolerance and respect for the thought of others . . . in the name of democracy and liberty.'[36]

Barat was far closer to the truth than he ever probably realized. In 1966 the *New York Times* ran an article on CIA operations that contained the revelation that '*Encounter* magazine, a well known anti-Communist intellectual monthly with editions in Spanish and German, as well as English, was for a long time – though it is not now – one of the indirect beneficiaries of CIA funds through arrangements that have never been publicly explained.'[37] The article caused outrage, particularly in the Third World, although in Europe the CCF and *Encounter* tried to ride out the protests. Nabokov issued a statement denying that the CCF had 'ever knowingly received support, directly or indirectly from any secret source'. Kristol, Lasky and Spender wrote to the *New York Times* that they knew 'of no "indirect" benefactions'.[38] Legal action was threatened by the CCF, but the London *Times* did not include any mention of *Encounter* in its reportage and it seemed that the story had died.

In early 1967 the CCF and *Encounter* received a second blow. A small radical monthly magazine published in San Francisco called *Ramparts* had uncovered how the CIA had used various charitable foundations as routes for covert funds. The focus quickly widened as CIA conduits were identified and the CCF once again found itself in the firing line as even such a notable non-Communist as Walter Lippmann called for the abandonment of the CIA's 'totalitarian method'.[39] Then, in May, further – unquestionable – light on the involvement of the CIA was cast by ex-CIA bureaucrat Tom Bradon, who wrote an article for the *Saturday Evening Post* entitled 'I'm glad the CIA is "immoral".'

Bradon joined the CIA in 1950 as assistant to the deputy director of the CIA, Allen W. Dulles, at a crucial point in the agency's development. Like IRD, the CIA was confronted with the threat of the Soviet 'Peace Offensive'. Bradon recalled, 'It seemed to me that this organization [the CIA] was not capable of defending the United States against a new and extraordinarily successful weapon. The weapon was the international Communist front.'[40] Bradon's strategy was to fight fire with fire. Late one day he went to see Dulles. 'I told him I thought the CIA ought to take on the Russians by penetrating a battery of international fronts.'[41] Dulles agreed, and three months later the International Organisation Division of the CIA was established to conduct a centralized offensive against the Soviet fronts. Central to the strategy were what became know as the non-Communist left (NCL). In the midst of the anti-Communist hysteria then sweeping the United States, Bradon recognized that 'the very people who many

Americans thought no better than Communists – were the only people who gave a damn about fighting Communism.'[42] Within the context of the Cold War there was a clear need to ensure the support and acceptance of Western intellectuals for a US inspired agenda, which included 'commitment . . . to a strong, well-armed, and united Western Europe, allied to the United States, which would stand as a bulwark against the Soviet bloc; support for the Common Market . . . [and] . . . advancing the cause of NATO.'[43]

It was a need that the British had also perceived, and Brian Crozier, who later worked for the CIA as well as IRD, has suggested a British dimension to the origins of the CCF. 'The British had suggested to the CIA that it would be a good idea to provide a broader intellectual haven for Western writers. . . . The Americans had responded with characteristic generosity, and the CCF was born in 1950.'[44]

Bradon, whose article was written in defence of the CIA's methods, made the revelation that the CIA 'had placed one agent in a Europe-based organization called the Congress for Cultural Freedom. Another agent became an editor of *Encounter*.' Bradon continued, 'The agents could not only propose anti-Communist programs to the official leaders of the organizations but they could also suggest ways and means to solve the inevitable budgetary problems. Why not see if the needed money could be obtained from "American foundations"? As the agents knew, the CIA-financed foundations were quite generous when it came to the national interest.'[45] One of them, Michael Josselson, resigned as executive director of the CCF.

Despite apparent editorial independence and in spite of frequent pressure applied from Paris, 'For Josselson the important thing was to have editors in whom he had confidence; the problems could then be sorted out as they arose.'[46] Unlike Soviet propaganda fronts, the CIA fronts were not expected to follow every twist and turn of US policy. The men who set them up had a much more sophisticated conception of how their operations would work. In his 1967 article, Bradon outlined the golden rule: 'disguise the extent of American interest; protect the integrity of the organization by not requiring it to support every aspect of official American policy'.[47] According to the minutes of a meeting held in 1968 of the Discussion Group on Intelligence and Foreign Policy (those present included representatives of the CIA, including Allen Dulles, businessmen, reporters, and military representatives), Richard Bissel of the CIA observed 'It is notably true of the subsidies to . . . cultural groups that have recently been publicised that the Agency's objective was never to control their activities, only occasionally to point them in a certain direction, but primarily to enlarge them and render them more effective.'[48]

What problems there were between the CCF and the editors of *Encounter* were, as often as not, tactical disagreements rather than disagreements over what the magazine was trying to achieve. In defence of criticisms that the magazine was not strident enough in its approach in 1955 Malcolm Muggeridge wrote, 'I can quite see that the Congress might wish it to be more specifically and voluminously ideological, but I am equally certain that, given the circumstances prevailing in this country and in Asia, this would be a mistake and would undermine the magazine's very real utility.'[49] The debate ended with general agreement that *Encounter* should sharpen its political edge.[50]

As well as raising criticisms of *Encounter* with Spender and Kristol in 1955, Josselson asked Norman Jacobs, chief political commentator on The Voice of America, to prepare a report on *Encounter* and its perceived failure to combat British anti-Americanism. Jacobs' report praised *Encounter* as the best of its kind in the English language but he did complain that it failed to combat the cliché that all Americans were 'barbarians' and that *Encounter* did not present its readers ' . . . with a sympathetic understanding of the role America must play as leader of the free world coalition'.[51]

Encounter survived the revelations of CIA involvement in 1966 and 1967. Although Stephen Spender resigned, Melvin Lasky remained as editor, insisting that he was not a CIA agent. Under the direction of Josselson, *Encounter* had found a new sponsor in the form of the International Publishing Corporation, which published the *Daily Mirror*, and broke its financial dependence on the CIA. That this support had been necessary is clear. According to Ray Cline, a former CIA executive, the magazines, including *Encounter*, that were born out of the CCF 'would not have been able to survive financially without CIA funds'.[52] During the early 1950s, according to Tom Bradon, the CIA 'budget for the Congress of Cultural Freedom . . . was about $800–$900,000, which included . . . the subsidy for the Congress's magazine *Encounter*.'[53] By the mid-1950s the CCF was being subsidized to the tune of around $1 million a year.[54] The covert funding of the CCF lasted until at least 1966, and that of *Encounter* until 1964, when its finances were placed on less embarrassing foundations as it became clear that the CIA connection would soon be exposed.

Over the following ten years the sheer extent of CIA propaganda operations including CCF gradually became apparent. In 1976 the Congressional Pike Committee outlined the extent of these operations: 'Activities have included support of friendly media, major propaganda efforts, insertion of articles into the local press, and distribution of books and leaflets.'[55] By the late 1960s, media and propaganda projects were absorbing over a third of the CIA's covert action budget. The emphasis was on clandestine propaganda, infiltration and manipulation of youth, labour and cultural organizations.' Included in the propaganda arsenal was Radio Liberty and the Voice of America which by 1950 was transmitting around 850 hours per week in over thirty-four languages as part of the international propaganda campaign.[56] The extent of these programmes was such that the CIA found itself operating in areas that, according to Tom Bradon, the Russians had not even entered. Bradon has, for example, been unable to identify an operation similar to that of *Encounter* carried out by the Soviets in Western Europe.[57]

These operations must be seen as complementing other CIA covert operations as well as those run by IRD. During the immediate postwar period, they were concentrated in Western Europe owing to the perceived threat of Communist expansion through indigenous Communist Parties and included subsidies to political parties, individual leaders and trade unions. For example, in 1947, in response to strikes led by the Communist-led French trade union Confédération Générale du Travail, Jay Lovestone and Irving Brown had helped to organize a non-Communist union, Force Ouvrière. This supposedly independent, 'free' trade union was soon being financed by the CIA.[58] Lovestone had been the leader of the American Communist Party before the war, but had switched allegiance to the US government for whom he worked during the war. According to Richard Fletcher, 'Through its network of front organizations, magazines, an subsidies, the CIA in the late fifties and early sixties had a decisive effect on socialism throughout Western Europe, and in Britain in particular.'[59]

Individually, the various CIA operations were probably not enough to make a decisive impact on any one country's political landscape, but, cumulatively, the effect could be enormous, as extreme cases like Chile demonstrate. As Richard Bissell recognized, 'Covert intervention is probably most effective in situations where a comprehensive effort is undertaken with a number of separate operations designed to have a cumulatively significant effect.'[60] In Britain the CIA was no less active than elsewhere.

The CIA helped to set up and fund numerous youth organizations in opposition to established international organizations, which were perceived as being Communist fronts. These included the International Student Confederation and the European Youth Campaign, which was almost entirely funded from the CIA purse. Pro-US politicians, notably in Italy and Germany, were also generously funded and their campaign's were backed by those of the CIA. Left-wing politicians found themselves outspent or even smeared by CIA dirty tricks. Most of those politicians supported by the CIA were not on the right wing of the political spectrum but were right-wing Social Democrats. As Michael Ivens, ex-head of the right-wing pressure group, Aims in Industry, complained: 'The CIA's decision, in the '60s certainly, was that there was no future for the conservative parties in Europe, they were washed out, they were finished. So therefore they ought to back the labour parties, the social democratic parties, this kind of thing.'[61]

The *bête noire* of the British radical left, Brian Crozier was to make another astonishing appearance in the publicity surrounding the CIA's activities. In 1975 the British *Time Out*, then a radical London listings magazine, obtained a memo written in 1968 addressed to the Director of Central Intelligence, Richard Helms. The memo was an operational summary for a CIA propaganda front based in London called Forum World Features (FWF). According to the memo:

> Forum World Features is an international news feature service located in London and incorporated in Delaware whose overt aim is to provide on a commercial basis a comprehensive weekly service covering international affairs, economics, science and medicine, book reviews and other subjects of a general nature. In its first two years FWF has provided the United States with a significant means to counter Communist propaganda, and has become a respected feature service well on the way to a position of prestige in the journalism world.[62]

The FWF had its origins as a media off-shoot of the CCF. The CCF had had three features services: Forum Information Service based in London and Preuves-Informations and El Mundo en Español based at CCF headquarters in Paris. Forum, which had developed from an earlier CCF information service, Information Bulletin Ltd in around 1960, was managed by an American book editor called Mier Mindlin. The editorial director was Melvin Lasky. The service was provided free, usually copyright cleared, and was presented as 'a service for friends, editors, and writers who follow the world-wide issues of cultural freedom'.

Most Forum writers were European and mainly British. They included Rita Hinden, who in the early 1960s was editing the right-wing Labour journal *Socialist Commentary*, financial journalist Douglas Evans and, on one occasion, a radical academic at London University's School of Oriental and African Studies, Malcolm Caldwell. Caldwell, whose specialist area was Indonesia, was asked to write a piece on Sukarno. His article, in which he had attempted to convey a sympathetic understanding of Sukarno's anti-Western nationalism, appeared in an Indian newspaper with a completely different angle. He was outraged and told *Time Out* that 'they actually added material without telling me and completely changed the slant of the story, turning it into a smear'. An article by Douglas Evans that was critical of the Common Market was rejected as too technical.[63]

In early 1964, Anthony Hartley of the CCF approached Brian Crozier with the offer of a job. The CCF wanted Crozier to take over the CCF's features services and to commercialize them. Crozier refused but agreed to visit South America to meet local representatives of the CCF affiliate and to compile a report on the CCF's Spanish language service. As well as producing two articles for *Encounter*, Crozier covered the area for the *Sunday Times* and the BBC.[64] A year later, the CCF renewed its approach to Crozier. Despite disagreements about the degree of independence from the CCF that the new service would enjoy, Crozier agreed. In his fascinating autobiographical history, *Free Agent*, he revealed that his acceptance of the offer was prompted by his knowledge that the CCF was a CIA operation. He wrote that his MI6 contact and friend, 'Ronald Frank', had told him that the CCF was CIA.[65]

The new press service, FWF, was set up in offices on Kingsway in London with a holding company called Kern House Enterprises Inc, registered in Delaware as a front for CIA funding. Initial finance was provided by a terminal grant from the CCF and an estimated $100,000 provided by the CIA via Kern House Enterprises, owned by ex-US Ambassador to London John Hay Whitney. In charge of the sensitive financial management of the operation was Charles Johnson, whom Crozier soon discovered to be CIA.[66] Another CIA man involved was 'case officer' Gene Gately, the FWF's vice-president and treasurer.[67]

The free service was dropped, although low rates were maintained for Third World editors. The staff, who had been restricted to Mindlin and a secretary, were increased to more than twenty. New services, including Chinese and Spanish, were started and new writers of a more conservative political stance were brought in by Crozier including Anthony P. Hartley of *The Economist* and Henry Farlie of the London *Daily Mail*.[68]

The main target area for FWF's material was the Third World. The FWF provided two types of article: longer, signed pieces and shorter, unsigned pieces on current news or research. By the time FWF was launched in January 1966, it had obtained some forty contracts for the service, including one from the *Sydney Morning Herald*. According to Crozier, the aim was to provide 'first-class background coverage to pre-empt space that might otherwise go to Communist disinformation. There was no ban on selling the service in Western countries, apart from America, but this was not the main point of the exercise'.[69] By the late 1960s the FWF was providing a service that was no longer limited to news media in the Third World. In Britain the service was taken by the *Guardian* and the *Sunday Times* and the FWF had become 'perhaps the most widely circulated of the CIA-owned news services.'[70]

An early contributor to the service who witnessed the change from Forum to FWF was American journalist Russell Warren Howe, who in the late 1950s covered Africa for the *Washington Post*. In 1958 Russell was invited to a CCF seminar on 'Progress and Representative Government' in Nigeria by Melvin Lasky. Following the seminar, which he attended, Russell was contacted by Mindlin, who asked him to contribute to the then Bulletin service. Russell agreed and over the next seven years contributed about thirty articles. Russell later wrote, 'I was included, with my *Post* credentials and free-spirit, liberal, but non-Marxist analyses of African affairs, to give balance and credibility to a service whose basic aim, presumably, was to counter Communist propaganda.'[71]

In June 1966, an article by a right-wing Polish émigré was put out by the FWF. The story, on Soviet influence in Somalia, purported to show that Moscow was supplying Somalia with 150 MiG-17 fighter-bombers. It was taken and printed by the *Guardian*. However, as *Time Out* pointed out, 'The real Somalian Air Force has perhaps 12 MiGs'.[72] Russell recalled that he had told Gately at the time that the story was 'bullshit', but it had gone out nevertheless.[73]

Crozier had also brought in BBC radio producer John Tusa as editor. Crozier recalled that 'Tusa had produced many of my own talks and discussion programmes, and I thought highly of him.'[74] Tusa was, like Russell, unwitting of the CIA connection and, despite Crozier's high regard for him, Tusa soon became a problem. According to Crozier, 'I had become increasingly critical of what seemed to me to be a pro-Soviet and anti-American bias. There were also, it is true, articles reflecting the American and Allied viewpoint, but it was clear that John Tusa and I were out of harmony on the definition of "balance".'[75] Years later, Tusa recalled being given a lecture by Crozier on the threat of world Communism when Crozier returned from a meeting in New York with Whitley and Gately.

The December 1966 meeting in New York was a key event. Gately left, and it had been made clear that, unless Tusa improved, he would have to go. According to Russell, 'it was also apparently decided that Forum should tell the "US side" of the Vietnam story.'[76] Crozier's CIA contact officer in London suggested, as a replacement for Tusa, Cecil Eprile. Although not considered particularly talented, Eprile told Crozier that, 'if appointed, he would be absolutely loyal to me in my absence and at all times. I offered him the job and he gave me [Crozier] no cause to regret it.'[77] Eprile demonstrated this to Tusa shortly before Tusa resigned and returned to a successful career with the BBC. Tusa 'was about to send out a positive piece about Soviet rural clinics. Eprile, Tusa said, "hit the roof", insisting on cuts, and leaving nothing that suggested that the Soviet system had any merits.'[78]

By 1970 Russell was worried by the increasingly political slant that the FWF was adopting. 'I could see that it was now taking a decidedly conservative slant – pro-Nixon, hawkish on Indochina, with articles urging "caution" on South Africa. There were frequent pieces by Crozier's highly conservative *Economist* friend, Robert Moss . . . and Lynn Price, a former Foreign Office man with a cold-war stance.'[79] The FWF was, by this point, not limiting itself to the provision of a features service, material for which was sometimes supplied by IRD via Crozier, but had gone into the book publishing business, just as IRD's output of books was declining.[80] Crozier recalled that IRD's

'Background Books series . . . was still useful, but I envisaged something sharper and stronger, with greater impact'. Crozier approached his MI6 and CIA contacts to discuss the project, of which they approved, the CIA agreeing to pick up any extra costs. In discussions with his unwitting publisher at Secker & Warburg the general title of *World Realities* was agreed and Crozier persuaded Lord Gladwyn to contribute the first edition, *De Gaulle's Europe or Why the General Says No*. Other editions in the series included *The Future of British Foreign Policy* by Max Beloff and *The Future of Soviet Foreign Policy* by Britain's ex-Ambassador to the USSR, Sir William Hayter.[81] The most controversial book to come out in the series was *Chile's Marxist Experiment* by ex-*Economist* journalist Robert Moss. A friend of Crozier and a regular contributor to the FWF, Moss visited Chile at the FWF's expense and wrote the book in 1972, conducting his research in the midst of a massive CIA campaign to destabilize Allende, Chile's Marxist president who had been democratically elected in 1970. Crozier recalled, 'The destabilization of the Allende regime in Chile was probably the last successful covert action undertaken by the CIA before the disaster of Watergate. I played a modest part in it, willingly and in what I considered a good cause.'[82] The CIA suggested a book on Chile and Crozier had commissioned Moss to write it.

The importance of the CIA's propaganda operation, which was coupled with economic destabilization, in preparing the way for the military coup that overthrew Allende was recognized by Moss who later wrote that 'The survival of a powerful opposition press and radio network in Chile was crucial to Allende's final defeat; it is scarcely an exaggeration to say that this was the nerve centre of the political opposition to Marxism.'[83]

CHAPTER FIFTEEN

The Fat Years: the 1960s

When the 1960s arrived, IRD found itself, once again, under the direction of Ralph Murray, who returned to the Foreign Office from a posting at the Cairo Embassy. Murray's new appointment was as joint superintending Under-Secretary of the Foreign Office's information departments together with Patrick Dean. The head of IRD was (later Sir) Donald Hopson. He had taken over the department in February of 1958, replacing John Rennie. Hopson, a highly decorated wartime commando had joined the Foreign Service in 1945. He had previously worked in IRD as assistant to John Peck in the early 1950s. Sheridan was still energetically in charge of the editorial section, wheeling and dealing with his shadowy contacts. In 1961 his cover as a 'public relations consultant' finally fell by the wayside when he received his one and only mention in the Foreign Office year book as an assistant head of IRD. Sheridan worked in the section, assisted by Josephine O'Connor Howe and H.H. 'Tommy' Tucker, both former journalists. Tucker had worked on both regional papers and the *Daily Telegraph* before joining the Foreign Office in 1951. Following a period with the Treasury's Economic Information Unit, Tucker would spend much of his career in IRD, before leaving in 1974 to become director of British Information Services in Canberra.

When Sheridan died relatively young in 1964, Tucker took over his job. Brian Crozier, whom Tucker persuaded to join IRD in 1964, recalled Tucker in his autobiography: 'Tommy, six and a half feet tall, and thin to match, had started as a journalist, then married into the Foreign Office. He was now, at thirty-eight, the youngest Counsellor in the foreign service. He was also shrewd and highly skilled.'[1]

O'Connor Howe joined IRD in 1952 at the instigation of her friend, John Peck. Following Oxford and a course in journalism, she had spent the war working for the Inter-Allied Information Committee, later the United Nations Information Office. After a year in the Hague for the Foreign Office, she worked on a freelance basis and for the International News Service. One of her jobs in IRD was as the editor of IRD's publication, *Digest*.

Another senior IRD figure of the period was Christopher 'Kit' Barclay. He started working for the Foreign Office in 1946 and served in Iraq, Egypt and Bonn, before joining the Information Policy Department as its adviser on the Middle East in 1953. In 1960 he served a year in Beirut as regional information officer before being transferred to IRD in 1961. In 1962 he became its new head, when Hopson left to become Ambassador to Laos. It was under Barclay's stewardship that IRD reached its zenith. By the mid-1960s it had about 400 staff – rather more than the original sixteen when files had to be stored in the bathrooms of Carlton House Terrace. The department had moved to new accommodation at Riverwalk House, a modern twelve-storey office block on the South Bank of the River Thames and rather distant from the rest of the Foreign Office. By now IRD's official budget was in the region of £1 million per year.[2] The real budget was far greater.

According to some IRD officials, however, IRD's size did not always translate into effectiveness. Norman Reddaway, who was to take overall responsibility for IRD in the early 1970s, recalled that, 'During the sixties IRD became fat and sluggish, unlike the days of its "lean team" of the late fifties. Its FCO Head from 1962–66 excelled at raising new, mostly secret vote money, for "research".'[3]

Whatever its value for money, during the 1960s, all of the IRD operations were at their peak. The news agencies were engaged in a last great flourish and the book publishing empire put out more volumes in the period than in any other. IRD continued to concentrate on its standard themes. Attention was paid to exploiting and attempting to widen the Sino-Soviet split. In April 1960 the split became a chasm when Mao allowed a series of polemics to be published in connection with the ninetieth anniversary of Lenin's birth. The Chinese accused Krushchev of 'revising, emasculating and betraying' Lenin's vision by endorsing cooperation with the West, the inevitability of war and the possibility that the Communists could come to power by non-violent means. IRD exploited the split and did everything in its power to open the wound wider. Organizationally, reflecting the increasingly worldwide scale of the Cold War, IRD was divided into two sections in 1958. From then on one section dealt with the Soviet bloc and another with areas of interest to IRD outside Eastern Europe.[4]

The department was still organized in terms of geographical desks, but, although its prime purpose was still the Soviet Union and the Eastern bloc, the development of the Third World as the main arena of the Cold War led to greater interest in IRD. Indeed, according to senior IRD officials, the Third World was taken 'extremely seriously' and the Vietnam War led to the significant growth of the South-East Asia desk.[5]

IRD material dealing with the Third World multiplied, but all with the same slant. For example, an IRD paper entitled 'East German Spearhead in Africa', dated August 1960, reported that, 'Current activities in Africa by several Communist States reflect international Communism's declared aim of extending its influence throughout the world.' It pointed out that 'The Communists are exploiting the inevitable reaction of newly-independent peoples against the former Colonial powers.' The briefing cited as evidence that an academic 'Institute in Leipzig . . . maintains "close links" with a number of developing countries.' Also, 'Since the beginning of 1959 at least 12 East German trade delegations have visited Africa.'[6]

In the early 1960s IRD also became involved in supporting wider media projects in the 'private' sector, including TV programmes which were for the first time becoming relevant as propaganda tools. When the government changed in 1964, Wilson's trusted ally, George Thomson presided over longer-term IRD activities, such as 'English by TV' in Iran, the Gulf, Sudan, Ethiopia and China. 'English by TV', started by the British Council in Tehran, was, taken up by IRD, broadcasting an English Language tuition programme to an estimated 100 million Chinese each week. The presenter, an

English girl by the name of Kathy Flower, was the best known foreigner in China. There was also disguised support for selected non-government organizations (NGOs), such as the Thomson and Ford Foundation.[7]

According to Sir Oliver Wright, a major concern was how to respond to Khrushchev's theory and offer of 'peaceful coexistence' between the Soviet bloc and the capitalist West. The offer of coexistence by Khrushchev, promoted by Soviet fronts around the world, from the late 1950s, was widely considered to be a continuation of Stalin's Peace Offensive following the Second World War. The potential success of Khrushchev's appeal prompted Christopher Mayhew into action. He had lost his seat in 1950 and ceased to be a Foreign Office minister. He had won Woolwich East in 1951 but, with his party, was out of power for thirteen years. Nevertheless, he kept in contact with IRD. Mayhew came up with the idea of 'coexistence Plus' in response and as a challenge to Krushchev's declaration that 'peaceful coexistence' was possible between the Communist and Capitalist systems, an idea that Mayhew believed the Soviets were having some propaganda success with. Mayhew explained that: 'What they meant by coexistence was not coexistence as you or I know it. It was the struggle without war between capitalism and Socialism in which all the forces of peace, freedom, etc. must be mobilised on the Socialist side to ensure the defeat of capitalism by non-military means. So I launched an alternative concept called coexistence Plus which meant coexistence plus ideological coexistence, and ideological coexistence is the exact antithesis of Marxism, at the same time it sounds rather decent.'

According to Mayhew, after he wrote an article in the *Guardian* about it, it was picked up by IRD, who 'did everything they possibly could to spread it'. IRD swiftly organized ministerial statements of support for the idea from the Conservative government. The Foreign Secretary, Alec Home, made a speech in its favour and it was taken up and pushed by the BBC Overseas Service. Publication of a 57-page book by Mayhew on the subject, by Bodley Head, was organized and IRD distributed 8,000 copies. Lord Mayhew believed that it was probably very useful in the Third World and claimed that this organized promotion of the idea provoked Krushchev to declare that ideological coexistence would be the death of Marxism.[8] The genesis and development of Mayhew's book is of some interest as its history illustrates how sponsored publishing could be integrated into a wider propaganda campaign using the various means at IRD's disposal.

Coexistence or not, 1962 was the year in which the Soviet Union and the United States took the world to the brink of nuclear conflagration. At the time, the Cuban Missile Crisis, despite Khrushchev's withdrawal of the missiles, seemed to indicate that an increasingly strong Soviet Union was ready to act even more belligerently than in the past. However, leading historians now believe that such a view was mistaken and that the Cuban Missile Crisis arose because Krushchev understood that the West was winning the Cold War. John Lewis Gaddis noted:

Kennan had predicted that its outcome would depend upon whether Western Europe and Japan . . . wound up within a Soviet or American sphere of influence. By 1961 that issue had been resolved: democratic politics and market economics had prevailed in the countries that counted. The Marxist-Leninist alternative retained its appeal in much of the 'third world', to be sure, but it lacked and capacity for coordinated action. Moscow might occasionally benefit from what happened there, as with Castro's revolution, but it could hardly create or control such opportunities.[9]

Following the crisis, a new kind of Cold War emerged. Soviet-American competition took on a degree of stability and predictability. Despite the intensification of the strategic arms race following the missile crisis, fuelled by the perceived humiliation of the USSR, the contest was conducted within a precise set of rules. These rules were codified in formal agreements, which included the Limited Nuclear Test Ban Treaty of 1963 and the Non-Proliferation Treaty of 1968. Equally important was the informal toleration of satellite reconnaissance (although there was not much either side could practically do about satellites). The Cold War evolved, at least at superpower level, into a 'peaceful' international system of military coexistence.[10] On the ideological level, as Gaddis recognized in retrospect, 'Moscow's economic, ideological, cultural, and moral example had largely lost its appeal by 1962, leaving only military strength as an effective means of projecting influence.'[11] Nevertheless, at the time this was not widely perceived. For good or for ill, the Communist bloc and the West were locked into an ideological struggle from which neither was prepared, or perhaps able, to escape. The war of words went on, nowhere more so than in IRD. Krushchev's climb-down over Cuba and his attempts to find rapprochement with the West led to his downfall. In 1964 a putsch was organized by hardliners, led by Brezhnev. The Soviet Union returned to a more confrontational stance, not only towards the West but also towards mounting deviationalism in its own satellite territories.

In this period IRD was particularly close to MI6. From 1966 until 1969 the Head of IRD was Nigel Clive. Clive was another appointment to IRD from outside the Foreign Office mainstream. Following wartime service with MI6 in Greece, where he worked with the resistance and the SOE, Clive became a full-time MI6 career officer. Although by definition a secret career, details have surfaced in relation to his role during the Suez Crisis, when he was MI6's Political Officer. A contemporary of Chris Mayhew's at Oxford, Clive had known and approved of IRD since its inception in 1947. Seeking out and exposing Soviet meddling was Clive's speciality and chief interest, making him particularly suited to his position as IRD's Head. A close focus was maintained on attacking and exposing Brezhnev's Soviet Union. According to one IRD official, 'It was a number one priority.'[12] The same official confirmed that, as in the cases of Cyprus and Kenya, IRD's interest in any given conflict or situation was in tracing and exposing any Soviet involvement, which was useful for ensuring the US 'understanding' of the British position.[13]

A major opportunity to go on the offensive against the Soviet Union was provided by the Soviets themselves when they invaded Czechoslovakia in 1968. The Soviet invasion may have been greeted with horror around the world, but in Riverwalk House it met with a far from negative reception. One senior IRD official recalled, 'I remember people turning round and saying "Oh, this is too awful for words." And I said, "From one point of view, from a Czech point of view I entirely agree . . . but from where I am sitting I am rubbing my hands. Proves how bloody right I've been all this time!"'[14]

MI6's relationship with IRD reached a new level with the appointment of Clive. Now MI6 had one of its own in charge of the department. Sanitized MI6 material continued to be used by IRD. Liaison was 'formal' cooperation rather than a structural relationship and, 'If MI6 wanted to get something out they would often go to IRD, depending on the matter in hand.' One IRD official also confirmed Brian Crozier's recollection that there was a small unit concerned with placing specific stories that needed to get out. 'It wasn't the only way in which MI6 and IRD were in contact. Across the board they were in contact, but of course this special department and MI6 were naturally in contact with one another.'[15]

During the 1960s the Foreign Office, reflecting the American line, began extolling the view that the non-aligned countries, particularly in Africa were the key to the balance of power between the West and Communism. It worried about the Soviet Union's increasing interest in Third World countries. The Future Policy Review of March 1960, which established the framework for British foreign policy in the 1960s, predicted that it was in the underdeveloped countries that the struggle between East and West would be most likely to continue.[16] Up to 1960, news in British colonial Africa was distributed mainly by British Information Service (BIS, run by the Foreign Office) and by the BBC. IRD needed to expand covert access to the press in the non-aligned countries. As we have seen in chapter nine the last wave of news agency fronts set up included Africa Features Ltd and World Features Services (WFS). Africa Features was described by the Kenya Press Directory (1968) as follows:

> Africa Features Ltd was incorporated in Kenya in August 1966. It is a subsidiary of a well-known international syndication service, INRAR Ltd, which is based in London. Africa Features was founded in the belief (adequately justified by the subsequent response) that there was a need for a mailed features service established in Africa by African journalists of the newspapers, radio stations and magazines of Africa.
>
> All articles and photo features are commissioned from African journalists in the following countries: Ethiopia, Kenya, Uganda, Tanzania, Zambia, Malawi, Swaziland, Botswana, Ghana, Nigeria and Sierra Leone. The company's office in London is responsible for commissioning articles from African journalists resident in London, Paris, Geneva, Vienna and Bonn.
>
> The company has two staff correspondents: one whose task is to rove Eastern and Central Africa, and the other who covers West Africa. The 2 staffers and all stringers operate under the direction of the service editor from his office in Nairobi.
>
> The service is provided generally on a contract basis – with a guaranteed number of feature articles' sent to subscribers each week. A special reporting service is also available to contract subscribers.
>
> In the short time since Africa Features was started, a gratifying number of news organizations in Eastern, Central and West Africa have become subscribers to the service. The features range from economic subjects to human interest articles, from sport and athletics to child care and women's specials. All of them relate directly to Africa.

According to the publicity, Africa Features was unique as the only Africa-based and African editorially staffed service on the continent serving the continent. The two staff correspondents at the time were John Dumoga, the West Africa correspondent, and Charles Kulundu, who covered East and Central Africa.

Dumoga, a Ghanaian, worked as one of the first black journalists in Kenya for East Africa Newspapers (in Nairobi) after Kenyan independence in December 1963, and then went back to Accra to be supervisory editor of the *Daily Graphic* and *Sunday Mirror* in 1966 and 1967. He joined Africa Features in January 1968. In the late 1960s he wrote a Background Book, *Africa between East and West*, which provides a flavour of the tone of his reports:

> In Africa, as elsewhere, Communism has presented itself as the only sincere ally of nationalism. Through propaganda, slogans, aid programmes, foreign policy pronouncements and smooth diplomacy, the Soviet and Chinese government are desperately trying to penetrate the African continent by their identification with African leaders and by equating Communism with nationalism, anti-colonialism and anti-neo-colonialism.[17]
>
> . . . The GPP under Nkrumah was closely patterned on the Communist model of a political party; it used Communist methods of organization – intimidation's, blackmail, character assassination, deceit, rigged elections, single lists of election candidates, and every other trick from the Communist book to win and retain power and finally imposed a merciless dictatorship on Ghanaians.[18]

Kulundu trained at the Commonwealth Press Union and gained a scholarship in 1962, before becoming a Kenya government press officer and editor on The Voice of Kenya radio. He also worked for East Africa Newspapers in Tanzania in 1966–7, joining Africa Features in May 1968. Although billed as African based and staffed, Africa Features' weekly file of material airmailed to clients was being edited, and in some cases written, in London in 1979. Addresses of field offices were given in Nairobi, Ghana and Nigeria.

WFS produced a similar file of material for clients, mainly in India, where it had an office in New Delhi. The Indian press director of INFA in 1978 reported that, in March 1978, Asia Features (India) Private Ltd[19] 'took over the Indian business of World Feature Services which is now a partner in the new venture. Daily bulletins in English and alternate dailies in Hindi are provided for subscribers.' A former Asia Features employee said that its material was taken by nearly every English-speaking paper in Africa, and a considerable amount of Asia Features and WFS copy has been traced in magazines with a Third World orientation published in Britain. Both in the African press and in Britain, this material was published without attribution – a procedure that is difficult to explain for a genuine commercial agency trying to build up its business. We emphasize that any journalist, employee or director may have been unaware of the MI6 and IRD roots of any of these agencies.

However, despite high points, such as IRD's role in the fall of Sukarno, one IRD official complained that, 'ministerial and official interest waned in the sixties.'[20] IRD was also subject to complaints and criticism from inside the Foreign Office mainstream, which held IRD in some suspicion. One critic who would later go public was Hilary King, Ambassador and Consul-General to Guinea in 1962. Prior to Guinea, King's career had taken him to Vienna, Washington, Moscow and Yugoslavia. While in Vienna, between 1951 and 1953, where he served as a Russian secretary, he had first come across IRD. King recalled in 1996 that he 'became aware not only of mountains of "unattributable" briefing papers, but also of British journalists who seemed to have some sort of hidden agenda as propagandists'. King was worried at the time by the quality of the sources used in IRD material. He recalled that 'they weren't choosy, and were quite happy to use unverified press clippings. They claimed to be using secret intelligence, but the secret intelligence in circulation was very often pretty poor stuff, deriving such verisimilitude as it had, for most recipients, more from the special Secret Intelligence forms it was printed on than from proven accuracy or careful screening.' He commented, 'Given the volume of the IRD output, I doubt whether systematic screening of all their texts would have been physically possible.'

In 1962, King had been faced with just such a possibility. He recalled, 'I once found in one of these briefing papers a hair-raising allegation about the country in which I was serving, and was paid to know about, which appeared flat contrary to all the evidence available. When I queried the source of this information, I was told that the IRD, of course, had access to secret information which I had not seen.'[21] The story alleged that Cuban revolutionaries were in Guinea training Black African guerrillas from all over Africa. King recalled, 'I had seen all the MI6's reports bearing on Guinea, and had reason to know the unreliability of the author of some of them.'[22]

Worried that information, which he considered of dubious veracity, was being passed off as fact, King set about checking out the origin of the story further. Among others, he contacted the Foreign Office Research Department, which also drew on classified information, and found that it was as puzzled as he was. 'After weeks of research . . . it was established that the only authority for the original report had been a few lines appearing in an insignificant foreign newspaper and nowhere else.' The newspaper was, in fact, a tiny south German publication. It is quite possible that the report, true or not, had been planted by IRD to lend credibility to the story.[23]

With growing criticism from within the Foreign Office, a less tense period of the Cold War raised questions over the future of IRD. It needed to find a broader agenda to justify its existence. Britain's increasing ties with Europe were to provide IRD with that new spark.

CHAPTER SIXTEEN

Indian Summer:
IRD and the EEC

In late 1972, Alistair (later Lord) McAlpine was recruited as treasurer for a discreet and high-powered pro-Europe lobby organization called the European League for Economic Cooperation (ELEC). It was only very much later that he discovered the reason for his appointment. 'A secret Foreign Office unit, closely linked to MI6, was set up to combat left-wing opposition to Britain remaining in Europe,' he said in his autobiography. This unit had been funding invitation-only meetings between senior media figures and pro-European politicians, diplomats and businessmen. These were regular, expensive and well-attended breakfasts at the plush Connaught Hotel.[1] This secret unit was, of course, IRD. Twenty-five years on, McAlpine was asked whether he thought it appropriate to have had civil servants involved in the European Economic Community (EEC) campaign. He said, 'Certainly not, particularly that sort of civil servant. It was a highly politicised campaign, there is no doubting it. I'm quite clear – if it is political, civil servants had no business to be involved in it.'[2]

The crunch had come, said McAlpine, when William (later Lord) Armstrong, then head of the Civil Service, found out about the unit and 'its dubious activities', which he considered 'scandalous'. He went to Prime Minister Ted Heath and demanded that the funds were withdrawn. As a result, ELEC took over running the breakfast meetings and fundraiser extraordinaire McAlpine was brought in.

★★★★

British and American intelligence services, it now appears, had a history of supporting Britain's entry into the EEC as a bulwark against the Eastern bloc. The CIA was used to preserve the British government's anti-federalist policies and encouraged Britain to enter Europe as part of 'the special relationship' to promote American interests within Europe. The CIA funded the European Movement, the most prominent extra-governmental group seeking to influence public opinion for a European community. Between 1949 and 1953, it was subsidized by the CIA to the tune of £330,000, channelled through the American Committee on United Europe (ACUE). Today, this would be worth more than £6 million. ACUE's board can now be seen to have been the alumni of the CIA, and the president of honour was the CIA director, Allen Dulles. CIA money continued to be paid into the coffers of the related European Youth Campaign until 1959.

In June 1970, Ted Heath's Conservative government had been elected with a pro-European manifesto. However, although the chances of securing entry through negotiations with The Six looked increasingly promising, the situation at home, in terms of securing the consent of the Houses of Parliament and the British public, appeared to be less so. In the country at large, opinion polls were strongly against membership in the period 1970–1. This appeared to have been, to a large degree, the result of disillusionment with Europe following the last rejection by De Gaulle. Nevertheless, disillusionment and opposition were not limited to the voting public, who had, after all, just elected a government for whom British entry was a principle policy. In reality, although the cabinet was packed with pro-Europeans, Heath presided over a party that was deeply ambivalent about the EEC. In February 1971, the whips calculated that 194 Conservative MPs were in favour, but 71 were doubtful and 62 against. In the party as a whole, the situation was even worse, with both pros and antis feeling the constituency parties to be hostile. In the Labour Party, anti-European sentiment was growing and, although an influential faction of the party was stridently pro-European, the bi-partisan, pro-European consensus was obviously crumbling.

During the campaign, Heath promised that membership would only occur 'with the full-hearted consent of Parliament and people'. Heath now faced the danger that, even were he to be able to overcome the primary obstacle of negotiating entry with The Six, he might find that Parliament, under constituency and public pressure, might reject the terms and block the British membership that he had so passionately fought for. Heath told the No. 10 Press Secretary, Sir Donald Maitland, to convene a meeting of senior information officers in Whitehall to find out what could be done.

According to IRD sources, 'Maitland told the meeting that "the Prime Minister is very keen to have an effective job done on what his policy is for Europe" and how mistaken people like Crossman and Shore and Walker-Smith were in saying that it was not in the interests of our country to go into it'. And the only people who were judged to be capable of doing something about this were IRD, so the whole thing was given to IRD to, as it were, advertise Ted Heath's policies for Europe."[3] IRD was to supply 'the main guts of the operation' to ensure support for entry.[4]

The civil servant chosen to run the covert pro-Europe campaign was Norman Reddaway, then Under-Secretary of State at the Foreign Office for 'Cultural Diplomacy', with a brief covering IRD and other Foreign Office information services. With his usual gusto, Reddaway set up a special IRD unit to propagandize in favour of British entry and counter those who opposed it. According to Reddaway, the unit, 'was extremely useful because although there was not much to say about Soviet Imperialism and the gulags, the researchers were extremely good at researching the facts about going into Europe'.[5] Its main writer was Foreign Office staffer H.H. 'Tommy' Tucker, 'a brilliant writer and shaper.'[6] The unit was drawn mainly from staff on IRD's West European desk and included IRD stalwart Josephine O'Connor-Howe.

The advent of détente and a more peaceful coexistence with the Soviet Union removed, to some extent, the apparent *raison d'être* of IRD. The European unit allowed IRD to move into broader areas, but using tried and tested methods. According to insiders, the unit worked closely with a number of pro-European politicians, to rebut the anti-European campaign in the media. IRD wrote and brokered articles through

Tufton Beamish MP. These were placed in the press. 'There was no shortage of MPs who were pleased to see something published under their name in *The Times* and elsewhere,' said one former insider. IRD launched a massive operation, relentlessly issuing briefings, articles and letters to the press and influential pro-Europeans. By all accounts the material diligently avoided the difficult questions of federalism and whether Brussels bureaucrats would be able to impose laws on the British people.

Placing pro-European material and close contact with the negotiators in Brussels enabled the unit to ensure wider dissemination through radio and television. The team also developed a technique that pre-dated New Labour's much touted rebuttal unit. If an anti-Europe article appeared in the media, IRD would place a detailed counter within hours, complete with the by-line of a prominent and consenting politician. One unit insider said:

> You might get a letter from Crossman in *The Times* saying that this [British entry to the EEC] was a load of rubbish. By about lunchtime you'd have a little brief on the weaker parts of Crossman's argument and that would go across to the broker and the broker would have half a dozen MPs who would like a seven out of ten chance of seeing their names in the paper. And so by that evening you would get something based on the brief going off to *The Times*. Well that gives you immediately half a million copies going world wide.

Material in the press convinced the broadcasters that they, too, should be covering the story. As the insider said, 'If you went to the BBC and said, "Look, for God's sake, make the case for Europe." They'd say, "Get stuffed. We don't do that sort of thing." On the other hand, if it has appeared in the papers then one can fairly ask whether the BBC are reflecting this for their audience.'

Reddaway and IRD also became discreetly involved in the non-government pro-European campaigning. Ernest Wistrich, a former RAF Polish section officer and failed Labour parliamentary candidate, had been appointed director of the British European Movement in 1969. According to him, he was approached by Geoffrey Rippon MP, then Chancellor for the Duchy of Lancaster and responsible for negotiating Britain's terms of entry into the EEC. Rippon asked Wistrich to run an overt pro-Europe campaign as the government could not be seen to be campaigning during the negotiations.[7] By this time the European Movement's budget of £550,000 per year was mainly donated by big business and prominent individuals like Sir Michael Sobell.

Starting in November 1970, the meetings of the European Movement's campaign group were held in its offices in Chandos House, Victoria, and were also attended by a representative of the Foreign Office. The presence of this civil servant was deemed sensitive enough to have it omitted from the minutes and deleted by means of an erratum slip when it was once included by mistake. Wistrich confirmed Reddaway's central role. 'Norman Reddaway was . . . head of the European unit in the Foreign Office. He had a particular European Desk I think at this stage.'[8]

Overseeing the various groups was a governmental coordinating committee, usually chaired by Tony Royle, now Lord Fanshawe of Richmond, who was then parliamentary Under-Secretary of State for Foreign and Commonwealth Affairs. These brought together a number of participants from all of the different groups, including IRD, to exchange ideas and ensure coordination.

A highly effective part of the campaign was organized by the ex-Director of Publicity for the Conservative Party, Geoffrey Tucker. Tucker took charge of Conservative Party advertising in 1959 and wrote the famous slogan 'Life's better with the Conservatives'. Don't let Labour ruin it!' It was considered a major aid in helping the Tory Party to come back to power in spite of the fact that the fiasco of Suez was still fresh in the public's mind. Tucker left the position following the Conservative's electoral victory in 1970, to return to independent public relations, but, as a convinced European, he suggested to Heath that a series of informal meetings should be organized to find ways of ensuring support for entry:

At the end of '70 after we had won the election I went to Ted and sat down with him and said 'The next big thing is Europe. I'm a pro-European, I've been converted to being a pro-European as against believing in the Empire'. But the public was apathetic. And I said to Ted 'Unless you can move public opinion, it will be very difficult for the pro-Europeans inside the Labour Party, let alone the pro-Europeans inside the Conservative Party to vote for Europe in the House of Commons, if you can negotiate the right terms, that we should go into Europe'. So Ted turned to me and said, 'Well Geoffrey, get on with it then.' It's a very curious thing that people do not believe that, in fact, it is enough for a politician to say to somebody, 'Well get on with it!' So I set off to do it.'[9]

These meetings were to be between 'insiders' from the government and Civil Service (including the negotiators) and 'outsiders' (such as media figures and opposition leaders). The frequent breakfasts were held in a private room at the Connaught Hotel. At a time when the cross-party consensus was breaking down, pro-Europeans from all parties were represented. Those from the Labour Party included Roy Jenkins, Roy Hattersley and the Deputy Secretary of the Party, Gwyn Morgan, who was then working for the European Commission. Also present was Michael Ivens, director of the right-wing organization Aims of Industry. They were usually also attended by Reddaway and Wistrich. Despite apparent differences and political antagonisms over different issues, the group was united by the overarching political aim to get Britain into Europe. Geoffrey Tucker said, 'I realized if we were going to get the vote in the House of Commons in favour of Europe, against the background of apathy and resistance, then we had to do something about the people out there and show them [the MPs] that the country was behind them.'[10]

The meetings usually involved twenty to thirty people, many of them newspaper reporters, including Majorie Proops of the *Daily Mirror*. By bringing in figures such as Nigel Ryan (from *News at Ten*), Ian Trethowen (managing director for BBC Radio) and Marshall Stewart (from the BBC Radio 4 *Today* programme) the media breakfasts were able to suggest pro-European programming for television and radio. Tucker allowed the media guests access to the EEC negotiators. 'Into the breakfasts came the people from Brussels. So the people who went to the breakfasts from the media got a briefing on what was actually going on day by day. So we were making news,' he said.

As a result of the breakfasts *News at Ten* started a series of five-minute specials on the EEC with a strong factual tone – television time that as advertising would have cost something like £1.25m in one month. Nigel Ryan said, 'I certainly met Tucker many times in the period as he was Heath's media man. I cannot specifically remember these media breakfasts in this distance of time but the ITN special items may have come out of them. These items would have been made with the usual editorial independence that ITN so fiercely guarded.'[11] Marshall Stewart recalled attending a number of the meetings, which he said he found useful to gather information 'at a time when there was a paucity of facts about the EEC'.[12] Tucker even claimed that, after pressure from the campaigners, the broadcaster Jack de Manio was removed from his job as a presenter of BBC Radio's *Today* programme because he was 'too anti-European'. However, Marshall Stewart denied the claim, describing it as 'bizarre'.

According to McAlpine, IRD secretly financed the breakfasts. Very few of the participants appear to have been aware of the involvement of IRD or its funds in the lobbying operation, although some of the campaigners had their suspicions. Ivens said that he suspected that it might have been funded by IRD. 'Tucker once told me that Ted [Heath] objected to the cost of the breakfasts,' he said.[13] Tucker said he thought that they had been funded by the European Movement.[14] Ernest Wistrich said that he was unsure where the money came from.[15]

Following withdrawal of government support, 'the flame was kept alive', according to Tucker, by Geoffrey Rippon and ELEC. Rippon had taken over the nearly moribund ELEC like 'a giant cuckoo', said McAlpine. 'Geoffrey Rippon told me: always choose a near defunct organization where the members have nearly all left as the vehicle for your covert operations.' Rippon had brought into ELEC many prominent European and British politicians, and businessmen including Valery Giscard D'Estaing, Douglas Hurd, Roy Jenkins and Lord Carrington. When Lord Armstrong had prevailed on Heath to cut IRD's secret subsidies, ELEC appointed McAlpine to find funds to keep the pro-Europe media campaign going. 'One matter I really do know about is how to organize a good breakfast. A choice of kippers, sausages, kidneys, scrambled eggs, bacon and tomatoes was laid on,' said McAlpine.[16] The breakfasts were to continue until after the 1975 referendum.

Heath's government was very sensitive about the media breakfasts. The most detailed account of the European Campaign is Uwe Kitzinger's book *Diplomacy and Persuasion*, which included a chapter on the meetings.[17] Kitzinger, an academic and pro-Europe movement activist from the late 1950s, was called twice to the Foreign Office by a senior Whitehall mandarin who told him that it wanted the whole chapter on them to be suppressed. Kitzinger was threatened with repercussions if he did not. The official claimed that he was concerned about the potential embarrassment for Labour MPs who had attended. Actually it seemed that it was really concerned about the role of civil servants who were taking a very decided line on an issue on which they should have retained neutrality. Kitzinger ignored the threats and the chapter was published.[18]

The effect of these overt and covert propaganda operations on public opinion quickly became apparent. Between late 1967 and early 1971, public support for entry had slipped from 65 per cent to 22 per cent. By July 1971, support was up to 28 per cent, and by August the *Financial Times* put it at 34 per cent for and 51 per cent against.

Perhaps more significantly, as opposition in the country waned and support grew, the opposition in Parliament crumbled; wavering MPs were brought into line under a barrage of propaganda and arm-twisting. In October 1971, Parliament voted by 356 to 244 to accept the conditions of entry. Some 69 Labour MPs voted against the whip. In January 1973, Britain joined the Common Market.

There is no further evidence of IRD involvement in the EEC campaign or the 1975 Referendum after Armstrong's order to desist. However, Conservative MP Sir Richard Body, who was joint chairman of the council of the 'Keep Britain Out' campaign, has said that Western intelligence services took a profound interest in the 1975 Referendum:

> At the very beginning of the campaign two CIA agents came to see me in the House of Commons. They were Anglophiles and they were very upset at the way their agency was going to interfere in the referendum campaign. They said a new head of station was going to be appointed who was not a normal CIA man, he was very well known in the federalist movement and they (CIA) were going to intervene in different ways, and they produced a substantial number of documents to verify what they were saying.
>
> I read these documents through and they seemed very hot stuff showing as they did that the CIA had been financing the European Movement since its inception. I showed them to one or two others and they agreed. However no newspapers would publish these documents, nor were they willing to interview the two CIA men. In the end I was reduced to *Time Out*, which then had a very small circulation.[19]

The *Time Out* story was published as 'Uncle Sam goes to Market'.[20] The documents told the basic story of how the CIA had covertly subsidized the early European Movement. The head of the station appointed to 'intervene' in the referendum campaign was Cord Meyer Jr, who had been one of the leading figures in the United World Federalists before joining the CIA. He was one of the CIA's most famous officials, with friends in high places. His first wife was a friend of Jacqueline Kennedy and her sister was married to Ben Bradlee, the editor of the *Washington Post*. There is no hard evidence that Meyer was sent primarily to make sure that the British stayed in Europe, but his tenure as head of station from 1975 to 1976 was not much longer than the run of the campaign. Body said, 'US Policy after the war had been in favour of the British joining the EEC. I think the Trojan House argument appealed especially to Kennedy and Kissinger and the Americans thought that by having the Britons in Europe would be more sympathetic to the Atlanticist point of view.'

Body also got intimation of other intelligence agency activity during the campaign: 'I was having dinner with a long time friend, a man I trusted totally, and who had intelligence connections. During the course of the meal he warned me that my phone was being tapped. He told me that MI5 was tapping the phones of anyone connected with former Labour MP Ann Kerr.'[21]

Ann Kerr had been the hard left-wing MP for Rochester, but had lost her seat in 1970. She was married to the prominent left winger Russell Kerr and was on the 'No to EEC' Campaign that Body sat on, but she attended only one committee meeting. 'Ann

Kerr was reputedly a Communist as was her husband who was an Australian. You have to remember at this time MI5 was obsessed by Communism. They thought that Ann Kerr was a fellow traveller and that the Soviets were supporting the No vote to leave Europe weak – so that the Soviets could walk into Germany and France. Therefore I was contaminated by having contact with her. My contact put it to me that I or any of my committee must expect to have our phones tapped.' Body has said that it is hard now to imagine the paranoia of that time. 'I think some of MI5 got wound up that the No vote was against the national interest. They were by no means alone. People in high places got very wound up over the issue. It was very difficult for the No campaigners to get their point of view over on the media. The BBC were the worst offenders.' Ann Kerr and her husband are now both dead.

Body has said that he is not aware of any Soviet money funding the No campaign. 'The Soviet Union subsidized *The Morning Star* by purchasing many thousands of copies. The newspaper was anti-EEC so it was reasonable for MI5 to assume that Moscow supported the No campaign. We had no Communists on the committee and I do not believe that Moscow or the Communist Party gave any money or help to the No campaign.' His view is reinforced by Sean Stewart, in 1975 working for Labour cabinet member Peter Shore: 'I thought the Civil Service was intensely disloyal. Peter Shore was my minister: most of my colleagues thought he was a "fellow traveller"; and Benn was a regarded as a Communist. You would not believe it, would you? In the whole of Whitehall, at the middle level, there was fear all over the place, and the "antis" [i.e. those anti-EEC membership] were being labelled as Communists and "fellow travellers".'[22]

In the 1975 referendum the British people voted to stay in the EEC. The impact of membership continues to be controversial. Ted Heath has frequently been accused since of not informing the British public of the full ramifications of joining Europe, especially over the loss of British sovereignty. For IRD the covert operations in favour of Britain's membership were considered highly effective and became feathers in the department's cap. Reddaway has described it as one of the department's most successful campaigns. Heath too thought it successful and asked whether similar IRD techniques could be applied to Ulster.

CHAPTER SEVENTEEN

Painting it Red: IRD and Northern Ireland

IRD's success during the EEC campaign for British entry in 1970–1 impressed Ted Heath; he saw the possibilities for discreet propaganda work. The most serious problem facing the government at that time was the recent explosion of violence in Northern Ireland, which had led to the deployment of British troops in the province in August 1969. In particular, the government was faced with the problem of how to respond to demands for a united Ireland, allegations of human rights abuses by the British Army, Irish American support for the Republican cause and Soviet propaganda characterizing the conflict in terms of British colonialism. Heath's government again saw a role for IRD. It was decided that the small rebuttal unit under Tommy Tucker should be maintained and turn its expertise towards rebutting what was seen as pro-Republican propaganda. The unit, based in London, used the same techniques that it had used so successfully against the anti-Europeans. According to one IRD source, a primary target for the unit's attention was the American senator Edward Kennedy, who had been writing what were perceived as pro-Republican and pro-IRA letters in the British press. Counter material was put into the media via various IRD contacts including Lord Wavell Wakefield.[1]

But IRD also played a role in Northern Ireland itself. At the beginning of the Troubles in the early 1970s, British intelligence was represented in Northern Ireland by the Secret Intelligence Service. MI6 is generally the overseas arm of British intelligence but the involvement of the Republic of Ireland in events made MI6 a convenient choice to carry out intelligence operations in the province.[2] During discussions with IRD, MI6 requested that it should be assigned some IRD experts to bolster its effort. One of the experts sent was Hugh Mooney, listed at the time as 'First Secretary, FCO'. Mooney arrived in Northern Ireland in 1971 and was given the title of 'information adviser to the general officer commanding'.

When Mooney arrived in Lisburn in 1971, the British propaganda effort was still in the process of development. When Northern Ireland had hit the headlines in 1969, the Army had found itself unusually exposed to the world's media. Previous counter-insurgencies, such as in Malaya and Cyprus, had demanded a propaganda strategy, but never before had the actions of the Army and the British government come under quite so much scrutiny or been so close to home. The Army also recognized that, in this conflict more than in any other, psychological operations would have to play a significant role. In his 1971 study of counter-insurgency, Gen Sir Frank Kitson, who in

1970 had been appointed commander for Belfast, wrote that, in situations of civil disorder accompanied by sabotage and terrorism, 'the operational emphasis will swing away from the process of destroying relatively large groups of armed insurgents towards the business of divorcing extremist elements from the population which they are trying to subvert. This means that persuasion will become more important in comparison with armed offensive action.'[3]

Initially the Army had responded to the media attention by setting up a network of press offices at headquarters and unit level. However, the development of events soon demanded a more concerted approach. By early 1971 the British Army, originally welcomed by the Nationalist community as offering protection from Loyalist attacks, was increasingly seen as the upholder of the status quo, the role of which, it appeared, was to contain the Nationalist community rather than protect it. The insecurity of the Catholic community and the lack of political progress facilitated the revival of the Irish Republican Army (IRA), and the first British soldier was shot on 6 February.

This was followed in August by the introduction of internment, which, owing to a lack of accurate intelligence provided by the Protestant-dominated Royal Ulster Constabulary, led to the imprisonment without trial of many political activists, as well as members of the IRA. Even worse, some people were mistakenly identified. Historian J. Bowyer Bell said 'The army was quite unprepared . . . property was ruined, innocent people hurt, the wrong men taken. . . . Hundreds of men were beaten and then jammed into cells . . . without charges . . . families howling at the gates, solicitors with papers, demonstrations through the British Isles, questions in Parliament, and hectoring editorials, and the whole thing on television.'[4] Internment was a public relations disaster on an international scale and only served further to convince the Catholic community that the British Army was the enemy. This increased sympathy for the IRA. For the British information services it was a turning point.

The IRA was itself split as to the correct policy to pursue. At the Sinn Féin annual conference at Ballsbridge in Dublin in January 1970, the division between the Official IRA and the Provisional IRA became overt. The Officials became increasingly radical in their politics, with a move towards Marxism, they moved away from the policy of armed insurrection. The Provisional IRA, with a relatively conservative Nationalist agenda, concentrated on organizing for war and offering protection for the Catholic community. As J. Bowyer Bell noted of the Officials, 'They might have an organization in place but all of their volunteers had to be made aware of the political implications of each act while the Provos had only to be taught to shoot.'[5] It was the Provisional IRA that emerged as the main antagonists of the British Army.

Responding to the increasingly difficult demands of the situation and, in particular, the need to present the British case, the information services were reorganized. The major innovation was the establishment of an Information Liaison, soon to become the Information Policy Department, headed briefly by one Lt Col Johnny Johnston who was soon replaced by Col Maurice Tugwell. Before his arrival in Northern Ireland, Tugwell, a paratrooper, had served as an intelligence officer in Palestine, followed by stints in three other areas where counter-insurgency methods were used: Malaya, Kenya and Cyprus. Tony Staughton, who had worked in Army information as both a soldier and a civilian, and had run Army PR in Northern Ireland since 1964, remained head of

Army PR. He was backed up by Maj Tony Yarnold, who had run an Army press office in Hong Kong during the Malayan Communist insurgency, and Colin Wallace, a civilian information officer whose local knowledge was considered invaluable. Next to the regular PR office was Information Policy under Tugwell. Journalist Paul Foot noted of the Army information services under Tugwell, 'Information policy was a separate unit working for the intelligence services but expected to work under cover of public relations. Its function was psychological warfare.'[6]

Staughton recalled that the new direction in information was accompanied by the arrival of new personnel: 'Immediately after internment, the IRA started to get the upper hand. And from that time on, the Foreign Office and the Intelligence people insisted on much more say in public relations.'[7] IRD was brought in to lend advice and guide propaganda policy: 'They sent over a man called Hugh Mooney – he was from a department of the Foreign Office called the Information Research Department. None of us ever knew what Mooney was about: who he reported to or what he was entitled to. All we knew was that they gave him a big house to live in and freedom to move at will throughout the barracks and Stormont.'[8]

Colin Wallace, who would end up working with Mooney frequently, remembered that Mooney 'was operating on his own before he got a post at Headquarters. He came in to Headquarters Northern Ireland, the Army Headquarters, under the title of Information Adviser to the General Officer Commanding, which was ostensibly a Foreign Office policy post, but was really a cover name. He had his own separate function initially, but then as Information Policy grew we all joined into the same suite of offices.'[9] According to Wallace, 'there was the Army Press Desk, which operated like a news room. It was manned 24 hours a day, series of watch keepers. And all the information coming in from the Army units all over the province was fed into that. Their job was dealing with factual information.' The offices of Information Policy lay across the corridor, 'and we were regarded as much more of a think-tank. . . . We also ran community relations, for example, "hearts and minds", classic psych-war type activity. But we did all these strange things which people could never quite work out exactly what. We ran the Army newspaper, in fact we created that. In addition to influencing public opinion we had to influence the soldiers opinions.'[10]

The effect of these developments quickly made itself apparent. As Bowyer Bell noted, 'Never after internment was the media treated so ineptly. The Army learned how to manipulate these observers with cameras or note books: briefings, special lunches, treats in London, tours and leaks and detailed kits were all ready. . . . The basic assumptions of the British view were . . . rarely questioned and even the more egregiously unpleasant policies found sympathetic ears.'[11]

As in most counter-insurgency situations, propaganda was never the province of one agency. Information Policy had a variety of personnel and sources representing various interested parties and departments. Northern Ireland was not a single IRD operation. IRD was a specialist area, but in the unit there were different elements, all having different inputs for different reasons.[12] Wallace's main sources of information for dissemination to the many journalists who were now visiting Northern Ireland on a frequent basis were MI6, IRD and Army intelligence. 'Each person had two or three different inputs. But in Northern Ireland the bulk of our day-to-day information, for my side, came direct from

Army Intelligence. We worked for Army Intelligence. I also worked for SIS which was my . . . main role initially, whereas Hugh Mooney had his input largely from IRD or from other sources in London which we never really knew.'[13] According to Wallace, 'the main thrust of IRD . . . was really the Cold War and therefore the bulk of our work was to create links between Irish terrorism and the Soviet bloc, or Soviet satellites.' Wallace observed, 'The whole idea of Soviet involvement was absolutely silly, but it was easy to understand in terms of the tabloids.'[14] Wallace claimed that, not only were IRD distorting political and public understanding of the nature of the 'Irish problem', but they were also distorting the facts themselves. This is vigorously denied by IRD sources involved at the time who claim that IRD was not wittingly involved in any of what, they admit, were black propaganda operations. Nevertheless, according to Wallace, 'most of the stuff we were doing was fictitious, which was supposed to be confusing the terrorists'.[15]

Disinformation, from whatever source, threatened to undermine Britain's own operations as well as those of the IRA. Wallace recalled that disinformation put out by Information Policy 'ran the danger of colouring our own intelligence operations, because an intelligence officer would come to us with reports which we had actually fed out'.[16]

In 1972 Colin Wallace and Hugh Mooney carried out a classic 'black propaganda' operation to 'prove' Soviet involvement in 'Britain's Cuba'. Wallace and Mooney approached Trevor Hannah, a Northern Ireland journalist working for the Ulster News news agency in Belfast. Wallace recalled that 'Trevor Hannah was [working at] . . . probably the most prolific of the local agencies. He covered for all sorts of people, he covered for the BBC. You tended to get troughs when nothing much was happening and people would pull out all their teams and he would be the sort of anchor man for God knows how many agencies.'[17] Wallace and Mooney sold Hannah a story of Russian submarines landing KGB-trained subversives off the coast of Ireland. Together they took the story to George MacIntosh, northern editor of the *News of the World*, and handed over 'proof' at a meeting at the Waldorf Hotel in London. In a Thames Television documentary for the series *This Week* in April 1990, MacIntosh recalled the meeting: 'There were various photographs. There was attached to the photograph a report from the pilot of the aircraft, the reconnaissance aircraft from which the photograph had been taken. Many other documents connecting eastern bloc countries with activities in Northern Ireland basically.' According to MacIntosh, 'Wallace told the story, Mooney confirmed it.'[18] Nevertheless, MacIntosh was careful enough to check out Mooney's credentials, confirming that he was a senior official at the Foreign Office. MacIntosh did not know of IRD until he was approached by David Leigh, the *This Week* reporter in 1990. With its authenticity confirmed by such an official and authoritative source, MacIntosh decided to run the story, splashing it on the front page under the headline 'Russia in IRA Plot Sensation'. Wallace said, . . . 'the Russian submarine, classic! IRD faked photographs taken by us. All the sort of peripheral back-up intelligence to support that was all produced by us. And that was again, a straight IRD operation.'[19]

Comments made by Michael Ivens, director of Aims for Industry, cast a little light on IRD activities in Northern Ireland at the time. According to Ivens, Reddaway 'was the sort of number one or number two at the Foreign Office who was head of communication and he'd do a lot of interesting stuff. Guns were unloaded in IRA boats.

Norman's people appeared miraculously to photograph the operation and it appeared in the *Express* or something like that. He's quite an operator.'[20] Senior IRD officials deny IRD involvement to this day. In fact, one IRD operative claims that the story and photograph came from Wallace and Army intelligence and that IRD involvement was minimal – that they had been as fooled as the public were.[21]

Perhaps the most serious allegation with regard to IRD in Northern Ireland is that, like MI5, it was involved in the dissemination of anti-Labour smear stories. According to Colin Wallace, an IRD official went as far as to disseminate material against Harold Wilson. As Stephen Dorrill and Robin Ramsay wrote in their book, *Smear!*, an unattributable briefing paper entitled 'Soviets Increase Control Over British Communists' was produced in the period before December 1973. According to Ramsay, Dorrill and Wallace, 'the briefing included annotations on it in the handwriting of Hugh Mooney'. The paper was concerned with the visit to Britain by a group of Soviet officials and included these passages:

> The Soviet [officials] paid tribute to the excellent contacts built up in the past between British Labour Party activists and the Soviet Trade Delegation in London. In particular they spoke warmly of the work done by Harold Wilson during his four years at the Board of Trade and his help in enabling the Soviet Government to purchase the latest Rolls Royce engines (Derwent and Nene) in 1947. . . .
>
> Needless to say the Soviet visitors forgot to tell their unquestioning hosts that the Soviet Trade Delegation for whom Wilson and his friends had played 'Santa Claus' was the front for Soviet Intelligence operations in Britain.[22]

The unmistakable aim of the briefing paper was to cast Wilson in a bad light. Whatever the source of this material, the withdrawal of IRD, according to Wallace and IRD sources, was a disaster for propaganda work in Northern Ireland. MI5 took over the coordination of the propaganda campaign, which was run by the director of B Branch of MI5 and Chief of Intelligence, Northern Ireland, from 1973 to 1975, Denis Henry Payne.[23] Wallace recalled:

> The problem . . . for most of us arose in 1973 when Hugh Mooney was withdrawn from Northern Ireland, because of a conflict with MoD, and also because MI5 took over the role of coordinating intelligence in Northern Ireland. Hitherto the senior intelligence officer had been an MI6, SIS officer. When the Security Service took over because of the inter-service rivalry, IRD, which was aligned with SIS, then lost its role and Hugh Mooney and his assistant were withdrawn. And this is when our operations were directed much more at the Labour Party and politicians and all kinds of strange things happened.

With the withdrawal of Mooney, Wallace lost access to IRD. From then on Wallace was forced to rely on the intelligence and security services. He recalled, 'I had . . . MI5 in terms of the way the overall policy was going and the SIS who, I suppose was my main source of information output.'[24]

Wallace and Information Policy output became increasingly political in nature, reflecting MI5's political concerns at the time. These, Peter Wright recalled, were moving towards British domestic politics: 'The Irish situation was only one part of a decisive shift inside MI5 toward domestic concerns. The growth of student militancy in the 1960s gave way to industrial militancy in the early 1970s. The miners' strike of 1972, and a succession of stoppages in the motorcar industry, had a profound effect on the thinking of the Heath government. Intelligence on domestic subversion became the overriding priority.'[25] MI5 was increasingly concerned that the major targets of the KGB were the Intelligence Services, the Civil Service and, increasingly in the 1960s, the trade unions and the Labour Party.[26] These concerns were increasingly apparent in the material that Wallace was being asked to put out. Wallace recalled, 'The whole thing was very heavily loaded in terms of the infiltration . . . of the Labour Movement by extremists and by the Soviets and all that sort of stuff.'[27]

Indeed, Wallace's allegations of a campaign run by MI5 officers against the Wilson government followed the revelations of Peter Wright. Wright alleged that, as early as 1968, there had been an attempt by MI5 officers to smear Wilson.[28] However, Wright recalled, 'the approach in 1974 was altogether more serious. The plan was simple. In the run-up to the election . . . MI5 would arrange for selective details of the intelligence about leading Labour Party figures, but especially Wilson, to be leaked to sympathetic pressmen. Using our contacts in the press and among union officials, word of the material contained in MI5 files and the fact that Wilson was considered a security risk would be passed around.'[29] According to Wright, up to thirty MI5 officers were involved in the plot.

This material began to appear in Northern Ireland. According to Wallace:

> the earliest, what I would call overt political material was probably about October, November '73. And then really it intensified dramatically in the lead up to the general election. Beginning of '74, March, April. And then because it was a minority government . . . and there was quite clearly going to be another election very soon. The campaign, I think, against politicians intensified dramatically right through to . . . October '74 , the next election. And that period between the first and second elections was total and utter madness. I mean that was complete lunacy. Not an exaggeration, 90 per cent of my time was spent in political disinformation, totally, totally ignoring the terrorists.[30]

Wallace complained that, 'for six years I was employed by the Army in Northern Ireland to fight terrorism, but for part of that time I was mis-employed by MI5 to disseminate black propaganda against British politicians including Harold Wilson.'[31]

Since the 1970s, evidence confirming MI5 involvement in questionable counter-subversionary activity has continued to come out. In 1990 the European Human Rights Commission found MI5 guilty of smearing two British citizens associated with the National Council of Civil Liberties, considered a Communist front organization by IRD as well as MI5. As ex-Secretary of State for Northern Ireland and Labour politician, Merlyn Rees recalled, 'I had not the slightest idea that down the line was a desk officer who had NCCL as a subversive organization that had to be looked at. This is why the whole thing has to be cleared up. You cannot target people on the basis of an umbrella description. It cannot so be.'[32] Furthermore, in August 1996 a Channel 4 documentary featured Lord Hunt, ex-cabinet secretary to Harold Wilson, who confirmed that 'malicious malcontents' in MI5 had tried to smear Wilson. According to Hunt, 'There is no doubt at all that a few, a very few, malcontents in MI5, people who should not have been there in the first place, a lot of them like Peter Wright who were right-wing, malicious and had serious personal grudges, gave vent to these and spread damaging malicious stories about that Labour government.'[33]

Although IRD pulled out of Northern Ireland in 1973, the department's Western European desk continued its work on Northern Ireland. This included the handling of IRA defectors and the issue of briefings on the situation to press contacts. One such briefing paper was 'The IRA and Northern Ireland: Aims. Policy. Tactics'. When this was first put out is not clear, but a revised edition was published in October 1974. This 63-page briefing covered topics ranging from IRA front organizations to fundraising and extremist support for the IRA in Britain, linking the revival of the IRA to the activities of the New Left. Colin Wallace recalled, 'There's no doubt that IRD were certainly targeting the New Left, but that interpretation was very wide.'[34] IRD pointed out that the IRA had allowed the civil rights movement to function as a sort of Trojan Horse:

> The IRA leaders decided reluctantly to give a free run to the Northern Ireland Civil Rights Association (NICRA), which was founded in Londonderry in 1967 by a group of Socialists, Liberals, Trotskyists, Communists and Nationalists, to agitate for the rights of the Roman Catholic minority in Ulster. NICRA was an immediate success and by the end of 1968, under strong Trotskyist and 'International Socialist' influence, had disrupted conditions in Ulster. This was the IRA's opportunity and in 1969–70 it moved in on a situation which had been made subversively promising by the New Left.[35]

A serious concern of IRD was American funding for the IRA. IRD noted, 'Overseas aid, mostly from private contributions in the United States, has played a major role in financing the IRA's campaign. Since the current troubles began, Irish-Americans are estimated to have donated between one and two million dollars, ostensibly for "relief work" among the dependants of detainees. But contributions have been diverted towards the purchase of arms.' Wallace recalled that this area was also being covered by Information Policy in Northern Ireland: 'a lot of the work I was doing was aimed at preventing money, arms coming from America and all sorts of places.'[36]

IRD informed its contacts that 'American finance for the IRA first became significant when the activities of the original Northern Ireland civil rights movement of 1968–69 led to violent clashes between the mainly Catholic marchers on one side and the police and extreme "loyalists" on the other. Since then it has tended to fluctuate with events in Ireland, reaching a climax at such times as early 1972 when the riots in Londonderry received widespread attention in the world Press.'[37] The reference to riots in Londonderry was, of course, a reference to the events of Bloody Sunday – thirteen Catholics were killed when British paratroopers opened fire on civil rights protesters in Derry.

A subsequent tribunal, under Lord Chief Justice Widgery, gave a 'somewhat guarded exculpation of the troops'[38] – a verdict that has been consistently challenged and undermined ever since. However, at the time, the perceived needs of propaganda may have outweighed the requirements of justice. The events of Bloody Sunday were clearly approached with propaganda in mind. In 1995, the *Guardian* revealed that a seven-page confidential memorandum recording a conversation between Edward Heath and Widgery, dated two days after the killings, thanking him for agreeing to conduct the hearings, had been found in the Public Record Office. According to the memorandum, Heath reminded Widgery that 'It had to be remembered that we were in Northern Ireland fighting not only a military war but a propaganda war.'[39] The IRD paper also identified pro-Republican 'fronts' in the Communist tradition and civil rights organizations that had fallen under IRA influence. These included the Northern Ireland Civil Rights Association, the Irish Civil Rights Association and the Association for Legal Justice.

IRD also briefed its readers on IRA links with international terrorism, but, 'Although sporadic links have been have been established with Palestinian guerrilla organizations, separatist movements and European Trotskyists, there is no evidence that the IRA is part of any "terrorist international".'[40] Nevertheless, 'By 1972 Libya was becoming the main centre in the Arab world for Irish contacts.' According to IRD, 'Further Libyan involvement with the IRA was confirmed in March, 1973, when the Irish Navy arrested the Cypriot coaster, *Claudia*, as she was attempting to land a cargo of arms on the Irish coast. . . . The vessel's owner, a West German businessman and convicted arms smuggler, Gunther Leinhäuser, said he bought the guns from President Qaddhafi.' The source for the story was cited as the *Daily Mail*, dated 2 April 1973. Where the *Daily Mail* obtained the information is an open question, but a senior IRD official in the 1970s claimed that the department helped to prove the link between Libya and the IRA.[41]

But even though IRD had been removed from Northern Ireland and the increasingly dubious activities of Information Policy, it could not escape being caught up in the fallout. According to the IRD briefing, 'The central aim of the Provisionals and the claimed justification for their campaign of violence in the North is to force the withdrawal of the British military and political presence. Given a British commitment to withdraw, the Provisionals say they would call off the campaign and cooperate with the Army and the Protestant leaders to ensure communal peace; Irishmen would then negotiate future political arrangements in Northern Ireland.' However, 'secret plans captured from the Provisionals in Belfast in May, 1974, showed that they were not only aware of the possibility of civil war resulting from this situation, but were also prepared in certain circumstances to provoke it'. Indeed, 'IRA denials that the bombing campaign is intended to increase sectarian hatred are not supported by the plans', which were 'evidence that the Provisional IRA was preparing a major campaign.' The briefing correctly reported that 'The Prime Minister, Mr Harold Wilson, told the House of Commons on May 13 that there was an IRA plan to occupy parts of Belfast and carry out a "scorched earth policy".' The captured documents 'revealed "a specific and calculated plan on the part of the IRA, by means of ruthless and indiscriminate violence, to foment inter-sectarian hatred and a degree of chaos".'[42]

The origins of this IRA plan lay in the criticisms that had been levelled against it for its failure to defend Catholic areas in Northern Ireland in 1969, when, like Belfast's Divis Flats, they had come under attack from Protestant extremists. As a consequence, plans were drawn up for implementation in just such an emergency, whereby the IRA would evacuate the area in question under the cover of burning cars, lorries and buildings. The plans had been obtained by British Intelligence and passed to Colin Wallace in Information Policy in 1972, at which point Wallace had passed them on to the press. The *Daily Mirror* covered the story, and, as Paul Foot noted, made it clear that the 'Doomsday' plan was, crucially, a proposed reaction to a Protestant attack.[43]

However, in 1974, further documents, which added some detail, were found. These were passed to Wallace, who recalled, 'we were simply given the documents and told to prepare them for a press conference which would announce to the world that an IRA plan had been uncovered to blow up half of Belfast, including large areas occupied by ordinary people.'[44] Despite the plan being defensive, a fact that Wallace raised, Wallace, 'set to work to prepare those parts of the maps and documents which would reveal the IRA plan – and to take out anything in them which gave a clue to their defensive purpose'.[45]

On 13 May 1974, Wilson revealed the existence of the plans to a shocked House of Commons. A press conference at Stormont presented the selected documents to the media. A cautious Robert Fisk, then working for *The Times*, wrote of the find: 'If, as Mr Wilson has said, they represented a campaign that was about to be put into action, then the Provisionals, who have always claimed to be non-sectarian, emerge as an organization of awe-inspiring cynicism.'[46] This, no doubt, had been the intention.

Interestingly, the IRD writer noted that Moscow Radio had identified the 'scorched earth' story as a 'propaganda bomb'. For once the Soviets had got it right

Large sections of IRD's paper on the IRA made a guest appearance in a book entitled *The British Army in Ulster*, by former Scotland Yard press officer and Belfast journalist David Barzilay.[47] The book, published by Century of Belfast, came complete with photographs, including one of Colin Wallace. It had three reprints, the last in 1981. Barzilay told reporters at a reception for the book's publication in 1973, attended by senior members of Ulster's security forces, 'I've . . . tried to give a short history of the IRA, some of its objectives and details of some of its weaponry in order to let people see what troops were up against.'[48] Entire passages from the IRD paper were copied almost word for word.[49]

Another publication was a seventy-page booklet entitled *Fianna Fail – the IRA Connection*. Journalist Duncan Campbell who investigated the propaganda war in Northern Ireland, wrote that, 'Although it entirely lacks any details of its purported author or publisher, it provides astonishing details of phone calls and bank accounts allegedly used by Fianna Fail members.' The central allegation made was that four members of an Irish government committee, including the former Taioseach, Charles Haughey, were secretly collaborating with the IRA. According to Campbell, 'The style of writing and indeed the typography . . . is characteristic of Foreign Office Information Research Department publications both before and since.'[50]

CHAPTER EIGHTEEN

The Fall

One of the most significant developments in the anti-Communist propaganda war was the establishment of the Institute for the Study of Conflict in 1970. The formation of this new addition to existing private anti-left organizations, such as the long-established Economic League and Aims in Industry, both of which were concerned with industrial and labour issues, was a perceived gap in the market left by a retreating IRD and CIA. Brian Crozier, the ISC's founder, recalled, 'In the increasingly threatening situation, I saw a serious gap. Existing institutes or research centres . . . however worthy, were either too academic, or too neutral, or too heavily concentrated on hardware strategy. . . . The need, as I saw it, was for a research centre which would produce studies on the ever-widening range of groups and forces bringing violence, chaos and disruption into our societies, but always in the context of Soviet strategy.'[1]

The 1970s had begun well for IRD with the department moving into new areas of interest and meeting with considerable success, most notably with its contribution to the EEC campaign. Although there had been problems in Northern Ireland under the Heath government, with ministerial interest and support, IRD's future seemed secure. Nevertheless, by 1974, it had undergone considerable change and was much reduced in size, if not influence.

IRD had reached its peak, in terms of personnel, in the early 1960s. It had been cut down slightly both in 1964 and 1968, but it was not until 1970 that radical cuts began to be made. The first of these was made by Norman Reddaway, who returned to propaganda work as Supervising Under-Secretary for Information and Cultural Relations in 1970. Reddaway found IRD very different from the 'lean team' that he had worked with in the second half of the 1950s. IRD had become too big and was producing too much research without enough careful and effective exploitation of the material that it was gathering.

According to Brian Crozier, in 1973 IRD underwent cuts of a serious nature. These were driven by the Chief Clerk at the Foreign Office, Oliver Wright, who pressed for substantial economies in the department. IRD had received funding through the Secret Vote, so it had been able to spend without adequate accountability and had, in the past, exploited that fact. There was, therefore, a good case to be made. Crozier recalled:

There was much heated discussion, at the end of which it was decided that IRD should come off the secret vote. This automatically created the problem of absorbing the existing staff under the open vote. As many as one hundred personnel were taken into the Foreign Office but many others went into the Research Department. . . . It was a kind of administrative massacre, with broken careers, the disappearance of many specialists who would never be replaced, and general demoralisation.[2]

The cuts amounted to some 60 per cent, but do not appear to be reflected accurately in the figures provided to the House of Commons, which seem to contain only those on the official pay role. According to these figures, between 1971 and 1977 the official staff of IRD shrunk from 117 to 85.[3]

The cutbacks were causing IRD's Cold Warriors great concern. They believed that, at the time that their resources were being reduced, the 'Evil Empire' was growing in power and influence. Such complacency threatened the future of the Western world. In what was to be a portent of the future, the private sector moved in as the public sector retreated. The ISC had its origins in the Current Affairs Research Services Centre of the CIA news agency front, Forum World Features (FWF), but it was set up as an independent entity in 1970. The *crème de la crème* of professional Cold Warriors and IRDers moved to support Crozier. Leonard Schapiro agreed to join as chairman of the new institute, while ex-IRD pioneer, Adam Watson, joined the Founding Council. Other members included IRD contacts Max Beloff and Hugh Seton-Watson; Maj Gen Richard Clutterbuck from the Royal College of Defence Studies; Geoffrey Fairbairn, a historian at the Australian National University; Brig W.F.K. Thompson, military correspondent for the *Daily Telegraph*; and Sir Robert Thompson, who had headed the British Advisory Mission to Vietnam in the early 1960s.

To obtain funds for his new enterprise, Crozier approached his contacts in MI6, the CIA and IRD. Crozier recalled that all three initially agreed to put up some of the money. 'All three of them had agreed. CIA, IRD and MI6.'[4] However, then a problem arose and the Foreign Office withdrew its backing for the project. Crozier later explained, 'the new Permanent Under-Secretary at the Foreign Office, Sir Denis Greenhill, vetoed any British financial contribution to the Institute for the Study of Conflict. In the insider parlance of the Diplomatic Service at that time, Sir Denis Greenhill was a "better notter", with the standard characteristics: a distaste for stretching the rules, and for unwanted publicity. Faced with two British defections, the CIA decided to drop out as well.'[5]

Despite the distinct lack of funds for his new outfit, Crozier eventually managed to secure funding from international oil companies, like Shell and BP. His CIA contacts then put him in touch with Richard Mellon Scaife, heir and major shareholder in Gulf Oil, who not only took over the financing of the FWF but also funded the ISC to the tune of $100,000 a year.[6]

Although it refused to fund the ISC, IRD became both a customer and a source of information for the new organization. For example, in 1973, 'As a sign of renewed mutual confidence,' IRD commissioned a series of the ISC's 'Counter-Insurgency Studies'. Crozier recalled, 'I prepared a kind of manual for them on counter-insurgency and very sensibly it was divided into sections. Each one was numbered separately so they would give it out on a selective basis. Some people could see something but not something else, so that is the way it was done. That took some months and committee meetings and all the rest of it.'[7]

The policy of détente pursued by world leaders from the 1960s onwards opened up discussions between the West and the Communist bloc. It was a bid to ease the world away from constant confrontation and the potential of nuclear devastation. However, it had also opened up a split within the West between those who believed that the Soviets were prepared to coexist and those who believed that the Soviets were lulling the West into a sense of false security before they struck. Challenging détente became the ISC's over riding concern during the 1970s. Crozier recalled, 'Throughout my period as Director, the Institute for the Study of Conflict was involved in exposing the fallacies of "détente" and warning the West of the dangers inherent in a policy of illusion.'[8]

The ISC's critique of détente was eagerly picked up by sections of the press. For example, long-standing IRD contact R.H.C. Steed of the *Daily Telegraph* wrote an article in March 1973, illustrating, 'How détente opens the way to Soviet subversion.' The article in question was a review of an ISC study entitled *The Peacetime Strategy of the Soviet Union*, which, Steed explained, 'set out the essential facts of Russia's vast and well orchestrated campaign to overthrow Western governments by any means short of war.' Détente, he argued, brought relief to Moscow. 'Without lessening her military superiority she can reduce her crushing arms burden. She can also import the Western technology and capital assistance that she desperately needs for the modernization of her economy and the opening up of mineral and other resources.'[9]

A year later the ISC held an international conference, chaired by ex-IRD head Sir Ralph Murray, on the 'New Dimensions of Security in Europe'. The ISC 'Special Report', which contained the four study group reports presented at the conference, argued that 'The situation in Western Europe leaves no room for complacency. There is a dangerous conjunction of military weakness, half-heartedness towards political unity, economic crisis and social unrest.'[10]

A more extreme perception of détente was provided by Chapman Pincher. In his book *The Secret Offensive*, he described détente as a Soviet deception designed to cover increasing subversion and military build-up. According to Pincher, 'Brezhnev himself assured his co-conspirators that, like "peaceful coexistence" in the past, détente would not interfere with the long-term aims of active measures but would, in fact, provide a more favourable operational environment for them. . . . The military chiefs were told that if the West could be lulled into continuing "détente" until 1985, the Soviet Union would then be so well placed that it could take a much tougher line, especially as regards military intimidation.'[11]

The ISC was filling a role that an increasingly constrained and downsized IRD was no longer able to play. Adam Watson recalled, 'Obviously one had a very much freer hand. I think by then it wasn't just a question of getting out certain elementary facts. Indeed, I think one could say not that there was a need for exposing Soviet activities in the world, so much as that in a world where a press values its freedoms and doesn't like to depend on government for its information, it is obvious that there are considerable advantages in a private operation.'[12] Not only did a private propaganda organization have the advantage of apparent objectivity and disinterest, but it could also cover areas that state agencies were restrained from, or wary of, covering. One such area was domestic subversion and the activities of the British far left. This was a gap that the ISC was already in the process of filling. For example, it had already published a report in

November 1972 by Nigel Lawson, entitled 'Subversion in British Industry', targeted at companies as a means of raising further sources of finance.[13]

The report followed an approach by the ISC to the Deputy Director-General of the Confederation of British Industry, John Whitehorn, in January 1972. Following correspondence with Crozier, Whitehorn had drawn up a memorandum marked 'Strictly private and confidential' to send to leading industrialists. The proposed memorandum informed its readers that, 'During 1971 the President and Director-General off the CBI had talks with a number of heads of companies who are worried about subversive influences in British industry. . . . They have also been in touch with a number of organizations which seek in their different ways to improve matters.' Whitehorn pointed out that, while the State's security forces were concerned with illegal subversion, business had a legitimate interest in defeating the efforts of those whose activities ran counter to their interests but nevertheless remained legal. He then called for financial support for a number of private organizations whose work complemented the aims of business leaders. Interestingly, he commented that 'Their objectives and methods naturally vary; and we see no strong case to streamline them or bring them together more closely than is done by their present loose links and mutual cooperation.'[14]

The organizations in question included Aims of Industry, Common Cause Ltd, the Economic League, the Industrial Research and Information Services Ltd, and the ISC. The ISC's main activity, the memorandum explained, was subversive movements overseas, and 'It conducts special research under contract, especially overseas. This activity is of considerable interest to industry, in particular to overseas investors. Its overheads are £30,000 a year. It plans to take an increasing interest in the study of subversion at home, and has a research project on the drawing board on conflict in British industry to be carried out, if finance is forthcoming through through case studies of conflicts in the docks, shipbuilding, motor industry, and construction.'[15]

The ISC's first paper on subversion in British industry was followed by the special report 'Sources of Conflict in British Industry',[16] which, published as it was in the heat of a general election in 1974, caused considerable fuss. Crozier recalled, 'Just before polling day, the Institute's report . . . had been published with unprecedented publicity. . . . To our surprise, David Astor bought it for the *Observer*. . . . A whole page was devoted to the controversial last section of the report. Congratulations on my "uncanny sense of timing" reached me from friends and strangers.'[17]

The period 1970 to 1974 had been marked in the Labour Party by a definite swing to the left. By the time that Labour was elected in February 1974, Britain had entered a period of widely perceived crisis. According to Crozier, who believed that the new Labour government was 'deeply penetrated' by Communists, the advent of Labour power also caused a degree of disquiet within IRD. 'When Labour got in 1964 and again in the early 1970s, they were very worried. I mean the second time that Labour came in after Heath had collapsed as a result of the miners' strike, they panicked and without any orders from above they stopped issuing anything on parties in this country, which I thought was a disastrous decision. In fact, suddenly it became much more important that they should have this.'[18]

IRD's Whitehall bosses had become nervous about the political repercussions of its domestic counter-subversion role. 'Until the election, the Department (IRD) had been issuing regular and accurate reports on the rival Communist parties and on various Trotskyist groups. As soon as the news of Labour's narrow victory came, IRD suspended all its reports on subversion in Britain,' said Crozier.[19] IRD's civil servants, Crozier alleges, 'saw that the new government was closer to these problems than any previous government and they knew that there might be a bit of a scandal or . . . mass sackings or that kind of thing. I can understand why they did it. They regretted it, of course.'

But in some ways things went on as before. A former IRD researcher working in the department in the 1970s observed that, unsurprisingly, what his senior colleagues demanded were analyses that identified the failings of the Soviet system. When he had once offered the opinion that the Soviet education system had some merits, he had been firmly told that this was of no interest.[20] By the mid-1970s the relatively relaxed atmosphere that the department had had in the late 1940s and early 1950s had gone. According to one IRD deskman of the period, 'IRD officials themselves were screened from parts of what went on and ordered not to tell even other FO staff where they worked.'[21]

Then came an exposé that made IRD bosses even more nervous. In summer 1975 came the story in the radical London guide *Time Out* that had linked Forum World Features to the CIA.[22] Two months later, with Crozier as its common link, the ISC also came under the spotlight. Some 1,500 ISC documents came into the hands of journalists Phil Kelly and Steve Weissmann. *Time Out* reported that, 'the leak of literally hundreds of secret documents to *Time Out* revealed a CIA hand behind the London Think Tank, the Institute of the Study of Conflict.'[23] The tangled webs of the secret state were becoming exposed and investigative journalists were closing in on IRD.

The political climate was changing both nationally and internationally. The CIA's murky past was exposed to daylight in a series of congressional hearings. In 1976, the *New York Times* ran a leader on the CIA's involvement with journalists. 'Practically as well as philosophically, this was wrong. American readers have a right to assurance that the journalists are not in any sense accountable to unseen paymasters. And foreign sources of news and the international consumers of American news have a right to expect that government purposes do not influence the process of reporting and editing.' The idea that the intelligence services had an open remit was beginning to disintegrate and the question was raised: 'Were they sometimes detrimental to democracy?'

Similar questions were being asked in Britain. It was James Callaghan's Foreign Secretary in 1975, Anthony Crosland, who started to examine IRD. Crosland came from the right-wing Gaitskellite section of the Labour Party and could by no means be characterized as soft on the Soviet Union. One of those close to him at the time recalled, 'There was a report on the future of IRD, then under Ray Whitney. What IRD then did was unattributable anti-Soviet, anti-Communist propaganda. Only briefing against Communism, no other ideologies, not right-wing ones.'[24] Crosland was not impressed by IRD, which he felt inappropriate to the times. A colleague recalled, 'Quite frankly they were just Cold Warriors. We felt there was a need for an organization with a wider brief, so we gave them a sort of test. We asked them to write a broad philosophical briefing on South Africa. What they came back with was a briefing, *South Africa: the Communist Peril*. It completely ignored the bad behaviour of the Apartheid State. Obviously, they had failed to get the point entirely.'[25]

As he recalled, where IRD failed, for Crosland, was that it was only directed against the Communist threat. Crosland wanted something else. 'We wanted to do business even handedly, about all forms of tyranny and oppression.'[26] IRD and, for that matter, the ISC had trouble grasping the mood of the time. Although officially set up to campaign for social democracy, IRD's *raison d'être* had always been anti-Communism. It was thus ill-equipped to turn its attention to non-Communist dictatorships, criticism of which often came from the Soviet Union and the left. To many Cold Warriors, left-wing critics of South Africa were to a greater or lesser extent the witting or unwitting servants of Communism and Soviet policy. It was this analysis that in turn led to the failure of the Cold War professionals to understand the New Left as it grew during the 1960s. As far as they were concerned, you were 'either with us or against us'. They did not understand a generation whose motto was 'A pox on both your houses'. By the mid 1970s IRD was out of touch.

It is not known whether or not Crosland had intended to retain IRD in one form or another. In 1976 he died suddenly and his place was taken by a young right-wing Labour MP, David Owen. Owen, like Crosland, soon had his attention drawn to IRD. According to Crozier, following hostile questions about the ISC in the House of Commons, Evan Luard, a junior minister under Owen, looked into Whitehall contacts with the organization. According to Crozier, 'He sent for a list of recipients of material from the Information Research Department, saw my name on it, and alerted Dr Owen. Apparently alarmed, the future defector from the Labour Party took the momentous decision, in May 1977, to close down the Department. Thus the Labour Government had destroyed the only active instrument of counter-subversion in the United Kingdom . . . as a sop to the Left. The KGB had won, possibly when it least expected victory.' IRD, Crozier believed, which had been set up by Bevin to take on Communism, 'was now being destroyed by the very forces against which Labour had fought'.[27]

Chapman Pincher took a similar view when he wrote regarding Callaghan and Owen's decision to close IRD. He said: 'Their reasons have never been made plain but the Labour Government was in a phase when it desperately needed to pacify its far left to remain in office. It can be safely assumed that the Politburo was pleased.'[28]

There is some truth in Crozier's allegation. According to an adviser to Callaghan at the time, IRD's right-wing contacts were a factor in the decision to close the department.[29] Indeed, according to the *Guardian*, Owen confirmed that the 'private circulation list had become suspect'.[30]

However, concern with the political complexion of IRD's contact list was by no means the whole story. Another factor in Owen's decision was undoubtedly the need for reform and economies in the Foreign Office. Owen recalled in his autobiography, 'In 1976 Sir Colin Crowe undertook an investigation of the three information departments of the Foreign Office: the Information and Administration Department, IAD; the Guidance and Information Policy Department, GIPD; and IRD.'[31] Indeed, the whole of the Diplomatic Service was then under review, and, despite an extremely effective campaign by Foreign Office civil servants, the final White Paper cut the Research Department by 17 per cent, while overseas information staff were cut by 16 per cent.[32]

The result of Sir Colin Crowe's investigation was a review of IRD's terms of reference. The formal shift from a concentration on anti-Communism to a wider concern with British interests in general, in line with Crosland's thinking, was clear. In a memorandum written by Crowe in 1976, entitled 'Revised Terms of Reference for IRD', IRD had a positive role:

> to influence decisions being taken abroad in matters affecting our economic, defence and political interests and to persuade international opinion of our case where specifically British interests are at stake, e.g. Northern Ireland, Southern Africa, or in bilateral disputes to which the UK is one of the parties. Its major role however is defensive, exposing and countering of threats both to the home base, the UK, coming from abroad, and to the interests of our allies and alliances, notably the EEC and NATO. This defensive role carries with it the capacity to counter-attack, to counter activities which damage British interests abroad or hamper the acceptance of HMG's foreign policy.[33]

However, everyone knew that it was not going to work. Inside IRD the writing was on the wall. As an IRD member of staff recalled, 'It was clear that they were going to wind up IRD. There was a considerable amount of panic. There was graffiti in the toilets and people started to look for other jobs.' Internal secrecy, which had mostly prevented discussion about the department's history, began to break down. According to the same member of staff, 'We picked up through gossip what the origins of the department were – that was when things started getting shaky. It was only later I realised how disliked IRD was by the rest of the FO. . . . There was a suspicion of IRD people in the Foreign Office. There were about twelve old timers. As it became clear that major changes were imminent a last ditch effort was made to save the department. Then they began to talk about old times.'[34]

Indeed, there had always been hostility towards IRD from the Foreign Office mainstream. Many diplomats felt that IRD's activities were not suitable or useful. IRD insiders felt that this attitude was based on a simplistic reaction: that propaganda work was 'not for officers and gents'. Whether Owen was influenced by Foreign Office hostility to IRD is not known, but, as he told us, a more fundamental reason for closing IRD was the policy of détente. For many inside and outside government and the Civil Service, détente appeared to be a retreat from justified confrontation of the enemy. It was a retreat that some saw as outright surrender to long-term Soviet objectives.[35] Even such hard-line Cold Warriors as Henry Kissinger, who had persuaded Nixon to recognize the People's Republic of China and pursue the SALT I talks with the USSR on limiting strategic limitations, was increasingly seen as 'soft on Communism' by the Cold Warrior fraternity.

Supporters of détente took a radically different view. While some critics saw détente as a cover for further Soviet subversion, some old anti-Communists saw the situation quite differently. And for Owen:

> Détente meant something to some of us who fought for it against all the odds. . . . you started to put obligations on both sides of the Cold War. I think looking back it

was one of the most successful parts of the Cold War. The idea that it all started with Reagan is complete rubbish. The break-up of the Soviet Union has been a slow and steady process in which at different times you used different instruments.[36]

Later right-wing critics of détente would argue that both SALT I and SALT II gave the Soviet Union strategic advantages in the nuclear field. As for the Helsinki Final Act (HFA), as Paul Mercer argued, 'In return for some vague and, in the event, dishonoured commitments to the recognition of basic human rights, the Soviet Union gained political concessions, trading links and, in particular, greater access to Western technology.'[37] However, this was not how the architects of Helsinki saw it, attacked as they were for giving in to Soviet pressure. Owen recalled, 'We . . . believed in the dialogue. Openness and greater transparency, that's what we fought for. I now think it was successful, and through the '70s and '80s . . . the pressures we tried to bring on these people. They loathed it, they loathed the review conference of the HFA. They disliked intensely that they had signed a document which legitimated their practices being examined.'[38]

Indeed, the Helsinki Final Act, far from being a victory for the Soviets, as some of them believed at the time, was the beginning of the end. As Richard Davy noted in his study of détente, 'the Final Act as it emerged was almost the opposite of what the Soviet Union had wanted. Instead of endorsing the status quo, it was a charter for change. Instead of legitimising the Soviet sphere of influence, it legitimised Western intrusion into it. Instead of making frontiers immutable, it specifically affirmed the principle of peaceful change.'[39]

Within IRD, steeped as it was in the darker side of Soviet policy, there was also concern about the new policy. According to Crozier, IRD officials were 'worried and sceptical' about détente.[40] An IRD Background Brief expressed similar sentiments. The paper on détente, dated November 1975, over a year into the new Labour administration, echoed ISC papers and right-wing concerns. Entitled 'Two Standards on Détente', the briefing argued that 'Analysis of Soviet and East European comment since the close of the Conference on Security and Co-operation in Europe (CSCE) on August 1, 1975, shows the Communist-ruled countries continuing to interpret détente and peaceful coexistence as allowing, and even assisting, the promotion of Communist revolutions throughout the world.'[41] As historian Peter Hennessy remarked in an article written in 1983, 'a frequent complaint from the more détente-minded in Whitehall was that: "We have one foreign policy, IRD has another".'[42] Although IRD briefings were, by definition, not government policy, factual briefings implicitly attacking the policy were undoubtedly giving ammunition to the opponents of government.

However, other sources who have had close involvement with IRD have made more serious allegations regarding the department's demise. A slightly different conclusion is suggested by Colin Wallace: 'Labour ministers including David Owen . . . discovered by various means that some of the material being run against the Labour Party during the '70s emanated from IRD. Now there may be very good other reasons why it was curtailed, but someone who was very close to David Owen, a former MP, came to see me round about '87 and we were going through a lot of the material and he actually told me that he had discussions with David Owen about this and he was quite sure that it was.'[43]

Owen made no mention of this to the authors, but said that he was concerned over the unclear line of accountability that IRD had developed as a result of its close links with MI6. This is the action desk for 'black operations' whose existence former IRD staff denied for so long. MI6's accountability, like the Diplomatic Service, runs through the Foreign Secretary, but, as Owen pointed out, 'It is a completely different channel and you keep it separate and it is better to have it clear right down through the system. Once you get it into this cloudy area, then things can happen which are not right and some things happened that were not defensible or right, in the climate of the 1970s . . . I uncovered quite a few things that quite shocked me and that's why I made it absolutely clear this had to change.'[44]

What might once have been appropriate, was not appropriate in the era of détente as far as Owen was concerned: 'In the late '40s, '50s you could take a pretty tough stance and you could be pretty unscrupulous. You were up against something that hadn't tempered. From Krushchev onwards there was a difference. How much of difference was open to argument. But how you handled it mattered.' Owen was concerned that IRD's existence would be revealed, and its activities cause a scandal and give ammunition to the Soviets. 'If . . . you are lecturing on democratic procedures and accountability and these things, you had to have your house in order if you were to carry any conviction.'[45]

In his autobiography, Owen recalled his decision to close IRD: 'In May 1977 I agreed that there should be a comprehensive reorganization and IRD was closed . . . and a new department was formed out of the remainder. The aim was to achieve greater clarity and end the grey area, which for too long had escaped proper scrutiny, falling neither in the open area of diplomacy nor in the closed area of spying.'[46] Owen reduced IRD down to a small general-purpose section renamed the Overseas Information Department (OID). To detach the research element of IRD from its capability for covert action – the point at which Owen felt the line between IRD and MI6 had become blurred – the covert capability of IRD was removed and incorporated into MI6. 'That was the big change, the covert element – the head of the covert unit was no longer accountable to the head of OID.'[47] Exactly who the head of the covert unit was, and what he had found so shocking, Owen would not make clear.

Lord Mayhew said of the closure, 'In 1977, I think I banged into David Owen and said "What are you doing getting rid of my baby IRD?" And he said, '"Well, it was getting very big you know and of course the Communist threat was not what it was." I think that it probably expanded its sphere of operations too far. I mean, there is a limit to what you ought to do with taxpayers' money and I think perhaps some governments were tempted to use IRD for their political purposes. I don't know, I'm only guessing.'[48]

The closure of IRD was done, as ever within the Foreign Office, discreetly in April 1977. The role that IRD had played during the Cold War only began to be revealed in 1978 with a series of major media exposés. In an article in the *Guardian* on 27 January, entitled 'Death of the Department that never Was', written by David Leigh, IRD's 'world-wide propaganda network' was revealed for the first time.[49] The *Guardian* article was followed the next weekend by a more detailed article in the *Observer* by a team of researchers led by Richard Fletcher, entitled 'How the FO waged Secret Propaganda War in Britain'.[50] While the first gave an overall outline of IRD's history and demise, the second focused on IRD's links with book publishers in Britain and Ampersand. These articles were followed by several others, including critical pieces in left-wing magazines like the *Leveller*, which linked IRD's operations to the recently discredited operations of the CIA.[51]

Not surprisingly, the Soviet press agency, TASS, made as much mileage as it could out of the revelations. Immediately following the article in the *Guardian*, TASS reported that 'another political scandal' had been exposed in Britain. Despite the fact that independent British journalists had uncovered the story, TASS claimed that 'the IRD's carefully concealed activities demonstrate that the freedom of the press, which the defenders of Western democracy so persistently vaunt, has again failed to withstand a confrontation with reality'.[52] Nevertheless, the decision was, Leigh argued in 1978, 'the logical culmination of moves to bring the organization . . . under firm political control, and abolish its furtive Cold War attitudes'.[53] IRD's 'special tasks', as referred to in internal reference books at the time, had been brought to an end.[54]

The left-wing magazine the *Leveller* pointed out that the difference between IRD and CIA media operations was 'the CIA, nominally at least, did not try to affect US politics through propaganda. . . . But the IRD effort was in part deliberately directed at influencing public opinion at home'.[55] Attributing the demise of IRD to 'the collapse of the social-democrat conservative "broad right" coalition which underpinned it', the *Leveller* argued that, 'As the right has moved further right, its anti-Communism has become too hysterical even for Labour Ministers: like the late Anthony Crosland . . . or Dr David Owen.'[56]

Mayhew, interviewed by David Leigh, came quickly to IRD's defence. Echoing Sefton Delmer's characterization of black propaganda as defined by a hidden source, Mayhew commented, 'We certainly did absolutely nothing to distort or twist the British media. . . . It was only black propaganda in the sense that our work was all undercover.'[57]

A few old IRD friends came to defend it from the exposure from the liberal press. American theatre critic and polemicist Milton Shulman, writing in the *Evening Standard*, said at the time, 'The complex explanations for this decision include the Foreign Office's need for economy, suspicion amongst certain Labour Ministers about IRD's contacts and a desire to further the atmosphere of détente between Russia and the West.' Shulman, who had himself been asked by Stephen Watts to write one of the Background Books, said, 'It seems to be both pusillanimous and short-sighted that just as our economic condition is about to put us back into a position of real power and influence in the world, our expertise at disseminating a fair and factual picture of ourselves as well as combating Communist propaganda aimed at subverting our institutions should be discouraged and curtailed in the transitory names of economy and détente.'[58]

Richard Fletcher continued to uncover more of IRD's hidden past. On the day before the *Observer* published the January 1978 story, Fletcher met up with a close friend of Col Sheridan's. This former SOE officer had once taken wartime sibs to Churchill's bunker under Admiralty Arch for the 'Old Man' to approve. Fletcher said, 'He was a sick man and was obviously keen to tell me something: he said he had never spoken to anyone about these things before, not even his family. Before I left he said: "I'll give you a clue. One word – Britanova. Follow this up and you'll be surprised where it will lead you."' Britanova led to the unravelling of the whole MI6/IRD news agency operation. However, IRD had still not lost its potential for political embarrassment. Some months later, Fletcher was commissioned by Sean MacBride of UNESCO to tell the IRD story. He wrote the paper entitled 'Free Flow of News' and delivered it to MacBride. Its opening paragraphs read:

> The current debate on freedom of the press is largely conducted in terms of generalities. This is mainly due to a lack of detailed empirical studies as to how the media actually operate, as against how the various protagonists imagine that they function.
>
> Gerald Long of Reuters is quite right in asking those who allege that the press is manipulated 'to tell us how the manipulation is brought about, how it works, to give us some examples of it'.
>
> This paper, a historical study of some of the methods used by one ex-colonial power to present a favourable image of itself in the Third World, looks at one aspect of the larger problem of the world flow of news. It is hoped that it will prompt other researchers to examine in more detail some of the further questions that it raises.

Gerald Long been challenging Third World critics to demonstrate manipulation by Western media. As Fletcher proved in his paper, Reuters had been closely involved in such manipulation. This, you might think, would be grist to the UNESCO mill. Not a bit of it. They did not print it, although they had paid for it, because they did not want to upset the British or American government, which at the time were refusing to pay their crucial annual UNESCO dues. An edited version of the paper eventually appeared in the *Guardian*, setting off more interest in IRD's activities.

Lacking IRD's covert faculty, finance and numbers, IRD's successor, the OID, was a pale shadow of its predecessor, its output no longer appreciated by those who had benefited most. Crozier has commented that, 'Unlike the IRD papers . . . the origin of the new service was stated on each paper issued. The "unattributable" rule, which had proved so effective in the past, had gone.'[59] Nevertheless, the OID continued to issue IRD-type briefings, for example, on Northern Ireland.[60] In 1988 the Foreign Office was forced to admit and correct mistakes in an OID Background Brief entitled 'The Provisional IRA International Contacts Outside the United States'. The briefing, sections of which appeared in the national press, smeared, among others, writer Liz Curtis as one such IRA contact. Writs were threatened and the Foreign Office backed down.[61]

The need for IRD's more covert skills had also not gone. In the 1980s, as détente gave way to renewed confrontation and the decision to station US Cruise missiles on British soil provoked confrontation with a revitalized CND, the precedent of IRD attracted renewed interest. In 1981, concern at the success of CND's propaganda campaign led ministers such as Douglas Hurd, Minister of State at the Foreign Office, and Peter Blaker, Minister of State at the Ministry of Defence, to seek a means of responding. Following discussions, Hurd and Blaker agreed to set up a small unit, specifically concerned with CND and defence issues.[62] Crozier remembered that 'It was resurrected very briefly. And on a smaller scale . . . but it only lasted, as far as I know, about a year . . . the man who ran it was Peter Blaker . . . As far as I know it wasn't even named, or maybe it was part of the other Information Department, anyway, I mean, in terms of volume of stuff that was distributed it was no more than about two percent of the old material.'[63]

Crozier, like other ex-IRD officials, had been advising both Blaker and Margaret Thatcher to set something up to counter CND and internal subversion. In 1978 a recommendation made by Shield, a body made up of members Crozier, Conservative MP Stephen Hastings, ex-MI6 man Nicholas Elliott and banker and SOE veteran Harry Sporborg, to advise Thatcher on foreign affairs, intelligence and domestic subversion, advised the establishment of a Counter Subversion Executive. According to Crozier, the suggestion was discussed at a meeting with Thatcher and Peter Carrington. 'I asked for reactions to its functioning in the margin of the Foreign Office, as IRD had done, but Carrington . . . would have none of it. There was indeed little logic in handling subversion from a foreign ministry, but then that was what IRD had done, successfully enough within its limits.'[64]

A small unit, set up along IRD lines in 1981, appears initially to have established contact with the British Atlantic Committee and Conservative MP Ray Whitney. The latter had been the last head of IRD and its scaled-down successor the OID until 1978, when he resigned to fight a by-election in the safe Conservative seat of High Wycombe. According to ex-IRD officials, the unit was quite effective until Blaker, who oversaw the operation, was succeeded.[65]

If IRD had gone, many of its principles continued to be applied. Those who had served or had contact with the secret department had learned skills that would continue to be used to control and manipulate information, both at home and abroad. A generation of Cold Warriors, whose skills had been honed in the war with Hitler, passed their skills on to a successor generation who have learned the merits of rebuttal, selectivity and spin in imposing their own version of events on the general public.

Conclusions

> The most generally held concept of propaganda is that it is a series of tall stories, a tissue of lies, and that lies are necessary for effective propaganda. . . . Anyone holding that conviction is extremely susceptible to propaganda, because when propaganda does tell the 'truth', he is then convinced that it is no longer propaganda.[1]

What is to be made of IRD? How effective was it? And what did it achieve? Estimating the success of any propaganda operation or agency, except commercial advertising where triumphs can be measured in financial terms, is extremely difficult. Norman Reddaway considers several IRD operations to have been major successes, most notably IRD's campaign against Sukarno in Indonesia. According to Lord Mayhew, IRD had no organized machinery for measuring the impact of its propaganda. However, he was sure that it had an effect, notably in the Labour Party where 'IRD's propaganda coincided with a considerable defeat of the extreme Left'; and in the trade unions where IRD material 'stiffened the backbones of trade union leaders who were anti-Communist'.[2] In part IRD had succeeded in the task it had been set by Mayhew. By promoting and supporting specific intellectuals, politicians and trade unionists it helped shape and define the political consensus for a generation. That consensus, which reached from the right-wing of the Labour Party across to the far right of the political spectrum, was defined by its anti-Communism. It is notable that when, in the 1970s, that anti-Communist alliance began to come apart, the consensus which had been reached in much of the rest of British political life, for example on the welfare state, also began to break down.

Overall, although few specific operations can be identified where a particular effect is clear, the evidence suggests that IRD's influence was enormous. While the Background Books, for instance, never produced a classic or world bestseller, overall through all its myriad outlets IRD influenced journalists, academics and the public's perception of the Cold War. Whether this could have been achieved with a less covert operation is debatable. Certainly, there seems little reason why campaigns like that to expose the horrors of the Soviet gulag could not have been conducted openly. However, although an open department distributing attributable material could have been just as effective, in that case at least, it seems clear that as long as journalists were willing to follow the rules, the unattributable nature of IRD's material was its strength. Information and exclusives could be directed solely to those who would make appropriate use of them. And while to the man in the street it appeared that a diverse range of media were separately coming to similar conclusions about Communism and the nature of the Cold War, in fact much of the media was singing from a hymn sheet which was provided by IRD. For this the media itself must accept a degree of responsibility. While there is no doubt that many journalists individually were in tune with Foreign Office thinking, to rely on IRD as a major source, as many did, was complacent. With respect to colonialism and Northern Ireland, the portrayal of these troubles as extensions of the Cold War distorted reality and prevented ordinary people from grasping the real issues at stake.

Most importantly, by organizing a constant stream of anti-Communist material into the media machine IRD could manipulate the media's focus towards issues, events and aspects of any given situation of its own selection, encouraging a polarized perception of the world as divided between Communist and anti-Communist. A perception of the world upon which the Cold War thrived. And although it is almost impossible to estimate the degree to which the media's focus was distorted during the Cold War, given IRD's close collaboration with the United States' own far greater propaganda offensive, it clearly had an effect, however unquantifiable.

This inquiry is necessarily imperfect. The veil of secrecy behind which governments so often hide their activities is not easily drawn aside. But it is clear enough from the material that in the late 1940s the British government set out secretly to influence its own people and the press of the world to its own ends, and laid careful plans to this effect. In 1992 two Britain-based academics, Scott Lucas and Cate Morris asked a number of pertinent questions in a paper on IRD: 'How much of the material in the "independent" British press and the BBC was "planted" by a government body that was not accountable to Parliament or, arguably, the cabinet? At what point did "anti-Soviet" operations turn into an "anti-anti-British" campaign? Who controlled the implementation of "subversion": the Cabinet, the Foreign Secretary, permanent Foreign Office officials, MI6, or another group?'[3] Although to a great extent these questions remain unanswerable in detail, it is perhaps appropriate to offer some tentative responses. The evidence so far suggests a considerable amount of IRD material found its way into the British media, despite the claim by ex-IRD officials that 90 per cent of its work was directed abroad. Secondly, IRD was an anti-Communist propaganda operation, but as almost all opposition to Britain during the Cold War was defined within its framework, in which opposition and criticism of the West would by definition benefit Communism, to be anti-Communist was to be anti-anti-British. Finally, from the limited evidence available, it appears that while the day-to-day work of IRD was overseen by permanent civil service officials, campaigns to subvert domestic or foreign enemies seem to have demanded political approval from the Foreign Office Minister responsible. However, exactly where the line was drawn at any given time and how the machinery which linked IRD with MI6 and MI5 worked remains partially unclear. Nevertheless, Lord Owen's comments suggest that in his view IRD had, in the past, overstepped the line.

Former IRD officials emphasize that their material was accurate and factual. Indeed, Mayhew accused IRD critics of failing to produce evidence of a single lie or fabrication. Most of IRD's output was indeed true and accurate. However, it was selective, delivered with a careful spin. Propaganda with impact is not to be found in lies delivered in stilted language. It is far more effective and likely to be found in the propagation of selective truths – a set of facts which on their own appear compelling, but which ignore evidence suggesting any alternative explanation. Truth, or facts, which the British propagandists discovered during the Second World War proved potentially a far more effective weapon than lies and untruths which might backfire. IRD's Cold Warriors applied the lesson with considerable effect, even to the extent that the journalists and organizations which they serviced treated them as a normal research department.

Although IRD was closed in 1977, its spirit lives on in many ways at the intersection between politics and the media. Any organization that can propagate its message in such a way that it appears to be a consensus reached by diverse opinion, yet is really a script written by one person or group of people, ultimately threatens to distort public perception of any issue. Consequently, such attempts deserve attention whether they are made by government ministers, or media proprietors. As Jacques Ellul, the French social and political philosopher, noted, 'When the eyeglasses are out of focus, everything one sees through them is distorted.'[4]

Appendix

We include here a typical IRD background briefing as an example of the department's work. It can be found at the Public Record Office, reference FO975/33.

FOREIGN OFFICE,
S.W.1

30th August, 1949.

CONFIDENTIAL
PR.2502/8/913

THE COMMUNIST 'PEACE OFFENSIVE'

We are sending you with this letter a copy of a paper, for use in publicity and elsewhere, on the Communist 'peace offensive'. Topicality is given by the Communist-inspired peace congress which will start in Mexico City on 5th September, and by the one which has just ended in Moscow; other examples were Wroclaw (September 1948) and Paris (April 1949).

2. In view of the great importance which the Kremlin attaches to this movement, you should make every effort to make widely known the real motives behind it. The Secretary of State has directed that attention should be given to this matter.

3. This paper is sent to Iron Curtain posts for information only.

Yours ever,

INFORMATION RESEARCH DEPARTMENT.

THE COMMUNIST 'PEACE OFFENSIVE'

Why is it that the Kremlin has recently become so interested in 'peace'? Why have instructions gone out that 'peace congresses' should be held wherever possible – in Paris, New York, Moscow and now Mexico City?

'Peace' is submitted by the Kremlin to the same test as any other policy – does it in present circumstances forward the world revolution? If it does, it will be for the time being, and just so long as it suits the Kremlin's purposes, the party line; but, if the situation changed, war would be pursued with equal enthusiasm. To understand the reasons behind these present tactics, and to see how peace propaganda is designed purely for countries outside Communist control, it is only necessary to look at the main lines of Soviet world strategy.

Soviet Strategy.

The basic pronouncements are to be found in the leading textbooks of Communism, e.g.

> 'We are living not merely in a state, but in a system of states, and the existence of the Soviet Republic side by side with imperialist states for a long time is unthinkable. One or the other must triumph in the end. And before that end supervenes a series of frightful collisions between the Soviet Republic and the bourgeois states will be inevitable. That means that, if the ruling class, the proletariat, wants to hold sway, it must prove its capacity to do so by this military organisation . . .'
>
> ('Problems of Leninism', page 160)

This was originally said by Lenin in 1919, and is quoted in Stalin's essay 'On the Problems of Leninism' (first published in 1926), followed by the remark 'clear, one would think'.

This work now appears in his collected 'Problems of Leninism' which is compulsory reading for all Communist Party members throughout the world as a guide both for theory and action; it is obligatory for study in all Soviet schools. Further to prove its present-day relevance one might quote from just one of the tributes which appeared in practically all Soviet journals on the 25th anniversary of the publication of a course of lectures entitled 'The Foundations of Leninism', which now forms the introduction to 'Problems of Leninism'. 'New Times' (No. 19, May 4th, 1949), the official Soviet propaganda weekly with a world-wide circulation said: '. . . every line strikes today . . . as trenchantly and as telling as it did a quarter of a century ago . . . this work is as true and applicable in the conditions of today as it was in the conditions of a quarter of a century ago when it first appeared'.

Works that the Kremlin considers out of date receive very brusque treatment. The official 'Large Soviet Encyclopaedia' is to be completely revised; since the great purges many of the biographical articles read rather unfortunately. The stenographic reports of the early Plenums of the Communist Party have been completely suppressed, since some parts of them do not agree with the officially approved Party history. 'Problems of Leninism' has never been revised and is never likely to be.

War, however, is something to be thought about much more seriously today than it was in the '20s when it may have seemed that a Communist revolution was about to sweep across the world. Besides, the North Atlantic Treaty has issued a severe warning to any power which may have been thinking of any low-cost military adventures. In fact, the potential threat carried by the Soviet armed forces, so far from advancing the Communist plan, has resulted in a very great drawing together and stiffening of the democratic camp. What Stalin has called the 'objective conditions' for success do not at present exist.

In 'The Foundations of Leninism' (1924), however, Stalin also out-lines the broad strategy to be followed by Communism in the third stage of the revolution, i.e. after it had been accomplished in the U.S.S.R. He writes:-

'Objective: to consolidate the dictatorship of the proletariat in one country, using it as a base for the overthrow of imperialism in all countries. The revolution is spreading beyond the confines of one country; the epoch of world revolution has commenced'.

('Problems of Leninism', page 69).

This revolution, however much Communists may try to deceive people by calling their aims 'democratic' or 'progressive' has no connection with the revolution that social democrats went. If we look at the programmes of revolutionary parties of 100 years ago, we see that at our present stage we have accomplished and in many cases far surpassed them. A revolution has already taken place in this country, and is still in progress. Certain people do not seem capable of recognizing a revolution when they see one, merely because it is not accompanied by fighting at barricades, famine and purges. Our revolution will continue just as far and just as fast as the majority in this country wish and the realities of the situation permit.

We have all observed the so-called 'revolutions' in Eastern Europe since the war. These meant the imposition of the ready-made dictatorship of a minority backed by the reality or threat of Soviet armed force. A more suitable title for them would be 'prefabricated revolutions' or 'steps in Soviet imperialism'.

(To prove this, we have only to listen to Communist spokesmen. Revai, the Hungarian Communist leader, has recently said, when analysing to his Communist Party how they obtained power:-

'in the beginning we were a minority. Nevertheless, we had a decisive influence in the armed forces. Our strength . . . was increased by the existence of the Soviet Union and the presence of the Soviet Army on whose support we could always rely'.

The Central Committee of the Communist Party of the Soviet Union said, in its letter to the Central Committee of the Communist Party of Yugoslavia on 4th May, 1948:-

'. . . the Soviet Army came to the aid of the Yugoslav people . . . and in this way created the conditions which were necessary for the Communist Party of Yugoslavia to achieve power. Unfortunately, the Soviet Army did not and could not render such assistance to the French and Italian Communist Parties.'

In its number of August 11th, 1948 the authoritative Czech Communist Tvorba read:-

'The Tito group declared that they were able to build socialism with their own strength, which means without the help of the Soviet Union and the other Peoples' Democracies. They also denied the <u>decisive role which the Red Army played</u> in setting up the Yugoslav People's Democracy.

Experience has shown that the participation of the Red Army in liberation is the decisive factor. This can be seen from events in France . . . where the main factor was missing.'

In Czechoslovakia the Red Army put the Communists in control of the police and other key positions; and the Communists were in a position to stage the Putch of 1948 without actually calling back the Red Army, which merely stayed as a threat round the Czech frontiers.)

As we have already said, the North Atlantic Treaty has removed the 'objective conditions' for such assistance to be safely given to any further countries in Europe. Nevertheless an extremely frank statement that long-term Soviet strategy remains still the same has recently come from a uniformed major of the Soviet Military Administration in Berlin. Speaking in a series of lectures on 'Bolshevik Strategy and Tactics' on 30th May, Major Patent said:-

'. . . the ultimate aim of Communism – world revolution – remains unchanged; only the means . . . change from the time to time . . . the decisive factor is correct timing. when the enemy is stronger, it is of no use kicking against the pricks. The time to attack an enemy and destroy him is when his forces, after an interval, have begun to disintegrate.'

It should be noted that Soviet majors do not use a House of Soviet Culture as a platform for airing their private views; lectures on Party strategy are meant as guides to action for the party cadres. Further, Major Patent was in full accord with that part of Stalin's 'The Foundations of Leninism' which deals with 'Strategy and Tactics'. In this section Stalin sets out certain rules of 'strategic leadership', of which the following is significant in this context:

'Manoeuvring the reserves with a view to effecting a proper retreat when the enemy is strong, when retreat is inevitable, when to accept battle forced upon us by the enemy is obviously disadvantageous, when, with the given alignment of forces, retreat becomes the only way to ward off a blow against the vanguard and to keep the reserves intact . . . the object of this strategy is to gain time, to demoralize the enemy, and to accumulate forces in order later to assume the offensive.'

('Problems of Leninism', page 74).

Soviet Tactics.
What then are Soviet tactics when their opponent is strong? They are to attempt by any and every means to isolate the democratic countries from each other, and governments

from their peoples. Communists will ally themselves with any movement, whatever its principles, so long as it will help them in reaching this objective.

(As Lenin said, in 'Left-Wing Communism – an Infantile Disorder':-

'. . . the most powerful enemy can be conquered only by exerting the utmost effort, and by necessarily, thoroughly . . . and skilfully taking advantage or every, even the smallest, rift among the opponents . . . and by taking advantage of every opportunity . . . of gaining a mass ally, even though this ally be only temporary, vacillating, unstable, unreliable and conditional'.)

If only the strength of the democratic countries should be sufficiently weakened, the 'objective conditions', where even a threat of force might be effective, would then exist. Every reasonable person wants peace and the Kremlin is making a determined attempt to use this universal sentiment for its own ends. Its tactics concerning peace are developed on three main lines, each of which consists of superficially attractive ideas to catch the unthinking or unwary.

(a) Armament expenditure.
The Kremlin, which has armed forces over 4 million strong and an armament industry of proportionate size, is making great efforts to show that in non-Communist countries any expenditure on such objects means impoverishment for the peoples in them; and that other governments should therefore at once stop spending their resources on such reprehensible matters.

(b) The horrors of atomic warfare.
The press in Communist-controlled countries takes the line that the atom bomb is extremely ineffective as a weapon of warfare; the Communist press, however, in non-Communist countries is frequently full of blood-curdling details of the horrors of a atomic warfare and the wickedness of the Americans in developing such a weapon. One is reminded of the remark that, if only the Soviet Government possessed large stocks of atomic bombs, what a powerful weapon for peace it would be!

(c) Neutrality.
The Kremlin has also declared that any forms of alliance or even friendship between democratic powers is extremely dangerous to the national independence of these countries, and puts them in great danger of becoming mere colonial appendages of the U.S.A. Unfortunately, it is becoming very widely realized that the term 'national independence' means to Communists 'support the Soviet Union right or wrong'. Also the years before 1939 have shown many people that 'neutrality' is always encouraged by those who would find it easier to pick off their victims one by one; until the time has come to absorb their prey such predatory powers are always very solicitous about their 'freedom' and 'independence'.

Soviet 'Peace Offensive'.
This tactical move is so important, however, that it requires closer study. The first

essential to realize is that 'peace' in the mouth of Communists and their supporters means something quite different from what we mean by it. This type of 'peace' might be defined as 'ANY STATE OF AFFAIRS, INCLUDING WAR, WHICH HELPS THE SOVIET UNION'. At the recent so-called 'Peace Conference' in Paris, the self-styled 'delegates' made great play with the horrors of war in Greece, Malaya and Indonesia. Such people as the Greek Government and the vast majority of the population, who were defending their own country, were condemned as criminal warmongers; the forces of peace were of course the rebels and such countries as Albania and Bulgaria which were supplying them with arms and bases. When a solitary British speaker remarked that it might be as well to deplore also the desolation of war in China, he was received in silence, and the French Communist daily 'Humanité', without quoting what he said, merely recorded that he made 'some remarks that did not receive the approbation of the congress'. On the news of the fall of Nanking, however, the 'delegates' stood and cheered for two minutes; in the Chinese war, of course, the Communist side was winning – a real triumph for 'peace'.

Further light on 'peace' is thrown by official Communist pronouncements. For example the Soviet 'History of Diplomacy' (published 1945) says:-

'To the same group of examples of the concealment of predatory ends behind noble principles also belong the instances of the exploitation of the idea of the disarmament and pacifist propaganda in the broad sense of the word for one's own purposes. From time immemorial, the idea of disarmament has been one of the most favoured forms of diplomatic dissimulation of the true motives and plans of those governments which have been seized by such a sudden "love of peace".'

An interesting statement on this subject was also made by the Communist Minister of Defence in Hungary, Farkas, who wrote in a leading article in 'Szabad Nep' on April 12th:-

. . . a certain pacifism has made itself felt within the ranks of our party, particularly lately. Slogans like 'we want no more wars' are very significant of this pacifism. First of all, therefore, we have to overcome this feeling of pacifism within our own party in order to be able to fight it down in the masses . . . a considerable feeling of paci-fism is reigning among our people, particularly among our women and peasants . . . we must, however, continuously point out to them that what they fear – war – is wanted by the imperialists'.

The serious dangers of pacifism have also been pointed out by 'Szabad nep' (13th June), when commenting on Revai's new Ministry of Popular Education and demanding the forcible elimination of Western culture:-

'. . . the positions of the enemy in this field are just as dangerous as if he held posi-tions in economic or political life. If we remember that in the enemy's arsenal we find such mental trends as cosmopolitanism and pacifism, it is clear that in this field too we must fight for . . . our freedom.'

This type of pronouncement is not new in Communist countries. Quite shortly after the end of the war the authoritative 'Soviet Literary Gazette' (28th December 1946) was announcing its policy in the following words:-

'We do not intend to abandon the war theme . . . we must write of war so that the generation of young people that comes after us can love arms.'

What are we to think of such statements as this?

We might also glance at a 'peace offensive' of the past. After Poland had been divided up in 1939 between the Nazis and the Kremlin, in accordance with the secret Stalin-Ribbentrop agreement signed before the war began, the Nazis issued peace proposals, which were supported by the Kremlin. Stalin said (Pravda 29th November, 1939):-

'It was not Germany who attacked France and Britain, but France and Britain who attacked Germany, thus assuming responsibility for the present war. The ruling circles of Britain and France rudely declined both Germany's peace proposals and the attempts of the soviet Union to achieve the earliest termination of the war.'

Communists in other countries took up their master's line. On 22nd February, 1940, Mr. Pollitt even fought a by-election at Silvertown on the slogan 'Stop this war'. From May 1940 the whole of Europe lay under Nazi control, and the British Commonwealth were the only group fighting against them. But Communists had forgotten about anti-fascism, about the extermination policy being carried out in Europe and the defence of democracy; Mr. Pollitt had also obediently forgotten his bold words of July 1939: 'an end to the mealy-mouthed pacifism which would lie down humbly and let Fascism wipe its boots on our bodies as a preliminary to trampling us down forever'. The Kremlin thought its policies would be forwarded by the cessation fo the war, and so Communists everywhere, castigating the British Government as imperialists and warmongers, were strongly for 'peace'.

22nd June, 1941, altered all this. When Russia was forced into the war by the Nazi attack, British Communist complaint now was that the Government was not prosecuting the war hard enough. The aggressors were now the Nazis, and Great Britain, for the time being at least, had been admitted to the circle of the 'peace-loving nations'. Only till 1945, however. After the war some of our policies seemed to stand in the way of Communist-sponsored 'revolutions' in various parts of the world. We therefore reverted to our role of warmongers; the Soviet Union again became the real and only force for 'peace'.

Doves over Yugoslavia.

The emptiness of the Kremlin's views about national independence are shown very clearly in their present quarrel with Yugoslavia. Few people would regard that country as any thing but a Communist police state, run with no less rigour and ruthlessness than the Soviet Union itself; the only unusual thing about Tito is that he would like to carry out his policy in his own way. The Kremlin therefore has no words of peace for him but says instead: 'it will not tolerate such a situation, and will have to resort to other more effective means to bring to order the un-restrained Fascist offenders'.

It is, in fact, a curious phenomenon that the 'peace offensive' <u>and</u> the 'war scare' both bear the trademark 'made in Russia'. Every medium of information within Soviet Russia warns the people there daily to prepare for a war to be launched against them; we cannot help recalling here the manoeuvres of another country which was so concerned to tell its population about the 'encirclement' to which it was being subjected. Further, since the recent Soviet jamming campaign against B.B.C. and Voice of America broadcasts, most Soviet citizens have been prevented from hearing anything which might cause them to realize that the war scare did not exist in the outside world.

The 'peace offensive' therefore is clearly shown for what it is – a cover for the furtherance of Soviet imperialism. Following the party directive given out at the 'Partisans of Peace' meeting in Paris, efforts were to be made to hold similar congresses in every country. We shall, unfortunately for their sponsors, be able to recognize them for what they are. They will not consist of serious discussions, at which the mistakes made at various times by all governments are impartially criticised and means of avoiding them in future considered; if they were, good democrats would be prepared to join in. Our whole system has been built up on our right to criticise others and their equal right to criticise us. But these 'conferences' in fact consist of prepared lectures denouncing everything connected with our system in the most violent and partisan terms and extolling the Soviet Union; the audience comprises a well-drilled band of Communist sympathisers, claiming to represent the nation, but – as their record in elections has shown – representing few but themselves; there will be a small handful of genuine people who have not yet realized, though they soon will, the purpose for which their enthusiasm is being exploited; every attempt is being made to shut out the smallest criticism of the Soviet Union. Democrats can predict what these meetings will be like. We have already set out exactly what their object is, and who it fits into Soviet strategy.

(Note:- all references to 'Problems of Leninism' are taken from the 11th edition, Moscow Foreign Languages Publishing House, 1947).

Notes

INTRODUCTION
1 *The Times* 28/1/64.
2 *Observer* 28/1/78.
3 Now foreign editor of *The Times*.
4 'The Department that never was', David Leigh, *Guardian* 27/1/98.

CHAPTER 1   Indonesia: Prelude to Slaughter
1 The brutal regime of pro-Western President, General Ahmed Soeharto was mildly rebuked for its human rights record by the Labour Foreign Secretary, Robin Cook, on his visit to Indonesia in the summer of 1997. The General, aged seventy-five had been in power for over thirty years.
2 *Political Killings by Governments: Mass Killings In Indonesia (1965 to 1966) and Kampuchea (1975 to 1979)* (Amnesty International Publications, 1983).
3 Andrew Roadknight, 'United States Policy Towards Indonesia, 1945–1949: A Conflict Between Rhetoric And Reality' (unpublished MA Thesis, University of Warwick, September 1995).
4 Roadknight, 'United States Policy Towards Indonesia'.
5 BBC, WAC, E1/2,074/1, 26 November 1959, p. 1.
6 PRO FO371/54052, 'British Foreign Policy in the Far East', 31 December 1945, cited in Roadknight, 'United States Policy Towards Indonesia', p. 12.
7 Roadknight, 'United States Policy Towards Indonesia', pp. 12–13.
8 Victor Marchetti and John D. Marks, *The CIA and the Cult of Intelligence* (New York, Dell Publishing Co., 1977), pp. 51–2.
9 BBC, WAC, E1/2,074/1, 26 November 1959 p. 1.
10 Julie Southwood and Patrick Flanagan, *Indonesia: Law, Propaganda and Terror* (London, Zed Press 1983), p. 10.
11 Budiardjo was a supporter of Sukarno and was imprisoned by the army of General Soeharto. She now lives in London.
12 Carmel Budiardjo, *Surviving Indonesia's Gulag* (London, Cassell, 1996), p. 42. These organizations were largely workers and peasants unions.
13 'Liquidating Sukarno' *The Times* 8/8/1986.
14 Ibid.
15 Interview with Hunter Wade by James Oliver 21/9/1996.

16 Tony Geraghty, *Who Dares Wins: The Story of the SAS, 1950–1980* (Glasgow, Fontana, 1981), p. 76.

17 Ibid.

18 Interview with Roland Challis by James Oliver 25/4/1996.

19 Budiardjo, *Surviving Indonesia's Gulag*, pp. 45–6.

20 Ibid. p. 59.

21 Ibid.

22 Private source.

23 Interview with Norman Reddaway by James Oliver 9/1/1996.

24 Ibid.

25 Interview with Roland Challis by James Oliver 25/4/1996.

26 Ibid.

27 'Tyranny Exposed: British role in Slaughter of 500,000', *Observer* 28/7/1996.

28 *Background on Indonesia*, B. 759, 7/10/1965.

29 Ibid.

30 *Political Killings by Governments* Amnesty International Publications. Gilchrist commented to London on the massacres that, 'I have never concealed from you my belief that a little shooting in Indonesia would be an essential preliminary to effective change.' Indeed, Gilchrist ensured that the Army could concentrate on eliminating the PKI by giving them a verbal assurance that Britain would hold back from military action in Borneo. See the *Observer*, 28/7/1996.

31 BBC Radio 4, 7 p.m. 3/8/1998.

32 Ibid.

33 Interview with Roland Challis by James Oliver 25/4/1996.

34 *Guardian* 2/10/1965.

35 Budiardjo, *Surviving Indonesia's Gulag*, p. 42.

36 Interview with Norman Reddaway by James Oliver 9/1/1996. The GCHQ intelligence also appears to have been passed by somebody to the Indonesian Army. See John Hughes, *The End of Sukarno: A Coup that Misfired: A Purge that Ran Wild*, (London, Angus & Robertson, 1968), pp. 112–165.

37 *The Washington Post* 21/5/1990.

38 Interview with Roland Challis; by James Oliver 25/4/1996.

CHAPTER 2   'Lies and Treachery': the Origins of IRD

1 M.R.D. Foot, *Resistance* (London, Paladin, 1979), p. 2.

2 Both MI5 and MI6 have been accused of conducting propaganda operations against the Labour Party during the interwar period. The most famous case is that of the Zinoviev letter, which recent research by Nigel West and former KGB agent Oleg Tsarev indicates was forged by a Russian agent working for MI6. See 'Our Secret Life' *Guardian* 12/3/1998.

3 Sir Fife Clark, *The Central Office of Information* (London, George Allen & Unwin, 1970), p. 27.

4 Charles Cruickshank, *The Fourth Arm: Psychological Warfare, 1938–1945* (Oxford, Oxford University Press, 1977), p. 9.

5 Philip Taylor, '"If War Should Come": Preparing the Fifth Arm for Total War, 1939–1945', *Journal of Contemporary History*, 16 (1981), 27.

6 E.H. Cookridge, *Inside SOE* (London, Arthur Balfour, 1966), pp. 5–6.

7 Ibid., p. 3.

8 Full accounts of the formation of the SOE are given in Cookridge, *Inside SOE*, and M.R.D. Foot *SOE in France* (HMSO, 1966).

9 Cookridge, *Inside SOE*, p. 37.

10 Ibid., p. 39.

11   M.R.D. Foot, *SOE: the Special Operations Executive, 1940–46* (London, BBC, 1984) p. 172.

12   Some 192 successful drops were made during the unsuccessful rising in August and September 1944, at a cost of forty-one aircraft. See Foot, *SOE 1940–46*, p. 191.

13   Foot, *SOE 1940–46*, p. 191.

14   Ibid., p. 200.

15   Quoted in Foot, *Resistance*, p. 137.

16   Cookridge, *Inside SOE*, p. 12.

17   Of the banking family.

18   Bickham Sweet Escott, *Baker Street Irregular* (London, Methuen, 1965), p. 125.

19   Foot, *SOE 1940–46*, p. 172.

20   J. Montgomery Hyde, *The Quiet Canadian* (London, Hamish Hamilton, 1962).

21   Richard Fletcher, 'Free Flow of News', published paper for UNESCO.

22   W. Stevenson, *A Man Called Intrepid* (London, Book Club Associates, 1976). This account has, however, recently been rubbished by Nigel West who has described it as 'almost entirely fictional'. See 'Our Secret Life', *Guardian* 12/3/1998.

23   Cruickshank, *Fourth Arm*, pp. 25–6.

24   Foot, *SOE 1940–46*, p. 24.

25   Sir Robert Bruce Lockhart, 'Political Warfare', Lecture at the Royal United Services Institute, 25/1/1950, *Journal of RUSI*, pp. 194–5. Anthony Eden had replaced Halifax as Foreign Secretary in December 1940; Brendan Bracken replaced Duff Cooper at the Ministry of Information in July 1941.

26   Lockhart, 'Political Warfare', p. 196.

27   Cruickshank, *Fourth Arm*, pp. 32–3.

28   Cookridge, *Inside SOE*, pp. 20–1.

29   Sefton Delmer, *Black Boomerang: An Autobiography* (London, Secker & Warburg, 1962), p. 14.

30   Ibid., pp. 74–5.

31   Cruickshank, *Fourth Arm*, p. 80.

32   Foot, *Resistance,* pp. 28–9.

33   Ibid., p. 30.

34   Cruickshank, *Fourth Arm*, p. 109.

35   Delmer, *Black Boomerang*, pp. 122–3.

36   Ibid., p. 123.

37   'Assault on Britain's "lie factory" by Jesuit', *The Times* 19/1/1978.

38   Ibid.

39   Cruickshank, *Fourth Arm*, pp. 110–11.

40   Interview with Sir Douglas Dodds-Parker by James Oliver 25/7/1997.

41   Cruickshank, *Fourth Arm*, p. 151.

42   David Stafford, *Britain and European Resistance, 1940–1945* (London, Macmillan, 1980), pp. 146–7.

43   Delmer, *Black Boomerang*, p. 168.

44   Ibid., p. 167.

45   Lockhart, 'Political Warfare', p. 197.

46   Cruickshank, *Fourth Arm*, p. 148.

47   Lockhart, 'Political Warfare', p. 197.

48   Delmer, *Black Boomerang*, pp. 163–4.

49   Cruickshank, *Fourth Arm*, p. 69.

50   Ibid., p. 34.

51   Lockhart, 'Political Warfare', p. 195.

52   PRO, INF1/724; Memorandum by International Broadcasting and Propaganda Enquiry 21/6/1939.

53   Philip Taylor, 'Techniques of Persuasion: Basic Ground Rules of British Propaganda During the Second World War', *Historical Journal of Film, Radio and Television* (1981), 57.

54   PRO, INF1/724; Memorandum by International Broadcasting and Propaganda Enquiry 21/6/1939.

55   Ibid.

56   Quoted in Cruickshank, *Fourth Arm*, p. 18.

57   Philip Schlesinger, *Putting Reality Together: the BBC News* (London, Constable & Company, 1978), p. 14.

58   Ibid., p. 27.

59   Quoted in Cruickshank, *Fourth Arm*, p. 181.

60   Foot, *Resistance*, p. 58.

61   Cruickshank, *Fourth Arm*, p. 69.

62   Ibid., p. 78.

63   Ibid., p. 101.

64   Quoted in Asa Briggs, *The History of Broadcasting in the United Kingdom,* vol. 3 (Oxford, Oxford University Press, 1970), p. 58.

65   Taylor, 'Techniques of Persuasion', p. 58.

66   Lockhart, 'Political Warfare', p. 196.

67   Quoted in Cruickshank, *Fourth Arm*, p. 186.

68   Interview with Sir Douglas Dodds-Parker by James Oliver 25/7/1997.

CHAPTER 3   Origins of the Cold War

1   L.Y. Gibianski, 'How the Cominform Emerged: the New Archival Materials', *Novaiia i noveishaia istoriia* (4, Jul–Aug 1993), 131.

2   Vladislav Zubok, and Constantine Pleshakov, *Inside the Kremlin's Cold War: from Stalin to Krushchev* (London, Harvard University Press, 1996), p. 110.

3   Ibid., p. 114.

4   Ibid., p. 119.

5   Denis Healey, *The Time of My Life* (London, Michael Joseph, 1989), p. 100.

6   Interview with Lord Mayhew by James Oliver 18/7/1995.

7   Interview with Norman Reddaway by James Oliver 9/1/1996.

8   Healey, *Time of My Life*, p. 103.

9   PRO FO371 56835, T. Brimelow, minute, 9/9/1946, quoted in Dianne Kirby 'The Religious Component in the Anglo-American Cold War Alliance, 1945–48'. A paper delivered at the conference 'Britain and the Cold War' organized by the Institute of Contemporary British History, July 1997.

10   Healey, *Time of My Life*, p. 106.

11   Lyn Smith, 'Covert British Propaganda: the Information Research Department 1947–77', *Millennium: Journal of International Studies*, 1 (1980), 68.

12   Interview with Norman Reddaway by Anthony Gorst and W. Scott Lucas, 1989.

13   PRO FO371/66371 N 9549.

14   Michael Nelson, 'The BBC External Services and the Cold War'. A paper delivered at the conference 'Britain and the Cold War' organized by the Institute of Contemporary British History, July 1997.

15   Kirby, 'The Religious Component in the Anglo-American Cold War Alliance, 1945–48'.

16   PRO FO371/5832, Warner Memorandum, 'The Soviet Campaign against those Country and our responses to it' 2/4/1946.

17   PRO FO371/56886/N12335/5169/38G, minutes of Russia Committee meeting, 3/9/1946
and 7/11/1946 cited in Tony Shaw, 'The British Popular Press and the Early Cold War', *Journal of Contemporary British History* (1998).
18   PRO FO371/56788/N12332, memorandum issued by N. Ronald 22/9/1946.
19   Note to Secretary of State from C.P. Mayhew, Mayhew Papers, 23/1/1947.
20   W. Scott Lucas and C.J. Morris, 'A Very British Crusade, The Information Research
Department and the beginning of the Cold War', in Richard Aldrich (ed.), *British Intelligence Strategy and the Cold War*, (London, Routledge, 1992), p. 90.
21   'Third Force Propaganda', paper to Secretary of State from C.P. Mayhew, Mayhew Papers 6/12/1947.
22   PRO CAB129/23, C.P.(48)8, 'Future Foreign Publicity Policy' 8/1/1948.
23   Smith, 'Covert British Propaganda', pp. 68–9.
24   Bill Jones, *The Russia Complex: the British Labour Party and the Soviet Union* (London, Manchester University Press, 1977), p. 136.
25   Interview with Lord Mayhew by James Oliver 18/7/1995.
26   PRO CAB129/23 'Future foreign publicity policy' Memorandum by Secretary of State for Foreign Affairs CP(48)8 4/1/1948.
27   Cited in Wayne Knight, 'Labourite Britain: America's "Sure Friend"? the Anglo–Soviet Treaty Issue, 1947,' *Diplomatic History*, 7 (1983), 270–2.
28   Kim Philby, *My Silent War* (London, Panther, 1968), p. 99.

CHAPTER 4   A Crusade Begins

1   Quoted in Smith, 'Covert British Propaganda'.
2   Norman Reddaway interview with James Oliver January 1996.
3   Annexe D, PR 2919/112/g, PRO FO 1110/277.
4   PRO FO 1110/176 Letter to Sheridan and Murray from McLaren 4/8/1949.
5   PRO FO1110/277, 30248.
6   PRO FO1110 174–177.
7   Foreign Office Historians, Note of Developments in 1949, IRD.
8   Interview with Fay Weldon by James Oliver 28 /11/1997.
9   Interview with Hugh Lunghi by Paul Lashmar 3/12/1997.
10   IRD, Origins and Establishment of the Foreign Office Information Research Department 1946–48. Historians: LRD 9 August 1995 FCO.
11   Ibid.
12   PRO FO1110/328; 'Information Research Department's Finances', 9/1/1950. The notes for the meeting, which are partially censored, note that the operation in question 'might even result in a small profit'. With regard to the employment of outside specialists, of which there were some thirty-five, it was noted that, 'If such a large number were shown under the heading of Information Research Department, the functions of that department would not stand up to examination, more particularly since many of its supposed functions could equally be performed by FORD.'
13   Robert Marett, *Through the Back Door* (London, Pergamon, 1968).
14   Private source.
15   Interview with Colin Wintle by Richard Fletcher, 1979.
16   Interview with John Cloake by James Oliver 10/12/1997.
17   Ibid.
18   Ibid.
19   Parrott, Cecil *The Serpent and the Nightingale* (London, Faber, 1977), p. 24.
20   Ibid., p. 47.

21   US National Archives, from London to Sec. of State. Top Secret. No 1993. May 20. 1949. 841.20200/5-2049.

22   Dianne Kirby, 'The Church of England in the Origins of the Cold War 1945–67' (PhD thesis, University of Hull, 1990).

23   The Vatican had been in disgrace for its failure to condemn Fascism, but was to achieve some redemption for its vigour in attacking Communism.

24   PRO FO 1110/22. CI(48)13 of 26/11/1948, PR 1250/23/913G,

25   Foreign Office Historians, Note of Developments in 1949, IRD.

26   PRO FO 371/71630.

27   Dianne Kirby, 'Church of England in the Origins of the Cold War'.

28   PRO FO371/71631.

29   Foreign Office Historians, Note of Developments in 1949, IRD.

30   These can now be seen at the Public Record Office, FO975.

31   Tony Shaw, 'The British Popular Press and the Early Cold War', *Journal of Contemporary British History* (1998).

32   Interview with Norman Reddaway by Anthony Gorst and W. Scott Lucas 6/1989.

33   Wesley K. Wark, 'Coming in from the Cold: British Propaganda and the Red Army Defectors 1945–52', *The International History Review* IX (1987), 50.

34   Interview with Lord Mayhew by James Oliver 18/7/1995. Authors' emphasis.

35   PRO FO1110/277, IRD Progress Report.

36   Andrew Boyle, *The Climate of Treason* (London, Coronet 1979), p. 347.

CHAPTER 5   Korea: a Hot War in a Cold War

1   US National Archives, Foreign Service Serial 93217/11/1948. British Record Group 59 (see note on sources at the end of report).

2   US National Archives, Under State Department Record code no. 841.202xx (xx is appropriate country code), RG59.

3   US National Archives, Henderson to Secretary of State no. 469 27/4/1949. 841.20245/4-2749, RG 59.

4   US National Archives, Enclosure to despatch No 347, Ap.27 1949. 'Cooperation with the United Kingdom on Anti-Communist Propaganda'. 841.20245/4-2749, RG 59.

5   US National Archives, From London to Secretary of State. Top Secret. No. 1674. 30/4/1949. 841.20200/4–3049 RC5.

6   US National Archives, Personal for Henderson from Kennan. Top Secret. May 9 1949. 841.20245/4-2749.

7   US National Archives, Humelsine to Souers, 15/3/1948 and PPS enclosure. 861.00/3–1548, RG 59.

8   US National Archives, New Delhi to Secretary of State. Top Secret. No. 737 25/6/1949. 841.20245/6–22, RG 59.

9   PRO FO1110/208 Despatch no. 20 of 24/6/1949, PR 1808/20/G.

10   US National Archives, Extract from a letter dated 6 January 1949 from the head of IRD, Foreign Office, to the British Embassy, 841.Z0246D/1-1049, RG59.

11   See, for example, US National Archives, US reports of meetings of British Defence Co-ordination Committee, Far East, at the time. RC 841.20, RG 59.

12   That is, J.B. Smith, *Portrait of a Cold Warrior* (New York, Putnam, 1976).

13   Interview with U. Alexis Johnson by Paul Lashmar, Washington DC 1995.

14   PRO FO371/84061 FK1015/125Murray to Lord President's Office, 4 /7/1950.

15   Interview with the authors, September 1997. Prior to June 1950 the United States limited

heavy weapons supplies to South Korea to prevent a rash attack.

16   PRO FO953/628 P1013/29 Minute from Warner to State Department, 9/5/1950.

17   Tony Shaw, 'The Information Research Department of the Foreign Office and the Korean War, 1950–53' *Journal of Contemporary British History* (1998).

18   Ibid.

19   Museum of Labour History, Labour Party International Department files.

20   Shaw, 'Information'.

21   PRO FO371/84178 FK1661/12. Minute by A. Rouse, 14/9/1950, FO371/87178 FK1661/14, IRD minute October 1950, FO371/84178 FK1661/17, notes to Lord Henderson, 8/11/1950.

22   Shaw, 'Information'.

23   Healey, *Time of My Life*.

24   For a much more detailed account of this, see Susan L. Carruthers, 'Korea: the Great Brain Robbery?', Paper presented at the 'Britain and the Cold War' conference, organized by the Institute of British Contemporary History, July 1997.

25   The authors have spent a good deal of time investigating the claims of germ warfare and feel that the matter is not conclusively resolved either way.

26   MOD *Treatment of British Prisoners of War in Korea* (London, HMSO, 1955).

27   PRO WO206/4014.

28   PRO FO953/635 P1013/10/G Burrows from Washington to FO, 9/8/1950.

29   Shaw, 'Information'.

30   PRO FO371/1063 P10122/22, Adam Watson telegram to IPD, 21/3/1951. FO371/1063 P10122/32 Circular from Morrison on Overseas Information Services, 14/8/1951.

31   Interview with Adam Watson by James Oliver 9/3/1998.

32   Carruthers, 'Korea'.

33   PRO FO1110/422.

34   Shaw, 'Information'.

35   Ibid.

36   Kim Il Sung was the self-proclaimed 'Great Leader' of North Korea until his death in 1996. He left behind an underdeveloped agrarian society run on the harshest Stalinist lines with little contact with the outside world. In 1998 North Korea was wracked by famine.

CHAPTER 6   Offensive: into the 1950s

1   Interview with Fay Weldon by James Oliver 28/11/1997.

2   Interview with Hugh Lunghi by Paul Lashmar 3/12/1997.

3   Interview with Fay Weldon by James Oliver 28 /11/1997.

4   Ibid.

5   Ibid.

6   Ibid.

7   Ibid.

8   Ibid. In spring 1951 IRD held a long-term planning meeting which set the anti-Communist themes it would concentrate on for its worldwide campaign. These were: Sabotage of Peace; Labour and Social Conditions (this to include 'The Impoverishment of the Workers'); Crime: Lack of Liberty: Kremlin Imperialism; Opposition to Nationalism; Hostility to Islam; Land Reform; Philosophic Background and Defeat Story. The target areas were in order of priority: South East Asia; India and Pakistan; Near and Middle East; Italy; Western Germany; France; Africa; South America; Scandinavia and Low Countries. (FO1110/305)

9   Interview with Hugh Lunghi by Paul Lashmar 3/12/1997.

10   Ibid.

11   Interview with Fay Weldon by James Oliver 28/11/1997.

12   IRD, B.291 *The Second Congress of the Rumanian Workers' Party (RWP)* December 1955.

13   IRD, B.423 *The Polish General Election; January 1957. IRD, B371 (R); Soviet Pre-Eminence or 'Proletarian Internationalism* August 1956.

14   Interview with Fay Weldon by James Oliver 28/11/1997.

15   FO1110/377; Letter from Jack Ward (Deputy High Commissioner, Wahnerheide) to F.R.H. Murray 18/1/1951.

16   PRO FO1110/377, 'Directive on Press Interviews with Soviet and Satellite Defectors in Care of Intelligence Division' 1951.

17   Quoted in John Lewis Gaddis, *We Now Know: Rethinking Cold War History* (Oxford, Clarendon Press, 1997), p. 210.

18   IRD, B. 341 *New Roads to Socialism* May 1956.

19   Gaddis, *We Now Know,* p. 210.

20   IRD, B. 393 *Can Rakosi Escape Trial?* October 1956.

21   W. Scott Lucas, *Britain, the US and the Suez Crisis* (London, Sceptre, 1996), p. 276.

22   IRD, B. 399 *Soviet Aggression in Hungary* November 1956.

CHAPTER 7   Nothing but the Truth: IRD and the BBC

1   Nelson, 'BBC External Services and the Cold War'.

2   IRD: Origins and Establishment of the Foreign Office Information Research Department 1946–48. Historians: LRD, no. 9 August 1995 FCO.

3   Gary D. Rawnsley, *Radio Diplomacy and Propaganda: the BBC and VOA in International Politics, 1956–64* (London, Macmillan, 1996). p. 16.

4   Interview with Norman Reddaway by Anthony Gorst and W. Scott Lucas June 1989.

5   Interview with Norman Reddaway by James Oliver January 1996.

6   IRD: Origins and Establishment of the Foreign Office Information Research Department 1946–48. Historians: LRD, no. 9 August 1995 FCO.

7   PRO FO371/56886/N12335/5169/38G. Russia Committee Meeting, 17/9/1946.

8   BBC, WAC, E2/324/1 3/1/1947.

9   *Observer* 18/8/1985.

10   Mark Hollingsworth, and Richard Norton-Taylor, *Blacklist: the Inside Story of Political Vetting* (London, Hogarth Press, 1988).

11   This was Alaric Jacob, a Labour Party supporter who was married to novelist and Marxist historian Iris Morley.

12   PRO FO1110/16/22 Ralph Murray, Minutes, 17/2/1948, cited in Hugh Wilford, *The Information Research Department: Britain's Secret Cold War Weapons Revealed* (unpublished paper, 1996).

13   PRO FO1110/16 PR10/10/913.

14   BBC, WAC, E2/324/5, 21/5/1952. R.H.K Marett appears to have been working in Information Policy in 1952. In September 1953 he was promoted to counsellor and appointed head of the Information Policy Department. In the early 1960s, Marett was supervising Under-Secretary overseeing IRD as well as the IPD.

15   IRD: Origins and Establishment of the Foreign Office Information Research Department 1946–48. Historians :LRD, no. 9 August 95 FCO.

16   PE 2030/55/967, PRO FO953/229A; PR 228/227/913, PRO FO1110/49.

17   PRO FO1110/16 PR377, Letter from Jacob to Warner of 28/5/1948.

18   BBC, WAC, E2/324/3, 11/7/1950. According to Stephen Dorrill and Robin Ramsay,

Kenneth Younger was a former senior member of MI5 who had run agents inside Communist organizations. See Stephen Dorrill and Robin Ramsay, *Smear: Wilson and the Secret State* London, Fourth Estate, 1991), p. 30.

19   PRO FO1110/84, PR 578/578/913 of 23/7/1948. FO1110/55, PR 1292/265/913 of 9/12/1948.

20   PRO FO1110/33. PR 902/71/913 Minutes of the Russia Committee, 14/10/1948,.

21   BBC, WAC, E2/324/2, 1949. Tangye Lean wrote to Ralph Murray on 18 October and received a letter from Murray with corrections on 17 November. See BBC, WAC, E2/324/2.

22   Nelson, 'BBC External Services'.

23   Report of 6/8/1958 to the Central Committee signed by L. Ilyichev, A. Romanov and G. Kazakov, CPA, Fond 5, Op. 33 Case 75, 163–7.

24   Smith, 'Covert British Propaganda', pp. 70–1.

25   Interview with Lord Mayhew by James Oliver 18/7/1995.

26   Michael Evans, 'MI6 Fed Cold War Propaganda to BBC' *The Times* 20/10/1997.

27   Smith, 'Covert British Propaganda', p. 73.

28   Ibid., p. 73.

29   He was later head of IRD between 1962 and 1966.

30   BBC, WAC, E2/324/4, 16/3/1951.

31   BBC, WAC, E2/324/4, 16/3/1951,

32   Ibid.

33   Grace Wyndham Goldie was the editor of *Panorama* and hired Woodrow Wyatt as a reporter in 1955

34   Interview with Norman Reddaway by Anthony Gorst and W. Scott Lucas 6/1989.

35   Interview with Gordon Waterfield by Richard Fletcher 21/11/79.

36   PRO FO 371/66370/N8114/271/38, Sir Orme Sargent to Sir M. Peterson, British Ambassador in Moscow 28/7/1947.

37   BBC, WAC R34/1580/1, Note by A.D. Dodds Parker, Foreign Office Minister 11/10/1956.

38   BBC WAC R34/1580/1, Note undated, but annotated as 'Late September or Early October', Top Secret.

39   W. Scott Lucas, *Divided We Stand: Britain, the US and the Suez Crisis* (London, Sceptre 1991), p. 287.

40   Nelson, 'BBC External Services'.

CHAPTER 8   The Medium is the Message: IRD and MI6

1   Interview with Fay Weldon by James Oliver 28/11/1997.

2   Interview with Lord Owen by the authors 10/1997.

3   Interview with ex-CIA officer by Richard Fletcher, Washington DC, 1979.

4   He took over from Maurice Oldfield. It must be said that Rennie was a Foreign Office career officer and not an MI6 career officer.

5   Ann Elwell obituary *Daily Telegraph* 1/1996.

6   On a number of occasions partisans, provoked by aggressive allied radio broadcasts, had launched campaigns against Nazi forces. Allied forces were unable to support these dangerous attacks and the partisans were overrun and destroyed by German forces.

7   CAB 130/37.

8   Anthony Verrier, *Looking Glass War* (London, Jonathan Cape, 1983).

9   PRO FO1110/226 PR1463/38/G Report by Warner.

10   BBC, WAC, E2/324/4, 23/2/1951. Information officers in Egypt put the respective audiences of the BBC, *Sharq al Adna* and Egyptian State Broadcasting respectively at 65, 35 and 100 per cent.

11   Ibid.

12   Richard Beeston, *Looking for Trouble* (London, Brasseys, 1997).

13   FO1110/235: PR118/38/G, PR119/38/G, PR120/38/G.

14   A number of sources assert that Tom Little was in MI6.

15   Jan Morris, *Conundrum* (London, Faber & Faber, 1974).

16   Selwyn Lloyd, *Suez 1956* (New York, 1978).

17   Swinburn had spent nearly thirty years in Egypt and had been a lecturer at Cairo University. When British subjects were dismissed from the university staff in 1952, he joined the ANA.

18   Keesing's Contemporary Archives (15083) 8–15/9/1956.

19   Lucas, *Divided*, p. 173.

20   USNA, RG59, CDF,774.00(W)/9–656, SANA to State Department, Despatch 189, 6/9/1956.

21   Lucas, *Divided*, p. 132.

22   Ibid., pp. 116–17.

23   Ibid., p. 132.

24   US National Archives, United States Office of Strategic Services documents.

25   Interview with Gordon Waterfield by Richard Fletcher 21/11/79 at Travellers Club, London. File 30/3-NA, Waterfield.

26   'News Agencies – their structure of operation' UNESCO 1953.

27   Interview with Bob Petty by Richard Fletcher 4/12/1980.

28   Verrier, *Looking Glass War*, p. 150.

29   Ibid., pp. 154–5.

30   Private source.

31   Extract from speech made by Denis Healey MP in the House of Commons; LPID; Eastern Europe; 3/11/1956.

32   Extracts from Mr Hugh Gaitskell's Speech; LPID; Eastern Europe; 6/11/1956.

33   Lucas, *Divided*, p. 276.

34   *Kodumaa* 13/10/1971, from FBI files see *Lobster* 16. Surprisingly, a lot of the statements made by Philby about MI6 after his defection were accurate where checkable.

35   This on the surface seems to be a wild claim, yet as late as the 1970s it was widely known in Fleet Street that many well-known journalists, especially foreign correspondents were close to MI6. How close and whether they were actually paid, we will probably never know. No one demonstrates the interchangeability between journalist and spy in his generation better than Philby, who, of course, after suspicion fell on him, became an *Observer* correspondent.

CHAPTER 9   Agencies of Change: the News Agency Network

1   Interview with Norman Reddaway by W. Scott Lucas and Anthony Gorst; June, 1989.

2   Tom Clarke had been editorial director of the *News Chronicle* until 1933. He was deputy director of the News Division of the Ministry of Information from 1939–40 and in 1941/2 he organized British propaganda in Latin America as a representative of Hulton Press. His activities were reported on with some amusement by the US State Department. Tom Clarke's *Word of the Englishman* (London, Hutchinson, 1942) explains his trip's objective: 'keeping alive the British journalism tradition' (p. 11) during and after the war.

3   This section is based on interviews with two former senior officers of the SOE in 1979, and Annual Returns at Companies Registration office, London.

4   Interview with Bob Petty by Richard Fletcher 4/12/1980.

5   Articles of Association NAFEN, NAFEN (Asia) Ltd and ANA (Cairo) Ltd.

6   *INFA 661 Press and Advertisers Year Book*, 5th edn, INFA (India News and Features Agency) (New Delhi, 1966).

7   Tom Little's friendship with Nasser was such that he even allowed Little to remain in Egypt for a year or so after Suez.

8   John Lawrenson, and Lionel Barber *The Price of Truth: the story of the Reuters £££ millions* (Edinburgh, Mainstream Publishing, 1985), pp. 99–101.

9   That is in charge of broadcasting to the Indian countries and Iran.

10   BBC *Yearbooks* and *Staff Lists* 1958–64.

11   Newspaper Press Directory, annual editions from 1955 to 1968.

12   Interview with Gordon Waterfield by Richard Fletcher 21/11/79.

13   David Leigh and Paul Lashmar, 'UK Propaganda Went on in Peacetime' *Observer*, 20/12/1981.

14   *Observer* 29/1/1978.

15   They also claim that no Reuters correspondent was appointed to an important post overseas without first checking that he was acceptable to the British Embassy. (Defenders of this practice say that it was essential for the correspondent to be on good terms with the embassy, as this would be an important source of news.)

16   According to some sources Onslow, after leaving the Foreign Office, went to work for Star or Globe News Agencies. *Lobster* 11.

17   Profile of Cranley Onslow by Andrew Roth, *New Statesman*.

18   No. 1095456, Registry of Business Names, London.

19   Little's friends portray him as a dedicated journalist specializing in the Middle East. He was also an anti-Communist and went on to be one of the founders of Brian Crozier's Institute of the Study of Conflict. See *Lobster* 11.

20   These were Glyns Nominees Ltd and a body called the Detur Fund. Glyns Nominees was the wholly owned subsidiary of Williams and Glyns bank. The Detur Fund gave an address in North London, c/o S.C. Rogers, Edgware, Middlesex, a Williams and Glyns branch man. It could not be traced in business, cooperative or charitable directories. INRAR made a total operating loss of £20,277 up to 1971.

21   James Holburn, telephone conversation with Richard Fletcher 13/7/1979.

22   Leigh and Lashmar, 'UK Propaganda Went on in Peacetime'.

23   134 Lower Marsh, London SE1.

24   Permanent Secretary, Ministry of State, Kenya, 1959–63.

25   Biographic details are from the *Kenya Press Directory* (MJB Productions, 1968).

26   Published by Constable in 1977.

27   D.R. Mankekar, *One Way Free Flow: Neo-Colonialism via News Media* (Clarion Books, 1978).

28   Richard Fletcher, 'British Propaganda since World War II – a Case Study', *Media, Culture and Society*, 1982.

CHAPTER 10   Imperial Adventures: IRD and the Colonies

1   PRO FO953/1695, John H. Peck to L. C. Glass; 22/6/1956.

2   PRO FO953/1695, John H. Peck to L. C. Glass 22/6/1956.

3   'Winning the war and losing the empire are the most immediately striking developments of the period'. See P.J. Cain and A.G. Hopkins, *British Imperialism: Crisis and Deconstruction, 1914–1990*, (London, Longman, 1993), p. 265.

4   Historian Andrew Roadknight noted, 'the United Nations (UN) Declaration on National Independence of March 1943 . . . committed colonial powers to setting timetables for the liberation of their colonies. On the face of it, by the middle of the Second World War, the US and its allies had agreed on the principle of independence for colonies and also on a mechanism for bringing it about.' See Roadknight, 'United States Policy Towards Indonesia 1945–1949.

5   David Fieldhouse, 'The Labour Governments and the empire-commonwealth, 1945–51' in Ritchie Ovendale (ed.) *The Foreign Policy of the British Labour Governments, 1945–1951* (Leicester University Press, 1984) p. 98.

6   Cain and Hopkins, *British Imperialism*, p. 279.

7   Ibid., p. 277.

8   Ibid., p. 280.

9   Brian Lapping, *The End of Empire* (London, Paladin, 1989), p. 202.

10   Michael R. Stenson, 'Repression and Revolt: the origins of the 1948 Communist Insurrection in Malaya and Singapore' *Papers in International Studies*, South East Asia Series, Center for International Studies (1969), p. 2. See also Michael R. Stenson, *Industrial Conflict in Malaya: Prelude to the Communist Revolt of 1948* (Oxford, Oxford University Press, 1970).

11   The PMFTU was an MCP 'front'. See Stenson 'Repression and Revolt', p. 5.

12   Lapping, *End of Empire*, p. 221.

13   PRO FO953/1637 'The Work of the Regional Information Office at Singapore'.

14   Ibid.

15   PRO FO1110/386; Minute by T.S. Tull 8 /1/1952.

16   Interview with John Cloake by James Oliver 10/12/1997.

17   PRO CO537/5698 'The Colonial Empire Today: Summary of Our Main Problems and Policies' CO Relations Department paper annex 5/1950.

18   PRO FO371/76005 Top Secret letter from J.H. Watson to O.H. Morris 1/12/1949.

19   Susan Carruthers, *Winning Hearts and Minds: British Governments, the Media and Colonial Counter-Insurgency 1944–1960* (London, Leicester University Press), p. 97.

20   Cain and Hopkins, *British Imperialism*, pp. 266–7.

21   Ibid., pp. 277–8.

22   Lapping, *End of Empire*, p. 209.

23   Carruthers, *Winning* p. 162.

24   Quoted in Carruthers, *Winning* p. 163.

25   Susan Carruthers, 'A Red Under Every Bed?: Anti-Communist Propaganda and Britain's Response to Colonial Insurgency' *Contemporary Record* 9 (2) 1995, p. 306.

26   Carruthers, *Winning*, pp. 161–2.

27   See Christopher Hitchens, *Hostage to History: Cyprus, from the Ottomans to Kissinger* (London, Verso, 1997), pp. 33–4.

28   Ibid., p. 36.

29   Ibid., p. 37

30   Ibid.

31   Quoted in Lapping, *End of Empire*, p. 390.

32   Ibid., p. 390.

33   PRO CO926/180 Cipher from Washington (Watson) to Foreign Office 13/8/1954.

34   PRO CO926/180 D.C. Hopson to D. Williams 16/8/1954.

35   PRO CO926/180 Sir P. Dixon, Inward Saving Telegram From New York to Foreign Office 16/8/1954.

36   PRO CO926/180 Note for UK Delegation to United Nations 8/1954.

37   PRO CO926/180 Hesmondhalgh to Cope 26/8/1954.

38   Carruthers, *Winning*, p. 205.

39   PRO CO296/180 Minute 18/8/1954.

40   PRO CO296/180 Minute 18/8/1954.

41   Lapping, *End of Empire*, p. 399.

42   PRO FO953/1695 Peck to Gray 13/7/1956.

43   Lapping, *End of Empire*, p. 390.

44   PRO FO953/1695 Minute M.E. Cox 17/7/1956.

45   'The BBC and Cyprus', *New Statesman* 14/12/1957.

CHAPTER 11   Spreading the Word: IRD Publishes

1   *Guardian* 11/7/1996.

2   'Orwell is revealed in role of state informer' *Daily Telegraph* 12/7/1996.

3   'Orwell's débutante friend tells of role in writer's "betrayal" list' *Guardian* 13/7/1996.

4   PRO FO1110/221.

5   PRO FO1110/221 PR920.

6   PRO FO1110/221 PR3361.

7   Phillip Deery, 'Confronting the Cominform: George Orwell and The Cold War Offensive of the Information Research Department 1948–50', *Labour History*, 73 (11/1997).

8   PRO FO1110/189 PR 1135/11/G.

9   PRO FO1110/189. Letter from Orwell to Kirwan 6/4/1949 p. 1.

10   *Guardian* 11/7/1996.

11   'Socialist icon who became Big Brother', *Daily Telegraph*, 22/6/1998.

12   *The Collected Essays, Journalism and Letters of George Orwell. Vol. 111 – As I Please 1943–1945* (Harmondsworth, Penguin, 1970), pp. 457–8.

13   Mayhew Papers, 6/12/1947.

14   The authors are grateful to David Chipp, formerly of the Press Association for lending them his copy.

15   Philby, *My Silent War*, p. 101.

16   PRO FO 1110/80 PR 523/523/913G, July 1948.

17   PRO FO1110/221 PR505 – Proposal to Organize Publication of Cheap Books, for Anti-Communist Publicity Purposes, sponsored where possible by Publishers with known Left affiliations.

18   PRO FO1110/221 PR1589

19   Correspondence between Dr J.E.M. Latham and the authors 1997.

20   British National Bibliography, 1951–1971.

21   Brian Crozier, *Free Agent: the Unseen War 1941–1991* (London, HarperCollins, 1994), pp. 51–7.

22   Arthur Bottomley, *The Use and Abuse of Trade Unions* (Ampersand, 1963), p. 85.

23   Smith, 'Covert British Propaganda', p. 177.

24   Letter from Bryan Magee to James Oliver 14/6/1975.

25   Letter from Michael Kaser to James Oliver 12/6/1995.

26   Interview with Adam Watson by James Oliver 9/3/1998. Watson discussed IRD's work with both Deakin and Brig Fitzroy Mclean, who followed Deakin to Yugoslavia. Watson recalled, 'those people had this operation [IRD] in their minds'.

27   Smith, 'Covert British Propaganda', p. 76.

28   Letter from Bryan Magee to James Oliver 14/6/1995.

29   *Observer* 29/1/1978.

30   Interview with Stephen Watts by Richard Fletcher 27/1/1978.

31   Filed at the Companies Registration Office, London.

CHAPTER 12   Internal Affairs: IRD's Domestic Campaigns

1   'Reds "Squander" Union £20,000' *Daily Mail* 15/11/1956.

2   Interview with Sir Douglas Dodds-Parker by James Oliver 25/7/1997.

3   Peter Wright, *Spycatcher*, (Australia, Heinemann, 1987), p. 55.

4   Dodds-Parker recalled of Reddaway, 'He'd just bring in a file and say, "We recommend this." It would be 6 p.m. or 7.30 p.m., and "The Secretary of State is unavailable and we want to get on with it quickly. Could you initial it?" It wouldn't be anything major. It was probably getting some – I don't like the word "tame" journalist – but there were people in the war, in the press, who were either on your side or they weren't.'

5   IRD sources maintain that this allegation did not come from them.

6   Victor Bailey, 'The "Spit and Polish" Demonstrations' in Victor Bailey, (ed.) *Forged in Fire: the History of the Fire Brigades Union* (London, Lawrence & Wishart, 1992).

7   'Trade Union Leaders Resign from Communist Party' *The Times* 14/11/1956.

8   'Chief Reds Meet All Day As Party Shrinks' *Daily Mail* 16/11/1956.

9   CAB 130/37.

10   See Peter Weiler, *British Labour and the Cold War* (California, Stanford University Press, 1988).

11   Dorrill and Ramsay, *Smear!*, p. 44–5. As noted, this is denied by Dodds-Parker.

12   Eric Shaw, *Discipline and Discord in the Labour Party* (Manchester University Press, 1988), p. 59

13   Mayhew Papers 11/5/1948, 17/6/1948 and 9/7/1948.

14   Healey, *Time of My Life*.

15   PRO FO1110/15 Letter from Denis Healey to J.H. Watson 2/11/1948.

16   Healey, *Time of My Life*, p. 109.

17   PRO FO1110/183 PR3217/8/9. Extract from SM/M (40) Second Meeting, 12/7/1949.

18   Mayhew Papers 24/3/1948.

19   John Demelis to William Green 28/2/1949 'Convention file 1948', papers of William Green, President of American Federation of Labor.

20   J.O. Rennie to Saul Rose 16/3/1955.

21   Woodrow Wyatt, *The Peril in Our Midst* (London, Phoenix House, 1956). At that time Phoenix House was sponsored by IRD to publish Background Books.

22   Frank Foulkes, President of the ETU in the 1950s. Frank Haxell, General Secretary of the ETU in the 1950s.

23   See Wyatt's unsigned article 'How Communists Run a Trade Union' *New Statesman* 7/12/1957.

24   Quoted in Henry Pelling, *A History of British Trade Unionism* (London, Penguin, 1992), p. 241.

25   John Lloyd, *Light and Liberty: the History of the EETPU* (London, Weidenfeld & Nicolson 1990), p. 457.

26   Private source.

27   Frank (later Lord) Chapple was a Communist who had left the CPGB over the Soviet invasion of Hungary in 1956.

28   Lloyd, *Light and Liberty*, p. 486.

29   'The Future of the ETU' *New Statesman* 7/7/1961.

30   Bottomley, *Use and Abuse of Trade Unions*, p. 41.

31   Lloyd, *Light and Liberty*, p. 470.

32   Aidan Crawley, 'The Hidden Face of British Communism' *Sunday Times* 28/10/1962, a four-part series reprinted as a pamphlet.

33   Interview with Lord Mayhew by James Oliver 18/7/1995.

34   Obituary of Sir John Peck *Independent* 20/1/1995.

35   J.H. Peck to Canon H. Waddams 29/9/1952 CFR papers.

36   For a full account see Dianne Kirby, 'The Church of England and the Cold War Nuclear Debate' *Twentieth Century British History* 4 (3) (1993), pp. 250–83.

37   Ibid.

CHAPTER 13   IRD's Fellow Travellers

1   Brian Crozier, *Free Agent*, p. 55.

2   Ruth Dudley Edwards, *The Pursuit of Reason: The Economist, 1843–1993* (London, Hamish Hamilton, 1993) pp. 900–1.

3   Ibid.

4   Interview with Brian Crozier by James Oliver 15/1/1997.

5   From documents supplied by David Benn.

6   Wark, 'Coming in from the Cold', p. 68.

7   Fyvel wrote a Background Book, *What is Culture?* In the early 1960s Fyvel wrote The *Insecure Offenders: Rebellious Youth in the Welfare State* for Pelican Books, primarily a study of the Teddy boy phenomena. In his biography he fails to mention his IRD work.

8   PRO FO1110/277 PR 2919/112/G, and FO1110/ 359, PR 110/5/G.

9   Smith, 'Covert British Propaganda'.

10   Obituary of Victor Zorza *Guardian* 23/3/1996.

11   Ibid.

12   Private source.

13   Interview with Norman Reddaway by W. Scott Lucas and Anthony Gorst, June 1989.

14   Penkovsky is attributed as providing some warning of the Cuban Missile Crisis.

15   David Leigh, 'The Department that never was', *Guardian* 27/1/1997.

16   Interview with Norman Reddaway by James Oliver 9/1/1996.

17   Crozier, *Free Agent*, pp. 57, 86.

18   Interview with Robert Conquest by Richard Fletcher 25/1/1978.

19   Letter from Lord Beloff to James Oliver 13/6/1995.

CHAPTER 14   A Mirror Image: the CIA

1   Peter Coleman, *The Liberal Conspiracy: The Congress of Cultural Freedom and the Struggle for the Mind of Postwar Europe* (London, Collier Macmillan Publishers, 1989), p. 1.

2   Iain Hamilton, *Koestler: a Biography* (London, Secker & Warburg, 1982), p. 190.

3   Paul Kennedy, *The Rise and Fall of the Great Powers: Economic Change and Military Conflict from 1500 to 2000* (London, Fontana Press, 1988), p. 480.

4   CIA History Staff, Cultural Cold War: Origins of the Congress for Cultural Freedom, *Studies in Intelligence* 1995.

5   Ibid.

6   Hamilton, *Koestler*, p. 28.

7   Coleman, *Liberal Conspiracy*, p. 27.

8   Ibid.

9   In his history of the CCF, *The Liberal Conspiracy*, Peter Coleman described how the hardline message was carried by Lasky, Koestler and their supporters through intensive caucusing and organization, through which they were able to maintain the initiative. See Coleman p. 27.

10   Ibid.

11   Ibid., p. 28.

12   Congress for Cultural Freedom, Press Release # p. 44 28/6/1950.

13   Ibid., p. 195.

14   Hamilton, *Koestler*, p. 201.

15   Coleman, *Liberal Conspiracy*, p. 9.

16   Interview with Michael Josselson by Richard Fletcher 5/5/1972.

17   Coleman, *Liberal Conspiracy*, p. 63.

18   Ibid p. 60. Josselson wrote to Spender that 'The Congress is not primarily interested in reaching readers in England and the US because a Communist or neutralist problem does not exist in those two countries.' See Coleman p. 61.

19   Hugh Wilford, '"Winning Hearts and Minds": American Cultural Strategies in the Cold War', *Borderlines*, I, 4 (June 1994), p. 321.

20   Coleman, *Liberal Conspiracy*, p. 59.

21   Ibid p. 77.

22   Conversation between Andrew Roth and the authors.

23   Coleman, *Liberal Conspiracy*, p. 185.

24   *Encounter* IV (6) 5/6/1955.

25   Ibid., XI (1), 11/7/1958.

26   Ibid., I, (1), 56 10/1956.

27   Ibid., IX, (2) 8/1957.

28   Coleman, *Liberal Conspiracy*, p. 77.

29   *Encounter* XVI (1) 6 1/1961.

30   Coleman, *Liberal Conspiracy*, p. 184.

31   Ibid., p. 12.

32   Ibid., p. 185.

33   Richard Fletcher 'How CIA Money Took the Teeth Out of British Socialism' in P. Agee and L. Wolf (eds) *Dirty Work: The CIA in Western Europe* (London, Zed Press, 1981), p. 193.

34   Recapitulation Des Seminaires CCF 30/3/3.

35   Fletcher, 'CIA Money' in Agee and Wolf (eds) *Dirty Work*, p. 193.

36   Hamilton, *Koestler*, p. 197.

37   Coleman, *Liberal Conspiracy*, pp. 222–3.

38   Ibid., p. 223.

39   Ibid., p. 226.

40   Tom Bradon, 'I'm glad the CIA is "immoral".' *Saturday Evening Post* 20/5/1967.

41   Ibid.

42   Ibid.

43   William Blum, *The CIA: A Forgotten History* (London, Zed Press, 1986), p. 115.

44   Crozier, *Free Agent*, p. 64.

45   Bradon, 'I'm glad the CIA is "immoral".' .

46   Coleman, *Liberal Conspiracy*, p. 61.

47   Bradon, 'I'm glad the CIA is "immoral".'

48   Marchetti and Marks, *The CIA and the Cult of Intelligence*, p. 336.

49   Coleman, *Liberal Conspiracy*, p. 70.

50   Ibid., p. 71.

51   Ibid., p. 72.

52   Blum, *The CIA*, p. 144.

53   J. Ranelagh, *The Agency: the Rise and Fall of the CIA* (London, Weidenfeld & Nicolson, 1986), p. 246.

54   Fletcher, 'CIA Money' in Agee and Wolf (eds) *Dirty Work*, p. 199.

55   P. Agee, (ed.) *CIA the Pike Report* (Nottingham, Spokesman Books, 1977), p. 190.

56   Philip M. Taylor, *Munitions of the Mind: War Propaganda from the Ancient World to the Nuclear Age* (Wellingbrough, Patrick Stephens, 1990), p. 224.

57   Blum, *The CIA*, p. 116.

58   Bradon, 'I'm glad the CIA is "immoral".'

59   Fletcher, 'CIA Money' in Agee and Wolf (eds), *Dirty Work*, p. 200.

60   Marchetti and Marks, *The CIA and the Cult of Intelligence*, p. 338.

61   Interview with Michael Ivens by James Oliver, 19/7/1996.

62   *Time Out* 20–26/6/1975.

63   Ibid.

64   Crozier, *Free Agent*, p. 52. Crozier also appears to have used the trip to collect information for MI6 at the request of MI6 official Ronald Franks.

65   Ibid., p. 64. According to a handwritten note on the 1968 memo to Helms, the FWF was 'run with the knowledge and cooperation of British intelligence'. See Steve Weissman, 'The CIA Makes the News', in Agee and Wolf, (eds) *Dirty Work*, p. 206.

66   Crozier, *Free Agent*, p. 68. John Hay Whitney also published the *International Herald Tribune*.

67   Weissman, Steve 'The CIA Makes the News' Agee, P. and Wolf, L. (eds) *Dirty Work: The CIA in Western Europe* London, Zed Press 1981 p. 206. According to Dorrill and Ramsey, 'It is probable, in our view, that the CIA's expansion in 1965 of the London-based propaganda front, Forum World Features . . . was a response to the political and financial pressure on IRD.' See Dorrill and Ramsey, *Smear!*, p. 110.

68   Russell Warren Howe, 'Asset Unwitting: Covering the World for the CIA', *More* (May 1978).

69   Crozier, *Free Agent*, p. 69.

70   Warren Howe, 'Asset Unwitting'.

71   Ibid.

72   *Time Out* 20–26/6/1975.

73   Warren Howe, 'Asset Unwitting'.

74   Crozier, *Free Agent*, p. 70.

75   Ibid., p. 73.

76   Warren Howe, 'Asset Unwitting'. According to Russell, Crozier 'ousted' Gately, but Crozier maintains that Gately was merely transferred to other duties. See Crozier, *Free Agent*, p. 71.

77   Crozier, *Free Agent*, p. 73.

78   Warren Howe, 'Asset Unwitting'.

79   Ibid.

80   Interview with Brian Crozier by James Oliver 15/1/1997.

81   Crozier, *Free Agent*, pp. 83–4.

82   Ibid., pp. 109–10.

83   *Guardian* 20/12/1976.

CHAPTER 15   The Fat Years: the 1960s

1   Crozier, *Free Agent*, p. 51.

2   Some £10,500,000 in today's money.

3   Letter from Norman Reddaway to James Oliver 25/10/1997.

4   Lucas and Morris, 'A Very British Crusade' in Aldrich (ed.), *British Intelligence*, p. 106.

5   Private IRD sources.

6   East German Spearhead in Africa B.588(R); IRD 18/1960.

7   Private source.

8   Interview with Lord Mayhew by James Oliver 18 /7/1995.

9   Gaddis, *We Now Know*, p. 261.

10   Ibid. p. 280.

11   Ibid. p. 279.

12   Private source.

13   Private source.

14 Private source.
15 Private source.
16 Ann Lane, 'Neutralism, non-alignment and British Cold War strategies 1958–1962' Paper given at the conference, 'Britain and the Cold War' organized by the Institute of Contemporary British History, July 1997.
17 John Dumoga, *Africa Between East and West* (Background Book, 1969), p. 114.
18 Ibid., p. 121.
19 8 Bhagat Singh Mang, New Delhi 110001.
20 Private source.
21 Letter from Mr H.W. King *The Times* 9/3/1983.
22 Letter to the authors 23/4/1998.
23 Conversation with Hilary King 27/6/1997.

CHAPTER 16   Indian Summer: IRD and the EEC

1 Alaistair McAlpine, *Once a Jolly Bagman* (London, Weidenfeld & Nicholson, 1997).
2 'Revealed: How MI6 men funded Euro Propaganda drive' *Sunday Telegraph* 27/4/1997.
3 Private source.
4 Interview with Norman Reddaway by Scott Lucas and Anthony Gorst, 6/1989.
5 Ibid.
6 Later disarmament co-ordinator, FCO, 1983–4.
7 Interview with Ernest Wistrich by James Oliver 19/12/1996.
8 Ibid.
9 Interview with Geoffrey Tucker by James Oliver 30/5/1996.
10 Ibid.
11 Interview with Nigel Ryan by Paul Lashmar 4/1997.
12 Interview with Marshall Stewart by Paul Lashmar 4/1997.
13 Interview with Michael Ivens by James Oliver 19/1/1996.
14 Interview with Geoffrey Tucker by James Oliver 30/5/1996.
15 Ernest Wistrich interview with James Oliver 1996
16 McAlpine, *Once a Jolly Bagman*.
17 Uwe Kitzinger, *Diplomacy and Persuasion: How Britain Joined the Common Market* (London, Thames & Hudson, 1973).
18 Private sources.
19 Sir Richard Body, 'The 1975 Referendum On Europe' *Contemporary Record* 10 (3), pp. 93–9
20 *Time Out* 23/5/1975.
21 Interview with Sir Richard Body by Paul Lashmar 1997.
22 Roger Broad and Tim Geiger, 'The 1975 British Referendum on Europe: a Witness Seminar' *Contemporary Record* 10 (2), 1996.

CHAPTER 17   Painting it Red: IRD and Northern Ireland

1 Private source.
2 Paul Foot, *Who Framed Colin Wallace?* (London, Pan Books, 1989), pp. 39–40.
3 Frank Kitson, *Low Intensity Operations: Subversion, Insurgency and Peacekeeping* (London, Faber & Faber, 1971), p. 199.
4 J. Bowyer Bell, *The Irish Troubles: a Generation of Violence, 1967–1992* (London, Gill & Macmillan, 1993), p. 229.
5 Ibid., p. 167.
6 Foot, *Who Framed Colin Wallace?*, p. 16.

7 Quoted in ibid., p. 17.
8 Quoted in ibid., pp. 17–8.
9 Interview with Colin Wallace by James Oliver 26/2/1996.
10 Ibid.
11 Bell, *Irish Troubles*, p. 230.
12 Interview with Colin Wallace by James Oliver 26/2/1996.
13 Ibid.
14 Ibid.
15 Ibid.
16 Ibid.
17 Ibid.
18 'MI5 on Trial' *This Week* 26/4/1990.
19 Interview with Colin Wallace by James Oliver 26/2/1996.
20 Interview with Michael Ivens by James Oliver 19/7/1996.
21 Private source.
22 Quoted in Dorrill and Ramsey, *Smear!*, p. 241.
23 'MI5 on Trial', *This Week* 26/4/1990.
24 Interview with Colin Wallace by James Oliver 26/2/1996.
25 Wright, *Spycatcher*, p. 359.
26 Ibid., p. 361.
27 Interview with Colin Wallace by James Oliver 26/2/1996.
28 Wright, *Spycatcher*, p. 369.
29 Ibid.
30 Interview with Colin Wallace by James Oliver 26/2/1996.
31 'MI5 on Trial', *This Week* 26/4/1990.
32 Ibid.
33 'Wilson was the target of MI5 'malcontents' *Guardian* 16/8/1996.
34 Interview with Colin Wallace by James Oliver 26/2/1996.
35 *The IRA and Northern Ireland: Aims, Policy, Tactics* 10/1974.
36 Interview with Colin Wallace by James Oliver 26/2/1996.
37 *The IRA and Northern Ireland: Aims, Policy, Tactics* 10/1974.
38 Kenneth O. Morgan, *The People's Peace: British History, 1945–1989* (Oxford, Oxford University Press, 1990), p. 333.
39 'Memo reveals "propaganda war" in Ulster' *Guardian* 10/11/1995.
40 *The IRA and Northern Ireland: Aims, Policy, Tactics* 10/1974.
41 Private source.
42 *The IRA and Northern Ireland: Aims, Policy, Tactics* 10/1974.
43 Foot, *Who Framed Colin Wallace?*, p. 94–5.
44 Quoted in ibid., p. 95.
45 Ibid., p. 96.
46 Quoted in ibid., p. 98.
47 David Barzilay, *The British Army in Ulster* (Belfast, Century, 1973).
48 'The Army in Ulster' *Evening Standard* 24/10/1973.
49 'How the British Army Wins Hearts and Minds' *Time Out* 14–20/10/1977.
50 'Still Dark in Paranoia Gulch' *New Statesman & Society* 9/2/1990.

CHAPTER 18 The Fall

1 Crozier, *Free Agent*, p. 86.

2 Ibid., pp. 104–5.

3 *Lobster* 16 (1988).

4 Interview with Brian Crozier by James Oliver 15/1/97.

5 Crozier, *Free Agent*, p. 89.

6 Ibid., p. 90.

7 Interview with Brian Crozier by James Oliver 15/1/97.

8 Crozier, *Free Agent*, p. 96.

9 'Softening up the West' *Daily Telegraph* 12/3/1973.

10 ISC Special Report 'New Dimensions of Security in Europe', ISC 5/1975.

11 Chapman Pincher, *The Secret Offensive* (London, Sidgwick & Jackson, 1985), pp. 239–40.

12 Interview with Adam Watson by James Oliver 9/3/1998.

13 ISC Special Report 'Sources of Conflict in British Industry', ISC 2/1974.

14 Crozier, *Free Agent*, p. 106.

15 Letter from John Whitehorn (CBI) to Brian Crozier 24/1/1972.

16 Ibid.

17 Crozier, *Free Agent*, pp. 107/8.

18 Interview with Brian Crozier by James Oliver 15/1/1997.

19 Crozier, *Free Agent*, p. 108.

20 Private source.

21 'Death of the Department that never Was'; *Guardian* 27/1/1978.

22 'CIA makes the News' *Time Out* 20–26/6/1975.

23 'Conflicting Accounts' *Time Out* 29 August to 4 September 1975.

24 Private source.

25 Private source.

26 Private source.

27 Crozier, *Free Agent*, p. 120.

28 Pincher, *Secret Offensive*, p. 314. In a footnote, Pincher also alleged that IRD may also have received money for its operations from the CIA. According to Pincher, his source for this was an MI5 informant who had told him that IRD had been wound up as a result of CIA involvement in the wake of the Watergate revelations. See Pincher p. 356. When questioned on this, Pincher was unable to expand or recall the allegation.

29 Private source.

30 'A Brief, Secret Glimpse' *Guardian* 16/6/1978.

31 David Owen, *Time to Declare* (London, Penguin Books, 1991), p. 348.

32 Peter Hennessy, *Whitehall* (London, Secker & Warburg, 1989), p. 272.

33 *New Statesman & Society* 3/3/1995 p. 15.

34 Private source.

35 See Crozier, *Free Agent*, pp. 96–7.

36 Interview with Lord Owen by the authors 7/11/1997.

37 Paul Mercer, *'Peace' of the Dead* (London, Policy Research Publications, 1986), pp. 87.

38 Interview with Lord Owen by the authors 7/11/1997.

39 Quoted in Michael Nelson, *War of the Black Heavens: The Battles of Western Broadcasting in the Cold War* (London, Brassey's, 1997), p. 138.

40 Interview with Brian Crozier by James Oliver 15/1/1997.

41 IRD, Background Brief 'Two Standards on Détente' 11/1975.

42 'Revival of Political Warfare' *The Times* 1/3/1983.

43 Interview with Colin Wallace by James Oliver 26 /2/1996.

44 Interview with Lord Owen by the authors 7/11/1997.

45 Ibid.

46   Owen, *Time to Declare*, p. 348.

47   Interview with Lord Owen by the authors 7/11/1997.

48   Interview with Lord Mayhew by James Oliver 18/7/1995.

49   'Death of the Department that Never Was' *Guardian* 27/1/1978.

50   'How the FO Waged Secret Propaganda War in Britain' *Observer* 29/1/1978.

51   'The Ministry of Truth' *Leveller* 3/1978.

52   'Another exposure – by TASS' *Guardian* 31/1/1978. Interestingly, this article was written by IRD contact Hella Pick.

53   'Death of the Department that Never Was' *Guardian* 27/1/1978.

54   Ibid.

55   *Leveller* 3/1978.

56   Ibid.

57   'Death of the Department that Never Was' *Guardian* 27/1/1978. Mayhew's reference to black propaganda is lamented widely among ex-IRD personnel as having given the wrong impression of IRD's work.

58   *Evening Standard* 7/2/1978.

59   Crozier, *Free Agent*, p. 189.

60   In 1981 the OID put out a revamped IRD briefing entitled 'Points at Issue'.

61   See '"Smears" row over briefing on IRA' *Guardian* 11/5/1988.

62   Private source.

63   Interview with Brian Crozier by James Oliver 15/1/1997.

64   Crozier, *Free Agent*, p. 143.

65   Private source.

CONCLUSIONS

1   Jacques Ellul, *Propaganda: The Formation of Men's Attitudes*, (New York, Vintage Books 1973) p. 52.

2   Interview with Lord Mayhew by James Oliver 18/7/1995.

3   Lucas and Morris, 'A Very British Crusade', in Aldrich (ed.) *British Intelligence*, p. 106.

4   Ellul, *Propaganda*, p. 61.

Bibliography

BOOKS

Ambrose, Stephen E., *Rise to Globalism: American Foreign Policy since 1938*, 5th edn, Harmondsworth, Penguin, 1988.

Andrew, Christopher, *Secret Service: the Making of the British Intelligence Community*, London, Heinemann, 1985.

Baker White, John, *True Blue*, London, Muller, 1970.

——, *The Big Lie*, London, Muller, 1957.

Barnett, Corelli, *The Lost Victory: British Dreams, British Realities 1945–50*, Chatham, Macmillan, 1995.

Beeston, Richard, *Looking for Trouble*, London, Brassey's, 1997.

Bloch, Jonathan and Fitzgerald, Patrick, *British Intelligence and Covert Action*, Dublin, Junction Books, 1983.

Blum, William, *The CIA: A Forgotten History*, London, Zed Press, 1986.

Boyd-Barrett, Oliver, *The International News Agencies*, London, Constable, 1980.

Boyle, Andrew, *The Climate of Treason*, London, Coronet, 1979.

Budiardjo, Carmel, *Surviving Indonesia's Gulag*, London, Cassell, 1996.

Butler, Ewan, *Amateur Agent*, London, Harrap, 1963.

Campbell, Duncan, *The Unsinkable Aircraft Carrier, American Military Power in Britain*, London, Michael Joseph, 1984.

Carruthers, Susan L., *Winning Hearts and Minds: British Governments, the Media and Colonial Counter-Insurgency 1944–60*, London, Leicester University Press, 1995.

Colby, William, *Honourable Men: My Life in the City*, London, Hutchinson, 1978.

Cookridge, E.H., *Inside SOE*, London, Arthur Baker, 1966.

Crawley, Aidan, *Leap before You Look*, London, Collins, 1988.

Crozier, Brian, *Free Agent: the Unseen War 1941–1991*, London, Harper Collins, 1994.

Curtis, Liz, *Ireland: the Propaganda War*, London, Pluto Press, 1984.

Daugherty, W.E., *A Psychological Warfare Casebook*, Baltimore, John Hopkins Press, 1958.

Deacon, Richard, *A History of the British Secret Service*, London, Fuller.

Delmer, Sefton, *An Autobiography: Vol. 1 Trail Sinister* (November 1961) *Vol. 2 Black Boomerang* (October 1962), London, Secker and Warburg.

Dodds-Parker, Douglas, *Political Eunuch*, Berkshire, Springwood, 1986.

Dorrill, Stephen and Robin, Ramsay, *Smear! Wilson and the Secret State*, London, Fourth Estate, 1991.

Endicott, Stephen, *James G. Endicott: Rebel out of China*, University of Toronto Press, 1980.

Farrar-Hockley, Gen Sir Anthony, *The British Part in the Korean War, Vols 1 & 2, Official History*, London, HMSO, 1990 and 1995.

Fergusson, Bernard, *The Watery Maze*, London, Collins, 1961.

Foot, M.R.D., *SOE in France*, London, HMSO, 1966.

Freeman, Lawrence, *The Evolution of Nuclear Strategy*, New York, St Martin's Press, 1989.

Fursenko, Alexsandr and Naftali, Timothy, *One Hell of a Gamble: the Secret History of the Cuban Missile Crisis*, New York, John Murray, 1997.

Fyvel, T.R., *The Insecure Offenders: Rebellious Youth in the Welfare State*, London, Pelican, 1961.

Gaddis, John Lewis, *We Now Know: Rethinking Cold War History*, Oxford University Press, 1997.

Healey, Denis, *The Time of My Life*, London, Michael Joseph, 1989.

Healey, Denis, *When Shrimps Learn to Whistle: Signposts for the Nineties*, London, Penguin, 1991.

Hitchens, Christopher *Hostage to History: Cyprus, from the Ottomans to Kissinger*, London, Verso, 1997.

Hollingsworth, Mark and Norton-Taylor, Richard *Blacklist: the Inside Story of Political Vetting*, London, Hogarth Press, 1988.

Holloway, David, *Stalin and the Bomb: the Soviet Union and Atomic Energy, 1939–54*, New Haven, Yale University Press, 1994.

Karalekas, Anne, *History of the CIA*, part of US Senate, Select Committee to Study Governmental Operations with Respect to Intelligence Activities, Supplementary Detailed Staff Reports on Foreign and Military Intelligence, Senate Report 94–755, 94th Congress 2nd session 1976.

Kitson, Frank, *Low Intensity Operations*, London, Faber & Faber, 1971.

Kitzinger, Uwe, *Diplomacy and Persuasion: How Britain Joined the Common Market*, London, Thames & Hudson, 1973.

Krushchev, Nikita, *Krushchev Remembers: the Last Testament*, Boston, Little Brown, 1970.

Lashmar, Paul, *Spy Flights of the Cold War*, Stroud, Sutton, 1996.

Lawrenson, Hohn and Barber, Lionel, *The Price of Truth: the Story of the Reuters £££ Millions*, London, Mainstream, 1985.

Leigh, David, *The Frontiers of Secrecy: Closed Government in Britain*, London, Junction Books, 1980.

Lloyd, Selwyn, *Suez 1956*, New York, publisher, 1978.

Lucas, W. Scott, *Divided We Stand: Britain, the US and the Suez Crisis*, London, Sceptre, 1991.

McAlpine, Alaistair, *Once a Jolly Bagman*, London, Weidenfeld & Nicholson, 1997.

Mankekar, D.R., *One Way Free Flow: Neo-colonialism via News Media*, town, Dell, 1974.

Marchetti, Victor and Marks, John D., *The CIA and the Cult of Intelligence*, town, Dell, 1974.

Mastny, Vojtech, *The Stalin Years: the Cold War and Soviet Insecurity*, Oxford University Press, 1996.

MOD: Treatment of British Prisoners of War in Korea, London, HMSO, 1955.

Morris, Jan, *Conundrum*, London, Faber & Faber, 1974.

Nelson, Michael, *War of the Black Heavens: the Battles of Western Broadcasting in the Cold War*, London, Brassey's, 1997.

Parrott, Sir Cecil, *The Serpent and the Nightingale*, London, Faber & Faber, 1977.

Peck, Sir John, *From Dublin to Downing Street*, Dublin, Gill & MacMillan, 1978.

Penkovsky, Oleg, *The Penkovsky Papers*, New York, Collins, 1965.

Philby, Kim, *My Silent War*, London, Panther, 1977.

Prados, John, *Presidents' Secret Wars: CIA and Pentagon Covert Operations from World War II through Iranscam*, New York, Quill, 1987.

Rawnsley, Gary D., *Radio Diplomacy and Propaganda: the BBC and VOA in International Politics, 1956–64*, London, Macmillan, 1996.

Richelson, Jeffrey T., *American Espionage and the Soviet Target*, New York, Quill, 1987.

Richelson, Jeffrey T.A., *Century of Spies*, Oxford University Press, 1995.

Rothwell, Victor, *Britain and the Cold War: 1941–1947*, London, Jonathan Cape, 1982.

Saville, John, *The Politics of Continuity: British Foreign Policy and the Labour Government 1945–46*, London, Verso, 1993, Appendix 2.

Shaw, Eric, *Discipline and Discord in the Labour Party*, Manchester University Press, 1988.

Slessor, Sir John, *The Great Deterrent*, London, 1957.

Stevenson, William, *A Man Called Intrepid*, London, Macmillan, 1976.

Strang, Lord, *The Foreign Office*, London, Allen & Unwin, 1955.

Sweet-Escott, Bickham, *Baker Street Irregular*, London, Methuen, 1965.

Taylor, Geoffrey, *Changing Faces: a History of the Guardian 1956–88*, London, Fourth Estate, 1993.

Taylor, Phillip, *Munitions of the Mind*, Glasgow, Patrick Stevens, 1990.

Walker, David, *Lunch with a Stranger*, London, Wingate, 1957.

West, Nigel, *A Matter of Trust: MI5, 1945–72*, London, Coronet, 1982.

Wyndham-Goldie, Grace, *Facing the Nation, Television and Politics, 1936–76*, London, Bodley Head, 1977.

Vansittart, Lord, *The Mist Procession*, London, Hutchinson, 1958.

Verrier, Anthony, *Looking Glass War*, London, Jonathan Cape, 1983.

Wright, Peter, *Spycatcher*, Australia, Heinemann, 1987.

Zubok, Vladislav and Pleshakov, Constantine, *Inside the Kremlin's Cold War: from Stalin to Krushchev*, Cambridge, Mass., Harvard, 1996.

ARTICLES

Adamthwaite, Anthony, 'The BBC's Response to Peace and Defence Issues, 1945–58', *Contemporary Record* vii (1993), 557–77.

Aldrich, Dr Richard, 'British Intelligence and the Anglo–American "Special Relationship" during the Cold War', *Review of International Studies*, 24 (1998), 331–351.

Broad, Roger and Geiger, Tim, 'The 1975 British Referendum on Europe: a Witness Seminar', *Contemporary Record* 10(2) (1996).

Carruthers, Susan L., 'Korea: the Great Brain Robbery', ICBH Conference: Britain and the Cold War, Senate House, London (July 1997).

Crawley, Aidan, 'The Hidden Face of British Communism', *Sunday Times* (28 October 1962) reprinted as a pamphlet.

Deery, Phillip, 'Confronting the Cominform: George Orwell and the Cold War Offensive of the Information Research Department 1948–50', *Labour History* 73 (November 1997).

Fletcher, Richard, 'British Propaganda since World War II – a Case Study', *Media, Culture and Society* (1982).

Gibianski, L.Y., 'How the Cominform Emerged: the New Archival Materials' *Novaiia I noveishaia istoriia* 4 (July–August 1993), 131.

Hennessy, Peter, 'The Secrets that will Stay Secret For Ever', *The Listener* 11 (September 1986).

Jenks, John, 'Fight against Peace: Britain and the World Peace Council', ICBH Conference: Britain and the Cold War, Senate House, London (July 1997).

Kirby, Dianne, 'The Church of England and the Cold War Nuclear Debate', *Twentieth Century British History* 4(3) (1993), 250–83.

——, 'The Religious Component in the Anglo-American Cold War Alliance, 1945–8', Institute of Contemporary British History conference 'Britain and the Cold War' (July 1997).

Knight, Wayne, 'Labourite Britain: America's "Sure Friend"? The Anglo Soviet Treaty Issue, 1947', *Diplomatic History* 7 (Fall 1983), 270–7.

Lashmar, Paul, 'Covert in Glory', *New Statesman* (3 March 1995).

Leffler, Melvyn P., 'Inside Enemy Archives: the Cold War Reopened', *Foreign Affairs* 75 (July/August 1996).

Lucas, W. Scott and Morris, C.J., 'A Very British Crusade, the Information Research Department and the Beginning of the Cold War' in Richard Aldrich (ed.), *British Intelligence Strategy and the Cold War* London, Routledge (1992), 85–110.

Mayhew, Christopher, 'British Foreign Policy since 1945', *International Affairs* XXVI(4) (1950).

Nelson, Michael, 'The BBC External Service and the Cold War' from the conference 'Britain and the Cold War' held at the Institute of Contemporary British History (July 1997).

Shaw, Tony 'The Information Research Department of the Foreign Office and the Korean War, 1950–53', *Journal of Contemporary British History* (1998).

——, 'The British Popular Press and the Early Cold War', *Journal of Contemporary British History* (1998).

——, 'British Feature Films and the Early Cold War' in Gary Rawnsley (ed.), *Cinema* Macmillan (in press).

Smith, Lyn, 'Covert British Propaganda: the Information Research Department 1947–77', *Millennium: Journal of International Studies* 9(1) (1980).

Van Courtland Moon, John Ellis, 'Biological Warfare Allegations: the Korean War Case', *Annals of New York Academy of Sciences* 666 (31 December 1992).

Wark, Wesley K., '"Coming in from the Cold" British Propaganda and the Red Army Defectors 1945–52', *The International History Review* IX(1) (February 1987).

Warner, Geoffrey, 'Collusion and the Suez Crisis' *International Affairs* (April 1979).

Weathersby, Kathryn, 'Soviet Aims in Korea and the Origins of the Korean War, 1945–50', *CWIHP Working Papers* 8 (November 1993).

——, 'To Attack or not to Attack? Stalin, Kim Il Sung and the Prelude to War' *CWIHP Bulletin* 5 (Spring 1995).

——, 'To Attack or not to Attack? Stalin, Kim Il Sung and the Prelude to War' *CWIHP Bulletin* 5 (Spring 1995).

——, 'New Russian Documents on the Korean War' *CWIHP Bulletin* 6 & 7 (Winter 1995/6).

Wilford, Hugh, 'The Information Research Department: Britain's Secret Cold War Weapons Revealed' (1996).

——, 'Britain, the US and the Cultural Cold War, 1945–1960' from the conference 'Britain and the Cold War' held at the Institute of Contemporary British History (July 1997).

In addition, all editions of *The Cold War History Project Bulletin* were extremely helpful.

OTHER MATERIAL

The authors drew extensively upon an archive of material on the IRD researched by a team under the direction of Richard Fletcher in the 1970s, which led to the exposure of the IRD's true function in 1978. The material includes biographies of IRD personnel and a large section on Ampersand, as well as the typescripts of interviews with Christopher Mayhew, Max Reinhart and Stephen Watts and many others. This archive contains, at present, probably the most detailed material on Ampersand and the Background Books series. It is now in the possession of Paul Lashmar.

Another archive containing substantial evidence confirming the relationship between the IRD and the Labour Party is the Labour Party International Department papers, which can be found at the Labour History Archive and Study Centre in Manchester.

The third archive that was investigated was the Public Record Office at Kew. Until recently the office held few identified IRD files. The Foreign Office held back the release of IRD files until 17 August 1995, when the majority of files for 1948 were finally released. A year later the material for 1949 was released. In early 1998 the material for 1950–1 was released; some material for the years 1948–51 is withheld.

Index

'revisionists' 112